FREE WOMAN

FREE WOMAN

Life, Liberation and Doris Lessing

LARA FEIGEL

BLOOMSBURY PUBLISHING
LONDON • OXFORD • NEW YORK • NEW DELHI • SYDNEY

Bloomsbury Publishing
An imprint of Bloomsbury Publishing Plc

50 Bedford Square　　　　1385 Broadway
London　　　　　　　　　New York
WC1B 3DP　　　　　　　　NY 10018
UK　　　　　　　　　　　USA

www.bloomsbury.com

BLOOMSBURY and the Diana logo are trademarks of Bloomsbury Publishing Plc

First published in Great Britain 2018

© Lara Feigel, 2018

British Library Cataloguing-in-Publication Data
A catalogue record for this book is available from the British Library.

ISBN: HB: 978-1-4088-7853-8
TPB: 978-1-4088-7854-5
EPUB: 978-1-4088-7855-2

2 4 6 8 10 9 7 5 3

Typeset by Newgen KnowledgeWorks Pvt. Ltd., Chennai, India
Printed and bound in Great Britain by CPI Group (UK) Ltd, Croydon CR0 4YY

For my friends

Contents

'I am interested only in stretching myself, in living as fully as I can'

Lessons from Lessing

There were too many weddings that summer. White weddings, gold weddings; weddings in village churches, on beaches, at woollen mills. Collectively, they seemed to go on for too long and to involve too much effort, whether it was the effort of the congregation to reach these much-loved remote places or the effort of the bride and groom to coordinate flowers, music, seating plans, personalised vows, home-made confetti and take-home marmalade. At all of them I chastised myself for my own mean-spiritedness and hypocrisy (I too am married, and once devoted a summer to it) but determined that at some point when not at a wedding I would work out why I minded it all so much.

I came closer to understanding my own truculence when I attended the wedding of a school friend while halfway through reading *The Golden Notebook*, Doris Lessing's 1962 exploration of the artistic and sexual life of a 'free woman'. Lessing's voice is powerful and it had taken hold of me, fifty years later, to the extent that it seemed to muffle the voices around me. I could hear her sentences in my ears as I sat below a hundred metres of tasteful Liberty print bunting that the bride, her sister and their mother (three intelligent and expensively educated women) had sewn by hand.

Troubled by the mental picture of a needle threaded, pulled through and along the fabric, back through, in again, back through, ad infinitum, I heard Lessing's central character Anna Wulf's pronouncement: 'I am interested only in stretching myself, in living as fully as I can.' For Anna, living fully means living freely. She has been married, and is prepared to marry again, but she's aware of the fragility of any relationship because love experienced authentically is dangerous. And she remains uncertain whether she's willing to allow a sexual relationship to define her place in the world.

Thinking about her, I realised that my main objection to these weddings wasn't a feminist one. I was certainly troubled by the ease with which we perpetuated the symbolism of the pallidly virginal bride being handed from one man to another, and perturbed in this case that it was the women who had done all that sewing. But it wouldn't have been much better if the groom had taken up needlework as well. What I minded more strongly was the apparent assumption that this remained the only way to live. Weddings celebrated on this scale seemed to take for granted a happy-ever-after of decade after decade of safely monogamous marriage, with appropriate numbers of children born at appropriate intervals along the way. They ushered in a world where work was a means to the ultimate end of enjoyable family life; where love was the 'love you' at the end of a phone call. I felt uncomfortable partly because it seemed to coopt everyone in the room into this vision and this made me claustrophobic, needing urgently to insist on my right to live fully, without quite knowing what I would want that to entail.

Sitting under that tasteful bunting, I was talking to two school friends at a table that had been emptied as people headed towards the dance floor. I asked them what they felt about this industrious celebration of love and was relieved to find that they were sceptical too, though one of them was preparing to get married a few months later and was even (occasioning more irritation on my part) planning to change her name. We were all aware that this was not what we'd had in mind when we read Virginia Woolf and D.H. Lawrence in adolescence, aware that we had once thought of love as something freer and more radical.

We remembered an evening during the summer of our A levels when the three of us had lain talking and drinking on the grass of one of their gardens and, as the sky darkened, each had confessed, to the surprise of the others, that we were still virgins. We had all had boyfriends, but we'd assumed an old-fashioned coyness in delaying the moment of deflowerment, partly out of fear and partly out of a reluctance to relinquish the independence of self-sufficiency, though I'm not sure we could have defined it so coolly at the time. Reared at a school where we'd been taught that girls could do everything and had no need of boys, we felt that there would be an element of self-betrayal involved in entering a state where we became dependent on the desire, approval and companionship of men.

As the band began to play in the adjoining room, I told them about *The Golden Notebook*; about Anna Wulf, who like us was in her mid-thirties, and her struggle to live as honestly as possible. I described what I saw as Lessing's central dilemma, and how it had helped me to see in retrospect what it was that we had feared would be lost once we had succumbed to a life of sex with men.

Anna wants to be free, believes that she cannot thrive as a writer or a woman if she does not exist independently of her lovers. But she cannot be happy without the love of a man and she cannot love fully unless she relinquishes control enough to lose herself in him. Sexually, she wants to be created by his desire; to have the pleasurably overwhelming feeling of experiencing his body as hers. Emotionally, she wants both to depend on him and to be needed by him so that together they can feel the vulnerability required to be transfigured by love. She is aware that the price for this transfiguration could be a loss of freedom. Indeed, she's prepared to accept that it might lead her to marry for a second time. Now, thinking about Anna as we rose to join the dancing, I thought that there might not be anything wrong with her acceptance of this, but that it was possible still to remember that it was a high price to pay, even while paying it, and that this required an ambivalence that seemed incompatible with all those metres of bunting.

I

Reading

This was the second time I had read *The Golden Notebook*. I read it for the first time as an undergraduate at Oxford in the late 1990s, when it did not make much impression on me. As a cheerfully capable nineteen-year-old student, I found Lessing's heroine unnecessarily lugubrious and found the failure in connection that characterised her relationships alienating. This meant that I had been curious rather than excited when I started it again. After Lessing's death, friends in their sixties and seventies had reminisced to me about what

Lessing had meant to them in their twenties and thirties. The women had read about their most intimate experiences in print for the first time; the men had discovered how women talked about men when they were alone together. This had intrigued me enough to send me back to the novel but I was surprised when I found it immediately enticing. Anna Wulf's world had become easily accessible, despite the great differences separating her time from mine.

The failures, the *longueurs*, even the moments of stylistic ugliness, all now seemed bravely realistic. Arguably, you cannot describe the daily life of an intelligent heroine without describing moments of boredom, irritation and alienation. The politics no longer seemed as distancing as they had done either. Lessing was describing Anna's commitment to communism as a personal leap of faith made by a woman desperate to believe that she can have some impact on her world. Anna, like her creator, was an idealist in an age when it appeared more possible to be idealistic than it ever had to me, one of 'Thatcher's children', growing up in an era of PR-driven pragmatic politics.

It seemed that Lessing was a writer to discover in your thirties; a writer who wrote about the lives of grown-up women with an honesty and fullness I had not found in any novelist before or since. The questions troubling Anna were questions that troubled me: how as a writer to write stories you believe in while constructing books with a beginning, middle and end that people would actually want to read; how as a woman to reconcile your need to be desired by men with your wish for sexual equality; how to have the freedom of independence while also allowing yourself the freedom to go outside yourself through love; or how, in Lessing's terms, to be a 'free woman' who is also happy.

Lessing's notion of the 'free woman' is at once alluring and frightening, because her free women seem doomed to disappointment. Anna observes that 'every woman believes in her heart that if a man does not satisfy her she has a right to go to another. That is her first and strongest thought, regardless of how she might soften it later out of pity or expediency'. This is freedom as sexual liberation; the kind of statement that the next generation of feminists took to be a sign of Lessing's commitment to Women's Lib. But if Anna is making the case for sexual promiscuity then she is making it inconsistently, because she is uneasily aware that in order to be satisfied she needs to be both desired and loved by a particular man.

She is convinced (and the sexual explicitness is astonishing, given that the ban on *Lady Chatterley's Lover* had been lifted only two years earlier) that women can only have vaginal orgasms with what she terms 'real men', and only when those men are allowing the possibility of mutual love. This may sound unappealing, but although in Lessing's formulation, real men are indubitably heterosexual, they are not quite as visibly macho as they might sound. They need not beat their chests or proclaim their sexual potency to the world; instead they need to be courageous in confronting the sexuality of women and loving and desiring them without fear. For Anna, such a man 'from the whole of his need and desire takes a woman and wants all her response'. If *The Golden Notebook* became a bible for strident feminists haranguing increasingly frightened men, then it was a bible that castigated men for not desiring women enough. In a way, Lessing was asking for more physical objectification rather than less of it, although the bodily adoration had to be entwined with an appreciation of the woman's mind.

What was compelling here was that Lessing placed sexual fulfilment at the centre of women's lives, while at the same time insisting on the urgency of their need to distance themselves from the expectations created by their sexual roles. Anna in bed is a traditional creature who needs to lose herself on the tide of male desire. Anna out of bed is passionately determined that she cannot be defined in relation to her lover. A similar paradox is present in relation to Anna's motherhood. There are moments when her daughter Janet is the centre of her physical and emotional world, when her whole body responds to the girl's smell and touch. But there are other times when she has to repudiate these feelings because she has to have a mental and bodily existence that is wholly independent of her child.

A significant element of my irritation that summer was frustration that the women I encountered at weddings seemed to define themselves foremost in relation to others. They began by identifying as part of a couple and then once a child arrived they identified themselves primarily as mothers. I often had a sense that their whole notion of life was now family life; that once the marriage had evolved to be more about triangular family love than sexual intimacy, all their need for intensity was fulfilled by their relationships with their children. And I half knew that I minded this so strongly because I was essentially one of them. Certainly I would look no different to the outside eye.

Of course, it was not this simple. Many of us were probably secretly imagining sex with men other than our husbands, or thinking about writing or painting something that could matter to us more than our children, or wondering how we might go about changing the world. But the point for me was that mothers with young children would rarely express this, or would only reveal it with guilt, where in *The Golden Notebook* Anna is completely open about the separation between her lives as a mother, lover and writer. This is in part the result of a compartmentalisation that both Anna and her creator see as a fundamental problem of their society, but I think it's more that she takes it for granted that in any moment she may be overwhelmed by feelings for the man she is in bed with or the book she is writing, to the extent that her love for her daughter recedes into the background. Similarly, however intense the love or the heartbreak she is experiencing in relation to a man may be, she is able to become an observer both of him and of herself when she sits down to write, moving fundamentally apart from him.

It seemed to me that Anna's refusal to define herself primarily as a wife, mother or lover was a significant part of the audacity of *The Golden Notebook*. I was starting to feel that there was a world that Lessing's generation and my feminist friends in their sixties and seventies had fought to bring into being that my generation seemed willing to let fall away. Crucially, this was a world in which it was more important to live fully than to live contentedly.

This doesn't mean that I was reading *The Golden Notebook* without uncertainty. But it was uncertainty that Anna herself shared in the novel. It may make us uncomfortable to watch her spending a whole evening cooking a breaded veal escalope for a man whom she knows is about to leave her; who turns out not even to be intending to come to dinner. But it makes Anna uncomfortable too. She is worried both that in seeking happiness in this way she is making herself less free, and that if she does not allow herself to love like this she will not be able to enjoy the sex she has freed herself for in the first place.

It was because of her inconsistencies, rather than in spite of them, that reading about Anna had enabled me to see my own world more clearly. She had allowed me to see my own sense of the inextricable nature of body and mind, of the personal and the political, as the basis for thinking about life. She was helping me to understand the questions I needed to ask, even if I was no closer to knowing the answers. And so, as the weddings continued into the autumn, I continued to read Lessing.

My reading had become more systematic now, and I wanted to write about her. But I couldn't yet imagine integrating my reading of Lessing into my life as an academic. This was the kind of urgent reading that was more characteristic of my book-fuelled adolescence than of my professional life and the feelings it was stirring up in me felt too illicit to be categorised as work. My identification with her had a naivety of a kind that I would discourage in my students.

I was convinced that the ingenuous hunger that she was inducing in me as a reader was a sign of her power. It didn't matter that her prose was uneven and that I was only occasionally seduced by her sentences. Many of them were rough-edged, workaday constructions, perhaps because Lessing like Anna Wulf distrusted surface beauty. If anything, though, the patchiness of the prose drew me in further, because it meant that I had to respond personally as well as aesthetically. It seems true of all the most enduring novelists, from Tolstoy to George Eliot to Lessing, that they illuminate our lives, and that we live differently as a result of reading them. It had been several years since I had encountered a novelist with this influence, or perhaps since I'd allowed myself to be shaped by fiction in this way.

I read the Martha Quest novels, where I found my own experiences of childhood (reading, yearning, arguing with my mother) alongside a less familiar experience that seemed recognisable, perhaps simply because of its intensity. Growing up like Lessing herself in the Southern Rhodesian bush, Martha discovers a kind of euphoric freedom in nature. Wandering beneath the vast African skies through the expanses of the Highveld, she encounters a liberation she cannot find with other people.

In the second novel, Martha becomes a mother, and here another aspect of my life played out. This was the most courageously graphic description of childbirth I'd ever come across and it was even more daring in its portrayal of maternal ambivalence. Lessing is particularly good at showing how deep, physical love for a child can coincide with a sense of irritated entrapment. I could certainly not conceive of leaving my own two-year-old child as Martha does and as Lessing herself had, but I could make more sense of this act now that I understood that it didn't simply result from a lack of mother love. It emerged from heart-breaking uncertainty and left its wounds of grief and guilt.

Then I read her autobiographies and memoirs and began to see the patterns where life was transformed into art and back again; to see that Martha and Anna were and were not Lessing and that sometimes the pain she refused to confront in her autobiographies could be channelled into her novels. I moved on to her books exploring madness – *The Four-Gated City* and *Briefing for a Descent into Hell* – and was excited to see Lessing experimenting with different modes of consciousness. This was very much of its time, though she didn't always admit the influence of R.D. Laing. But I liked the way that she saw madness as something people could experience together, as she had in Anna Wulf's relationship with Saul Green. Here was a form of love transformatively different from the love I was watching being celebrated at weddings.

I read *The Summer before the Dark* and was disturbed and moved by Lessing's portrayal of middle age. I was disturbed because she presented the sexual needs of the middle-aged woman as both urgent and unfulfillable. From Lessing's close friend Suzette Macedo, I learnt that overnight at the age of fifty Lessing herself had pulled her brown curls into an austere grey bun, uncrossed her legs and adopted the persona of a middle-aged spinster. She had just gone through the menopause and was frightened that soon she would be undesirable. Always uncompromising, she wanted to preempt this by cutting herself off from men.

I had now noticed that the image of a door being slammed was used throughout her novels and autobiographies, both literally and metaphorically. She elaborates on this image in her autobiography, where she uses it to describe her move to London at the age of thirty. 'Behind me a door had slammed shut. Doors had been shutting behind me all my life… I knew all about the mechanisms of the shut door, recognised it not by some loud external bang but what went on inside me.' She slammed the door on her own childish vulnerability when she cut herself off emotionally from her mother as a young girl; she slammed the door on her children when she abandoned them as toddlers; now she was slamming the door on her own sexuality.

I wanted to berate her for this, and to urge her not to do it so abruptly. It was clear how much it cost her from the grief and madness in her novel. But then I read *Love, Again*, her wonderful late novel about an ageing woman falling passionately, physically and shamefully in love with a younger man and I learnt that this was a novel written partly to survive the humiliation of Lessing's own unrequited passion for the composer Philip Glass, with whom she had collaborated on two operas.

Now it was Glass I wanted to rebuke, for failing to see what this return to sexuality had cost her. I wanted to ask him if he had read this novel and I wanted as a younger woman to stand up to an older man on behalf of the older woman that as a result of reading this novel I feared I would become. I didn't want Lessing to have been proved right in her certainty that for women to allow themselves middle-aged sexual need could only end in distressed rejection. But I was reading too compulsively fully to understand these thoughts. All I knew was that through Lessing I would eventually gain more understanding both of my life as it was currently lived and of the life that awaited me later on.

II

Dangling

As the new year began, I turned thirty-five, and celebrated quietly. 'Thirty-five is the end of youth,' a friend in his sixties announced. While his wife hastily contradicted him and told me how much younger my generation was than theirs had been, I thought that actually I was ready for my youth to be over. This was largely because of Lessing, who was teaching me about the possibilities of adult life. Shortly afterwards, I discovered that I was pregnant. Whatever moments of ambivalence I might feel about motherhood, I was certain in my desire for a second child, and had been for over a year. But two months later I learnt during a routine scan that I'd had a miscarriage.

I have since discovered that almost all the women I know with children have had a miscarriage at one time or another. However, as a result of what seems a ridiculous taboo preventing us from mentioning pregnancy before it's legitimised by the twelve-week scan, very few of them had told me about it. Partly because of this and partly because of my own rather absurd confidence that the gods were on my side, it had not occurred to me that there was any possibility this happily imagined baby was not going to be born that October.

I was filled with pregnancy hormones, which for two months had sent me leaping and crashing between happiness and fragility, unusually inward-looking and self-contained, smugly conscious of the growth occurring within my body and of the distance that this knowledge created between me and the rest of the world. Now it turned out that in fact there had been no growth; the tiny arms and eyelids I had imagined gradually and miraculously moulding their way into existence had not had a chance to develop; there was a mere sac that had ceased to live a month earlier. After three days of shock I started bleeding, and was surprised to find that the blood and pain came as a cathartic relief. I felt myself bleed my way back into my old body and, at the same time, into a new phase of adult life.

My confidence that I lived in a world that simply fell into place around me had gone and this loss, though painful, brought with it a tentative curiosity about the imperfect world that was taking its place. Since my schooldays I had seen life as a journey in which you desired to do things and then achieved them in an endless process of ascent. I had worked hard, passing one academic exam after another, acquiring a list of As and firsts. I had been energetically pleasing, making friends with increasing ease, being liked by my teachers, meeting my future husband at the age of twenty-one. Sometimes there were difficulties but I tried harder and found that by the age of thirty-one I had a child, husband, house, job and book; by the age of thirty-five I had another book and another child to come. Now it became clear that in fact this journey towards a destination did not go on for ever. As I put it to one friend, in the wake of the miscarriage, I had now reached the destination and had to wander around and locate myself in my new surroundings. It was the wandering that had to become the source of interest and pleasure, rather than the forward progress. 'You are dangling,' he said, taking the image from Saul Bellow's *The Dangling Man*. 'Real life is dangling.'

This was an exciting discovery but it was also frightening, because it meant that increased effort might no longer be the guarantor of increased happiness. And it seemed likely to entail more loss. I felt this most strongly in my marriage where, once we had lost the narrative of progress provided by the new pregnancy, we seemed to lose faith in each other. During the long year of trying to become pregnant, I had felt our confidence in the relationship wane. I had minded that my husband seemed to want to shout at me more often than he wanted to touch me, at least outside bed, and that his physical affection seemed to be directed more towards our son. He had minded that mentally I was always half in my work and that my vision of family life was one in which I might well spend a Saturday afternoon reading a book. More fundamentally, he minded that I had made him wait until I was ready to become pregnant with the first baby and then again with the second, though by the second attempt I was well aware that it might take us a long time.

These differences had been forgotten in the excitement of the new pregnancy and it had felt as though we were both relieved to lay our doubts about the marriage aside. Here at least, in the gratified desire for a second child, our wishes and mood easily coincided. At first the miscarriage, too, had brought us together. There had been a new tenderness in our touch and talk; I could hear the love in his voice when I called him at work and when he came home and greeted me in the evenings. There was also a collusive intimacy in our attempts to keep any knowledge of what was happening from our son. Quickly, though, we found that our grief manifested itself in divergent ways. I cried, pausing to write, or to go out and seek distraction by socialising. He returned with grim stoicism to ordinary life and turned his sadness into anger. On the eve of departing for a holiday that we'd both expected to be suffused with the optimism of my pregnancy, I bought some Lego for my son to play with while we were away. My husband, an architect who had honed his construction skills on Lego in his youth, hated the fact that the creatively versatile bricks of his childhood had been replaced by specific kits, allowing the child to build only one thing. He shouted at me for succumbing to this inferior modern trend.

As I waited out his anger, I tried to imagine what this felt like for him. This was rage at the imagined childhood we'd lost; anger at his own powerlessness in a marriage where it was my body that had the apparently arbitrary ability to create and destroy life, and my mind that dictated the timeframes within which this should happen. I retreated once again into comparing us to Anna and her lovers, and Martha and her husbands. There is plenty of impotent male rage in the Martha Quest books. Martha leaves both her husbands partly because they are unable to face their own vulnerability and can experience it only as anger.

Perhaps I, like Martha, would end my marriage. Perhaps I, like Anna Wulf (and, more uneasily, like my own mother), would end up as the single mother of one child. Though I had been so dismissive of those weddings the previous summer, I saw that I hadn't fully questioned my own place in the smug structures of middle-class life. Now I was prepared to depart from the tramlines to success that I'd followed obediently for so long; to join Lessing in asking if there were other models to live by and in seeking the freedom to try them out.

It was becoming clear to me that the book I needed to write about Lessing was a book about her preoccupation with freedom. At that moment, when I had to learn to find my own new sensation of airborne life enjoyably freeing, I needed her to teach me how to do so. I wanted to learn from her how to stand in the bush looking up at the sky and to liberate myself from the conflicting desires that stopped me being free. And I wanted to learn what it was like to crash through life, discarding ties, avoiding the actions expected by others.

When I talked about Lessing to other people, I was finding that what I liked about her was unusual. There were the elements of her life and writing that others admired: the award of the Nobel Prize and her crotchety reaction to it, her involvement in Zimbabwean politics, her ability to write about groups. And there were the elements that were generally seen as more problematic: her abandoning of her children, her restless and ultimately dissatisfied sexual life, her willingness to sacrifice almost everything for her writing, her tendency to go from one extreme position to another. Perhaps because of the particular circumstances in which I'd encountered her, these were the aspects of her that most interested me and that

I kept finding myself determined to make a case for. And they all seemed to relate to her urge for freedom.

In a century where questions of freedom were crucial, politically and socially, Lessing was one of the most compulsive of freedom-seekers. The words 'free' and 'freedom' are used throughout her work: probably more than she knew. Indeed, I was starting to see that Lessing was as obsessed with freedom as I was obsessed with Lessing.

This emphasis on freedom separated her time from mine. Though Western political leaders still liked to talk about the 'free world', freedom had become less of a popular mantra than it used to be. Politically, this seemed to be the result of the Cold War, when both sides claimed to offer freedom, continued in the twenty-first century when George Bush took the imperialist rhetoric of freedom to new levels. Personally, it seemed to be the result of the demise of free love, partly brought about by the AIDS epidemic in the 1980s. Also, perhaps as ordinary life had become relatively freer, more radical notions of freedom had been forgotten. Once sex before marriage, abortion and divorce had become more widely accepted, once women had greater opportunities for education and employment and were aided domestically by the input of 'new men', there was less need to seek freedom in radically different forms of life of the kind proposed by communism or by the first forms of feminism.

What I found most enticing about freedom as explored in Lessing's novels was that it is allowed to be contradictory. Communism is never presented as a straightforward answer because she doesn't forget the absurdity of this attempt to subjugate life to a system. Sexual liberation is never seen as an uncomplicated good because it is not often a source of happiness. This in part explains her frequent changes of opinion. It may have been a desire for liberation that made Lessing join political movements, but it was the same urge that took her away from them.

I don't think I was aware at that stage that these contradictions made freedom a more questionable, albeit perhaps also a more compelling, good. But I did see that it was clear from Lessing's own life as well as from her novels that there were tremendous costs involved in Lessing's attempts to live freely. My relationship with Lessing had begun with a process of identification, but gradually as I understood more about her life I also saw where we diverged, especially when it came to her tendency to cut herself off from people she had loved.

My confidence in my own invincibility had diminished after the miscarriage. Though during arguments with my husband, I fantasised about discarding ties, I was also frightened of losing them. I spent a week fearfully imagining what it would be like to lose my existing three-year-old son. When I was with him I found it hard not to touch and kiss him all the time. I rushed back anxiously to pick him up from nursery, not quite believing that he could have survived a day in someone else's care. Having imagined what it would be like to lose a child, I was more shocked than I had been that she could relinquish hers willingly.

Still, I remained convinced that leaving her children was, at least at that moment, a necessary condition of Lessing's bid for freedom. This was partly because of the world she lived in: because of the perceived impossibility of living as a single mother and because of communism, and its apparent incompatibility with the family structure. It was also because of Lessing's own tendency to slam doors. This was the only way she knew how to live. I had come to accept that a certain amount of wreckage was entailed in the life of the 'free woman'. I was left wanting to know if it was possible both to avoid wreckage and to avoid succumbing to the more puritanical aspects of my own age, or if this was an impossible and indulgent quest to live two lives simultaneously.

So this book emerged as an attempt to understand freedom as Lessing conceived it and as we might apprehend it now, politically, intellectually, emotionally and sexually. I didn't start with a definition of freedom: I wanted to begin by seeing how Lessing used the word, working up an understanding of the concept through observation. I wished to know if the free, intelligent world she tried to create is something we can have any hope of forging afresh, and if it will make us happy if we do. Why has it been so discredited, during the last few decades? Does freedom necessarily entail unbearable loneliness, as it does for Anna Wulf and seems to have done for Lessing? Is the only true source of freedom the existential feeling we can sometimes experience in nature?

If my obsession with Lessing had begun with her work, I was now equally preoccupied with her life, so I knew that I wanted to move easily between the two. Her attempts to be free tended to originate in her life, but then usually found expression in her books. This means that communism, free love, madness, Sufism can all be found in her work a few years after she tried them out in life. However, Lessing herself warned us against reading the novels autobiographically, reminding us that the relationship between art and life is a difficult one to understand. The novels did not simply document the life, even at their most autobiographical. Instead, they enabled her to take her explorations further than she could in actuality and to acknowledge truths too unpalatable to admit to the people around her (though she was unusually courageous in her willingness to be unpopular, not just with enemies but with friends). The novels permitted Lessing to experience the contradictions inherent in any attempt at freedom more fully than she could always do in her life.

I knew that this was my story as well as hers, and that I needed to allow my fascination with Lessing to take its own peculiar form. For me, this was becoming an exercise in learning how to live in a new phase of adult life, and using books as a means to do so. Avid readers are formed as much by books as by the people around them. This was true both for me and Lessing in adolescence; it was partly why I had identified so strongly with her portraits of herself in her youth. It's rarer for it to happen later in life, but it was happening to me and I wished to be conscious of the process.

I wanted to return to adolescence – both hers and mine – to learn about where her vision of freedom had come from and why it mattered so much. I wanted to track down her surviving lovers and to visit the places where she had felt most free. I knew that the book once begun would change me and that the vicissitudes of my own life would change what I wrote about in the book, and I hoped that my personal experiences would resonate with those of others, at different stages in their lives. 'Writing about oneself,' Anna states in *The Golden Notebook*, 'one is writing about others, since your problems, pains, pleasures, emotions – and your extraordinary and remarkable ideas – can't be yours alone.' Of course the impulse to tell your own story is rarely simply altruistic. We all have our own motives for doing it and in my case the writing quickly became its own force for freedom.

'This infinite exchange of earth and sky'

The Bush

'Every writer has a myth-country'

Lomagundi

I began in the bush. It was where it all started for her: that restless urge for freedom. The endless expanses of dry grass, dotted with stubby trees – this was a landscape that she characterised so often as 'free'. When she returned to Africa in 1956 after seven years away, she described wandering around the bush as a physical sensation of liberty:

> Sometimes I stopped the car and left it and went off into the bush and sat in the grass under a tree for the pleasure of being alone. I had not been alone in seven years. In London one can never be alone, not even with the doors locked and the telephone off the hook… But here, it seemed, I was breathing free for the first time since I left home. No one knew where I was. All around me, acres and acres of empty country.

Much later, in her 1992 book *African Laughter*, Lessing wrote that 'every writer has a myth-country', adding that 'myth does not mean something untrue, but a concentration of truth'. Hers was 'the old house built of earth and grass, the lands around the hill, the animals, the birds'.

Reading my way through novel after novel where she'd evoked the landscape of her childhood, I started to find it easy to visualise her house, forged from the bush to which it would one day return, its walls moulded from the thick red soil that coated the ground of the Highveld. I could see the young Doris's bedroom, with its door leading out into the garden that she refused to shut at night, wanting to listen to the drumming from the compound as she fell asleep and to see the hawks sliding motionless down the currents of air. She was usually the first in the house to hear the rains coming each year, awoken by the sound of the water as it turned the grass from brown to green overnight. The thatched roof leaked until it expanded enough to absorb some of the fluid, so she was supposed to move her bed out of the line of the drips. But she preferred to leave it where it was, allowing the water to trickle on to her bare limbs as she slept.

Kermanshah farm was on a hill in the Banket district of the maize-growing region of Lomagundi. The vicinity of the house had been cleared, making room for the garden that Doris's mother valiantly maintained. But then the habitation gave way to the veld, dipping into the mealie fields and then into mile after mile of virgin, uncut bush, interrupted by two rivers, the Muneni and the Mukwadzi, before rising again to the hills in the distance. She repeated the names of her hills a lot in her writing and I found them curiously compelling. They seem to have had a talismanic quality for her, writing about the bush from London. The Ayrshire

Hills in the north, the Hunyani mountains in the west and the Umvukwes, or the Great Dyke, in the east. This eastern range was particularly beautiful, visible from Doris's bedroom, where she could watch as the hills modulated from blue to pink to mauve.

The north-east of Southern Rhodesia was unusually unpopulated, even for such an empty country. Doris and her younger brother Harry often went whole days without meeting anyone as they ran across the plains or cycled into the hills, armed with guns with which they shot small game (pigeons, guineafowl) for their mother to cook. Harry tended to direct these expeditions, but when he was away at school Doris wandered alone, pushing her way through green aisles of mealie stalks to emerge triumphantly into the vleis and ridges of the bush, where she rambled from tree to tree with the wild pigs, porcupines and antelope.

There was one moment in particular that she came back to again and again, and it was a moment when the contrast between the freedom of the bush and the constraint of her house was thrown into relief. She was ten years old. She'd spent the afternoon, as she spent most afternoons, roaming in the bush, intently observing the chameleons and the changing light on the distant hills. Then it was time to come back to the farmhouse, where she found her parents sitting huddled in a cloud of cigarette smoke that seemed to contain all the disappointment of their failed hopes and ambitions. 'I won't', she said to herself. 'I will not be like that'. From now on 'I will not, I will not' became an urgent inner refrain.

Outside, she'd been exhilarated by the emptiness of land and sky. Inside, she felt constrained by the Liberty prints and Persian rugs with which her mother had attempted to stamp civilisation on to their surroundings. And she felt restricted by the will of her parents. Later she reflected that there was 'a dark grey cloud, like poison gas' brooding over her early years. Her father talked endlessly about the sights and sounds of the war they knew as 'the Great Unmentionable' in which he had lost his leg. Her mother stayed in bed for a year, complaining of a bad heart, and then emerged resigned to her new life in Africa but determined to remind her ungrateful children of all that she'd sacrificed for them. Gradually, her mother's trunk of evening dresses gathered moth holes and her father's dreams of success dwindled into elaborate attempts to mine gold on their land, his wooden leg banging as he climbed dangerously up and down mine shafts.

Doris was conscious of the weight of needing to succeed on their behalf and felt trapped by her mother's insistence that she was a sickly child. Maude Tayler guarded her daughter's body as though it was a possession, refusing to let her emerge into adulthood by making her wear the dresses of a young girl. Doris needed to escape, and the liberating emptiness of the bush enabled her to do so, though she was starting to realise that the bush itself would eventually become part of the snare.

There wasn't only the bush. Like so many children and adolescents who feel out of place at home, she escaped through books and daydreams. This may have been what made the bush compelling for me: the way that it came together with the mental experience of my own childhood, especially because she was so good at describing the intense pleasure of lying with a book in one place while secretly entering another world. I liked the way she remembered reading at that age as a physical experience. She read curled up on a mound of grain sacks in the corner of the storehouse verandah: *Robinson*

Crusoe and *Alice in Wonderland*, *Oliver Twist* and *The Jungle Book*. She read lying on her bed, eating oranges as she turned the pages of *Anne of Green Gables* and *What Katy Did* over and over again, lulling herself into a waking reverie. Most often of all, she read sprawled under the Muwanga tree at the bottom of the hill, on the boundary between the farm and the veld. Though the pale trunk had been scarred by lightning, the branches remained strong, thick with green leaves that formed a canopy of shade for the girl lying reading below them, the ridges of her spine tessellating with the roots protruding from underneath her.

Here she read Walter de la Mare's *The Three Royal Monkeys*, following the simian protagonists on their journey 'beyond and beyond, forest and river, forest swamp and river' into the open valley of Tishnar, easily able to imagine the seven peaks that rose before them, 'clear as amber or coral, still and beautiful in the sunrise', the Mountains of Arakkaboa. Then, as she moved from childhood to adolescence, she read Olive Schreiner's *The Story of an African Farm*. Gripped by a book whose setting seemed so close to her own, seduced by its heavy atmosphere of sexual longing, she found that her daydreams took the form of an erotic trance.

Lessing later wrote that the selective nature of memory made it hard to characterise her early life. She could say that she had spent her 'childhood, girlhood and youth' in the world of books. She could say with equal truth that she had occupied them with exploring the bush, watching and listening. Or she could say that she had passed her adolescence in a sexual reverie. 'You remember with what you are at the time you are remembering.'

In fact, I don't think these experiences were separate for her. That image of the Muwanga tree, which she came back to again and again in her fiction and memoirs, is an intensely physical one, and the experience of lying on its roots reading seems so much part of the experience of being in the bush. Reading and wandering through the veld, she was dreaming herself into a new world and a new embodied self. And the dreaming itself was often sexual. I don't think it's a coincidence that the young Doris was eating during much of the time that she read. 'You ingest images through your eyes, calories by mouth', she observed. She'd reminded me that the urgent reading of adolescence is strangely corporeal; the body isn't forgotten as you shift absent-mindedly from one position to another, so it seems natural that this imaginative hunger should bring with it physical and then sexual hunger. And in her case, the bush, reading and erotic daydreaming all became associated with freedom.

For me, the most powerful of Lessing's descriptions of her home was the first one she wrote. She'd described the African veld with extraordinary power in her first novel *The Grass is Singing*, written just after the war. But then in London in 1952, missing the bush, she returned to the very particular landscape of her childhood in *Martha Quest*. What's interesting here is that when we initially encounter Martha she's a grumpy adolescent who's unappreciative of the freedom of the landscape that surrounds her. We first see her aged fifteen, sitting on the steps reading a disquisition on sex by the sexologist Havelock Ellis, watched over by her mother and her friend, too bored to move though she is irritated by the conversation. She looks away from them to the bush, where she watches the land travel 'endlessly, without limit... like that hinterland to the imagination we cannot do without'. And she finds that the vast landscape is so familiar that it causes 'only the prickling feeling of claustrophobia', despite its limitlessness.

This is autobiographical. The ten-year-old Doris may have found the bush liberating, in contrast to the house, but by the time she was Martha's age it had become part of the life she felt she needed to escape. That's why reading was so necessary: imagining her way into alternative worlds was a mode of survival. For Martha, though, and I think this was also true for Doris, the bush regains some of its associations of freedom once it becomes part of her sexual awakening.

Meeting a man she's attracted to in town, Martha announces that she's planning to walk home through the bush, hoping it will make him invite her into his house. When he doesn't, she walks back anyway and finds that her encounter with the veld becomes a moment of release. Striding along, she is 'savouring freedom'. Gazing at a white-stemmed tree bathed in 'a magical sky-reflecting light', her heart moves in 'exquisite sadness' and she enters a timeless moment, more painful than ecstatic, with space and time 'knead[ing] her flesh'.

From this point Martha becomes more conscious of her body, hugging her 'sun-warmed arms' and gazing at her 'long and shapely legs'. It's in this state that she goes to her first dance, drinks enough to convince herself that the clumsy boy who kisses her is the man of her dreams, and then has a visionary encounter with her own naked body in the mirror, which gazes at her 'like a girl from a legend'. Walking home from the dance the next morning through the veld, she takes off her shoes in order to enjoy the pleasure of the mud squelching against her feet and then reads 'hungrily' for days, needing to find in books something to balance the intensity of her recent experiences.

It's only after she leaves the farm altogether that Martha understands what the bush has meant to her. Remembering the farm after she's moved to the city, Martha finds that the pang of lost happiness is 'so acute it shortened her breath'. But then she asks herself if there is any moment of her childhood she would choose to live again, and realises that there is not. Seeking freedom, she has escaped the constraint of her childhood in the veld, only to find that the landscape she left behind constitutes a lost form of liberty. Rereading the novel as I began to think more systematically about freedom, this seemed crucial to me because of the notion of freedom it introduced. It's customary to think of freedom as an absence of restriction or as a cornucopia of choice, but this was different. It was as an inner experience of endlessness.

II

'Because it is so empty we can dream'

The sea

I'd known from the start that I'd begin in the veld. What I didn't know was how preoccupied I'd become by childhood and adolescence, or how much I'd find myself reliving my own early years. As an only child, I grew up with a mother who shared Maude Tayler's tendencies towards self-sacrifice and towards infantalising hypochondria on my behalf. I used books to develop an intensely private, complex inner world in order to gain a space where I could move freely. I had nothing like the bush to escape into, but each summer we went to Wales to visit my grandmother, who lived on the coast, and I went for long walks along the beach, staring out at the sea, fascinated by the encounter with limitlessness.

Lessing's recollections of childhood brought back memories of standing on the beach, hypnotising myself by watching the waves rolling in towards the shore. I remembered repeatedly imagining that I was in the sea, that my body was propelled onward towards the freedom of the horizon. This was a necessary release from the confines of boredom. It was only in retrospect that I could see that the boredom enabled an imaginative escape that was a part of the freedom that I certainly didn't recognise as freedom at the time.

I now realised that it wasn't coincidental that it was in Wales that I located my first experiences of sexual curiosity. I remembered sitting on the floor of my pink-carpeted bedroom in my grandmother's house, repeatedly reading the sex scenes in a novel I had found in the bookcase. It was erotic rather than pornographic, suggestive of urgent desire rather than sexual fulfilment: a zip undone, a breast revealed and crushed in a hand, bodies pressed against a wall. After reading it, I started talking curiously to the men who came to the house, wondering if they were conscious of my eyes, breasts, hips, and wondering what I would have to do to make them so.

During these years, the walks along the promenade became charged with sexual fantasy. After a morning spent reading *Gone with the Wind* or *Jane Eyre* or André Gide's dreamy account of adolescent desire in *Strait is the Gate*, I would walk along the seafront willing into being a man who would combine the sexual forcefulness of Rhett Butler or Mr Rochester with the sensitivity of Gide's Jerome and imagining at length the conversations we would have. These dialogues went on for hours, continued as I sat staring at the sea, meandering between exposures of the soul and declarations of desire. The figures were too shadowy for the imaginings to take on a physical form, but there were glances and moments of touch, resulting in a heightened sense of the undulations of my own body. My memory of that dream-logged wandering now seemed like a physical memory of freedom.

I decided that it was time to go to the sea. In the months after the miscarriage, I'd found that I continued to need time to adjust to the revelation of contingency it had brought. My body, which for two months I'd thought of as containing life, felt unfamiliar. As I waited each month for my period, there was a kind of stasis that exacerbated the feeling of dangling.

I found it harder to talk to my husband about my grief. While I needed to continue feeling sad, his anger had dissipated. He now wanted us to create a narrative in which the abortive pregnancy would be subsumed into the new one that we assured each other would happen quickly. Reading about how many women experienced miscarriages, he reasonably urged me to think of it as an ordinary setback rather than a tragedy. I could see why he needed this and I wanted to grant it to him. I could see that the sense of powerlessness as time elapsed was even harder for him, without the localised feeling of progress created each month by the hormonal cycles. So I outwardly joined him in his optimism, while feeling increasingly alone with my stubborn sadness.

My isolation was made worse by the disappearance of a friend: a man in his seventies who loved me, while being content to do so from a distance. This distance had been bodily and usually geographical, but had not been emotional. Within a couple of weeks of our meeting at a party six months earlier, he had been writing me long, insightful letters about the people in my books which, as I responded, curious about his own experiences, had quickly become letters about ourselves.

He had a habit of taking off alone to wander slowly through large, flat landscapes. On discovering that I was drawn to the same edge-of-the-world beaches and estuaries, he invited me to join him. Once a month, we had met to walk along the flat empty seascapes of Norfolk and Suffolk where we both felt happily peaceful and, with an openness somehow made possible by our ages, seemed to hold nothing back about our past and present lives. We found that we shared a sense of ourselves as works in progress, engaged in a process of becoming that seemed to last beyond adolescence into adulthood and even old age.

There had been a moment of confusion, when we asked ourselves what all this meant. He wrote a bemused missive declaring love to the American voice on my GPS, who'd become a character on our expeditions. But then he realised, or wrote his way into accepting, that the openness we both valued was somehow predicated on the bodily distance that had characterised our encounters. So we agreed to continue the friendship in the form in which it had emerged.

When I had become pregnant, he was surprised to find that he experienced it almost as if it was happening to him, wanting to share in the emotional porousness brought on by the hormones, always there to amuse or commiserate in eloquent emails. During the miscarriage, he had visited me while I sat at home bleeding, both of us unnerved by this sudden transition from seascape to domestic interior, both now accepting that this strange form of still largely textual intimacy had become a necessity, though this acceptance entailed several days of fiercely logical correspondence on the difference between wants and needs.

Then, he had written to say that he was too ill with flu to be in touch. After a week without hearing from him, I wrote to a friend of his asking for news, and was told that he had been diagnosed with an advanced and inoperable cancer, but was expected to return home from hospital soon. Grief-stricken, I attempted to tell my husband more about this strange friendship that he had known about only in outline. He tried to sympathise, but it was hard for him to see how a man double my age whom I had met at a party only a few months earlier could have become someone who mattered enough to make me feel that I was falling again, just when I had thought I had reached the ground.

It was hard for me to understand too, but if anything explained it, then it was the intimacy of the written word. Writing late in the evening, effortlessly producing muscular paragraphs in which it seemed easy to find the right words to express thoughts and feelings that were rarely possible to see clearly, I had felt more myself than I usually felt in relationships that were dominated by conversation. It seemed to both of us, I think, that we had found a form of communication somewhere between thinking and speaking. The loss I now faced was the loss of the possibility of exposing myself and knowing that I'd be seen clearly, and loved disinterestedly and apparently unconditionally for what was seen. For those months, I had discovered that there were relationships in which faults became curiosities to be shared and mutually examined rather than judged, because it was taken as a given that the whole person was loveable. Because his gratitude for our unexpected connection had made me too conscious of giving pleasure to be grateful myself, I had realised how much all this had mattered to me only once it was gone.

I hoped now that I could find a way to experience on my own the pleasure in reading and writing that I missed so much with him. I wanted to turn my loneliness into the creative solitude I'd been remembering from adolescence. I spent several days compulsively reading and rereading *Martha Quest* and its sequel *A Proper Marriage*. Identifying with Lessing and Martha, reading too naively to differentiate between them, I was entering a contradictory state. I still yearned for another baby and found it painful when I encountered a mother leaning down with pleasurable familiarity to touch her baby's head, or was handed a baby to hold. I was still longing for emotional connection, either with my husband or with my dying friend. But in the absence of these possibilities, I was becoming more insistently drawn to the freedom that Martha discovers when she abandons her husband and children; I saw this as enabling an honesty that was becoming increasingly difficult for me in a life where I found it hard to talk about what I felt. So I allowed all my desires to converge in an urge for freedom. I wanted to escape husband, child and home and perhaps most of all to exchange the cramped London streets where I lived for the less constricting landscapes I'd walked in with my dying friend. I was yearning for the wide skies of East Anglia.

Periodically since having a child, I had left my husband and son at home and rented a cottage by the sea in which to write. It was always on the coast, which I had come to associate with the mental emptiness that for me was a large part of the pleasure of writing. This time, I went to Suffolk, where after arriving in the house I moved a desk to the window and sat looking out at the sea.

The brown, pebbled beach, the white-grey sky and the blue-grey water reminded me of the Welsh landscape I had spent all those hours staring at in my childhood. In Africa, Lessing gazed out on the deep reds and greens of an oil painting. I had spent much of my life looking out on to the subdued shades of a watercolour. But her descriptions of the bush still made more sense to me here than they did in the city. This was my 'myth-country'. It was the landscape I identified with endlessness: the horizon that was curtailed only because my eyes could see no further; the silence that was interrupted only by birds.

The sea started to flow south, drifting past me as though seen from a train window. My life at home now seemed far away. The missing baby and the missing friend felt like neither presences nor absences; they were floating, weightless, somewhere in the misty sky, along with all the emotions and thoughts that had been tangling insistently in my mind. I felt as though I had been there for years and would remain for years longer, not just for a week. I had been there for twenty-five years, since I had first looked out to sea and imagined that with each inward roll of the waves I was propelling myself further out, more a part of the life of the water than of the life taking place on the shore.

I didn't swim as a child. I only imagined it. My swimming, till I left home, took place in swimming pools. Swimming in the sea began later; began – coincidentally or not – shortly after sex, becoming a form of obsession, leading me to immerse myself in the water of any beautiful landscape I found myself in. Now, as much as ever, I felt the urge to plunge into it. I could imagine the feeling of the cold water on my skin, the sensation of my arms reaching forwards and my legs kicking behind me. But I had become lethargic. Thinking about adolescence had plunged me contentedly into the passive languor of those years. I fell asleep mid-sentence on the sofa, my computer on my lap. I gazed out apathetically at the drizzle, waiting for the sky to change colour, which it did when a storm came into view in the late afternoon.

The upper half of the sky was now swathed in dark grey, separated from the white strip below by a jagged line. The sea turned green, tapering into grey on the horizon, and the waves became more clearly defined, rolling towards me to break out of view, somewhere below the ridge of shingle. The rain stopped for a while and the sky whitened, now dotted with painterly clouds. I went out for a walk, wearing a cagoule that clashed with my skirt, enjoying adding to my sense of solitude by dressing badly, trying out invisibility as Lessing had in middle-age.

I walk fast when I'm alone, because I like watching the landscape rushing past, and because I like pushing my legs to the point where I can feel the muscles straining. Now I walked faster than usual because with every pace, away from the town, out along the seafront and then into the marshes, I was leaving the world further behind. I thought of Lessing, who paced up and down London at night when she lived there in her thirties and forties, longing for the bush. All her political campaigning in those years, her drive towards liberation of one kind and another, seemed to come out of that restless walking.

There was a middle-aged couple kissing on the seafront, their bodies blown towards each other by the wind. Usually I would instinctively imagine my way into the mind of the woman, grateful that love of this serious, mutually absorbing kind is not reserved for those younger than me. This time I walked past briskly, too detached from the world to identify with her, pleased that it had started to rain again and that my hair was sticking to my face as I walked, the fresh smell of the rain mingling with the salt of the sea.

It was not until the next morning that I ran outside, wearing the cagoule over my swimming costume to cross the shingle, and entered the water. I had closed the curtains at night and so there was an element of surprise in waking up to find that the sea was still there – a new confrontation with its vastness. In the early morning light the water sparkled; the beach was empty, the water colder than I had imagined. As I paddled awkwardly across the slippery pebbles, I told myself that it was better to leap forward into the waves than to ease in carefully, and then found that when I did this there were a few seconds when the cold was too preoccupying to experience my body immersed in a new element.

Then I was swimming, drawn out towards a horizon that seemed visible enough to be reachable, barely needing to move my arms and legs as I floated along on the outgoing tide. I turned to swim parallel to the shore, luxuriating in the freedom of weightlessness, observing my arms and hands as they moved through the water, which was more transparent than I had expected from its glittering surface. Warmer now, I drifted for some time, sure that the landscape seen from the sea was indeed the widest, freest landscape I had ever experienced. Turning to swim inland, I found that it required more strength to push against the tide and in towards the beach. As I thrust my arms and legs hard against the water like the oars of a boat, I took pleasure in my own strength, enjoying this experience of the body's power.

I thought of Doris Tayler first becoming aware of her body. She was standing in a corner of the bush with her rifle loose in her hands. She suddenly saw her legs – brown, slim, well shaped – as if for the first time and thought 'they are beautiful'. She pulled up her dress to her knickers to examine her thighs, filled with pride. 'There is no exultation like it,'

Lessing wrote looking back, 'the moment when a girl knows that *this* is her body, *these* her fine smooth shapely limbs'. This was the mood that I had regained and which Lessing describes so well: the sense of the whole body as expectantly sexual that somehow precludes the possibility of sex.

After a few days the sun came out and pulled me back into adult life. Spring had burst unexpectedly into a moment of early summer and the view from my window had become Mediterranean. Blue sky; turquoise sea; yellow beach. In the afternoon I put on a dress and walked along the seafront. It was filled with people and I was aware once more of myself in relation to them. For the first time since the miscarriage, I was conscious of the bodies of the men I passed, while willing them to be conscious of mine. In the afternoon light, my shadow had taken on the exaggeration of a sculpture, and I admired its elongated curves. At the end of the beach there was a sea wall, leading along the river. The grass was bright green now, and the water in the small pools beside me glistened. These could have been the vleis and long grasses of the African bush.

All too soon, it was time to leave. I was reluctant to return home because it involved leaving behind the strange adolescent freedom that I had recaptured. Arriving, I felt the usual flood of panicky relief on being reunited with my son, missing him more in retrospect than I had while I was away. But I also felt more than usually pressed in by the grubby Victorian houses that surrounded me and especially by our own house, which we'd moved into three years earlier intending soon to do building work that was delayed while we waited for my husband to complete the architectural plans.

He'd been progressing rapidly with these when I was pregnant and now had slowed down, so I was starting to feel resentful of the broken step and sagging bathroom floor, which could seem like they were intended to induce a retaliatory feeling of powerlessness. Most of the rooms were dark, with broken light circuits that we didn't bother to fix; the decoration in the sitting room had remained unchanged for forty years and I felt wrongly characterised by the aspiration of its crazily paved walls and chandeliers. None of this mattered when I was happy, and I frequently told myself that I was lucky to own a house at all. But the gloomy atmosphere and my inability to do anything about it added to my sense of passive stasis as I waited to become pregnant. I was also waiting to hear from my absent friend, who remained silent despite having returned home, apparently not wanting to be in touch with me. Seeking distraction from the growing feeling of emptiness, I found that I had a restless urge to seek out moments of connection with a complex constellation of friends and acquaintances. I enjoyed the excitement of transient intimacy – here, after all, was something that felt attuned to the freedom I was relentlessly investigating – while also longing for the restfulness of something more sustained.

I resolved that the following spring, after the rains had fallen and the grass had turned green again, I would go to the Highveld and locate the hill where Lessing's house once stood. For now, my attempt to understand freedom would have to remain cerebral; I would see what I could find in books. But next year I would walk across the plains she would crave for the rest of her life and would try to understand more about the nature of the freedom that is to be found in that flat emptiness of land and sky.

Lessing herself returned for that 1956 trip, leaving behind the confines of a London street much like my own. She was consumed by a need for the bush that had become a fever, 'latent always in [the] blood'. And when she stepped outside on her first night back in Southern Rhodesia, she found that the fever was at last assuaged. Standing in the rich red earth, looking up at the stars, she felt in touch with the soil and its creatures once more; lost in 'this infinite exchange of earth and sky'. Surrendering herself to the physical experience of freedom, she saw that her own utopian politics had been born out of this land, conceivable only because of the wild, boundless possibilities of adolescent reverie. 'Because it is so empty we can dream,' she wrote; 'we can dream of cities and a civilisation more beautiful than anything that has been seen in the world before.'

2

'She was free. Free!'

Womanhood

'My fourteenth was a make or break year, a sink or swim year, a do or die year, for I was fighting for my life against my mother.' This was a struggle to escape the blinkers of childhood, the constricting doom of the farm and the disappointment of her parents. It was a fight for freedom that was as physical as it was mental, and it included an effort to forge herself as a sexual being. Her legs pushed their way restlessly out of the house and into the world beyond; her breasts burst out of the tight garments of childhood. There's a furious energy in those images, as there is in her charging around the veld. Now she was on the point of abandoning the bush and seeking freedom in sex instead. But she was looking again for a form of physical freedom that could offer an escape from body and mind. And she was pursuing it with all the pent-up, restless vigour of adolescence.

After my return from Suffolk, I found that I was thinking a lot about my early sexual experiences, as well as Lessing's, and was wondering what relation they'd had to those adolescent walks along the beach. I was interested in the way that sex had led, with a relative swiftness that was more surprising given my time and place, to marriage, which surely I couldn't have expected to be any more freeing than she did, when she married at the age of nineteen. It was beginning to strike me how much my irritation with weddings was compounded by my perplexity at my own decision to get married in my mid-twenties. It wasn't that I was wondering why I had married this particular man, but that I was wondering why I'd got married at all at that point, given that I'd considered myself a feminist and was not even ready to have children.

Reading about Lessing's marriage made me realise that for her at least, marriage had offered a form of liberation. This, though, seemed to be a very different kind of freedom from the expansive weightlessness she sought in sex: something more like escape from constraint. In her case – and could this also have been true for me? – it was a chance to escape from her mother and from a life in which she was still defined more as a daughter than a woman. I was becoming particularly interested in the ways that the freedom of rebellion, conducted through sex and then through marriage, was related to but also at odds with the physical freedom of the sexual act.

For the adolescent Doris, the new stage of generational conflict began with illness. An attack of conjunctivitis at her convent left her claiming that she could no longer see properly. Surprisingly, her mother permitted her to drop out altogether. Returning home, Doris came down with a persistent fever and was sent to the mountains where, away from the battle with her mother, she recovered. Here she was given her first bra: a trophy of expectant womanhood that she wore proudly on her return, even after her outraged mother lifted her dress to reveal it to her embarrassed father, demanding that he should share her disapproval. Doris decided that from now on she would resist her mother's need to infantalise her daughter. Each week, she walked into town through the bush, carrying guineafowl that she'd shot. With the money given to her by the butcher, she bought material to make her own dresses.

Exulting in her own body in the bush, Doris was beginning to dream about sex. The feeling she describes is a liberating one. It's a symbol of the life denied by her mother. What was most interesting for me was that it seemed to open up the possibility of a new kind of epiphany that was related to the endlessness she encountered in the veld.

Looking back, Doris Lessing recommended controversially that some girls ought to be put to bed at the age of fourteen with men ten years older than they were, with the understanding that this 'apprentice love' would end. Hearts might be broken, but they were broken anyway; it would be a distraction from school, but this 'paragon of a loving mentor' would insist on homework being done. Her suggestion was unlikely to catch on in 1990s London, where she was writing her autobiography. But she was convinced that she'd inherited the longing of her sexually unfulfilled father and that this had left her in a dangerous trance from which she needed to be awakened.

The opportunity for both escape and sexual discovery was provided by a job working for the Salisbury telephone exchange. Although the work was boring, it brought a new independent life, dancing and drinking with the youth of the aggressively colonial Sports Club; a life of sundowners, hangovers and insistent communal frivolity. Lessing doesn't describe the moment when she lost her virginity in her autobiography, instead moving straight from isolated self-love to sex with her husband. Nine years later, she casually wrote to her lover John Whitehorn that she had been 'raped the first time (well practically)'. The briskly exaggerated tone of the rest of the letter makes it hard to take this claim seriously, but it suggests a troubling encounter. In *Martha Quest*, which is at its most directly autobiographical in describing this period of Martha/Doris's life, Martha loses her virginity almost by accident to a Jew called Adolph, whom she has befriended partly as a protest against the anti-Semitism of her Sports Club friends. Elsewhere she informed Whitehorn that her early sexual experiences were gained (like Martha's) with 'nice boys who wouldn't have sex' but wanted to fool around in cars, and a Jewish man who would, but then wanted to marry her.

Adolph taunts Martha by insisting that she will not go to bed with him. Defensively, she replies that there's no reason why she should not. He places her on the bed, kisses her more curiously than passionately, and carefully removes his clothes, folding them up in a pile. Martha lies passively waiting, wanting to avert her eyes from this unromantic spectacle but determined not to appear a prude. Adolph makes love to her 'using the forms of sensitive experience' in a manner both reassuring and chilling that leaves her mind untouched. While he's occupied with her body, she spends her time reconceiving the disappointing act to fit her imaginative ideal. Martha's hope for sex is that 'the quintessence of all experience, all love, all beauty, should explode suddenly in a drenching, saturating moment of illumination'. When this fails to happen, she reimagines it as a more exalted experience while waiting expectantly for another lover who will enable the illumination to occur.

I

'A drenching, saturating moment of illumination'?

Sex

Sixty years later, my hopes and disappointment when I lost my virginity were as extreme as Doris Tayler's. What is perhaps most surprising is that I knew little more than she did. Before she had sex for the first time, she had read a 1928 sex manual entitled *Ideal Marriage: Its Physiology and Technique* by the severely named Th. H. Van de Velde, M.D., a Dutch gynaecologist. Tracking down a battered copy of this book almost ninety years after its publication, I found it surprising in both its open-mindedness and its detail.

Starting with the premise that most marriages fail because of the sexual inadequacy of one or both spouses, Van de Velde reasonably suggests that marriage as an institution may have had its day. However, given that marriage is well suited for the raising of children, he thinks that it's worth trying harder at it, and offers instructions on how to do so. The 'ideal marriage' of his title is a relationship in which the spouses enjoy simultaneous orgasms easily, frequently, and in a variety of positions. They do this during pregnancy and almost immediately after childbirth; they do it even when tired, because both are adept at arousing the other through imaginative foreplay.

This is extensive knowledge. It's advice that would come in useful for many of us now. But Lessing told John Whitehorn that she had 'combined the most profound knowledge of technical details about sex with the most extraordinary innocence', suggesting that theoretical information does not lessen inexperience. The reader of Van de Velde's book knows that she can vary her sensation of pleasure by adjusting the position of her legs and buttocks, and knows too that through sex her soul can 'meet and merge' with the soul of her lover in ecstatic bliss. But it's hard to understand in advance exactly how these aspects of the experience will relate to each other, and this doesn't seem a problem that knowledge can solve. Indeed, even now, with so much pornography and technical knowledge easily available, it's possible to have no idea what sex will actually feel like.

'The first time I was kissed with an exploring tongue I was shocked and revolted beyond words,' Lessing wrote to Whitehorn, though she would have learnt from Van de Velde that 'from its lightest, faintest form', the erotic kiss could 'run the gamut of intimacy and intensity to the pitch of *Maraichinage*, in which the couple, sometimes for hours, mutually explore and caress the inside of each other's mouths with their tongues, as profoundly as possible'. It seems likely that the exploring tongue that entered Doris's mouth was less erotically sensitive than that of Van de Velde's ideal lover. Martha Quest finds her head bent back by a succession of men from the Sports Club in a 'thrusting, teeth-bared kiss' that is followed by an awkward apology, as though each kiss is a 'small ceremony of hatred'. My own memories of early kisses are more reminiscent of the revolving washing machine than of a profound caress. And my loss of virginity came in three stages, all in retrospect unsatisfactory.

At eighteen I too looked to sex for a freeing epiphany. I wished to escape childhood with its awkwardness and its constraint, and I hoped – though it was only now that I realised this – to find the kind of physical boundlessness I had experienced staring at the sea. Yet this background of romantic longing was combined with a wilful ignorance about the practical aspects of sex that was unusual for my generation, and which I now found rather embarrassing. Even my self-love was less easily erotic than that of the young Doris. At the time when Lessing was writing her account of the sexual needs of fourteen-year-old girls, I was fourteen and living around the corner from her in north London. It would have been easier for me to find a ravager than it was for her, but the idea would have horrified me. Unlike her, it would be a few years before I became an avid reader of D.H. Lawrence. I found him frightening in his insistent maleness and derived my erotic stimulation from the less embodied writing of Charlotte and Emily Brontë. For reasons that remain shadowy for me now, I was alienated from my body. I didn't investigate its crevices and I did not exult in the changes of adolescence. I was surprised and impressed later to discover that in their early teens one of my school friends had taught another to masturbate. I didn't attempt to do so until the third in a succession of pairs of inexpertly roving hands finally prompted my curiosity.

The first set of hands belonged to a boy I had kissed at a party, three days before my eighteenth birthday. He was not especially enticing but I wished, coldly, to gain experience so that it would seem more possible to go to bed with the boy who was. I could therefore hardly blame him for the lack of passion though, unlike Martha, I made no attempt to blend reality and fantasy. There were the rotating tongues, his acrid with cigarette smoke, mine moving obediently in response to his. There was a hand on my breast, dutifully accepted though I felt nothing in response. We repeated the experience a week later and I was taken to his parents' empty flat. Business-like, we negotiated how far we would go: I allowed him to roam freely around my body, though I kept my knickers on; I had very little interest in touching him. After a desultory half hour, I zipped up my dress and returned home to my virginal teenage room, unmoved by the experience but pleased nonetheless with my progress.

Where was my erotic feeling located? Those fantasies about Mr Rochester remained arousing, producing a kind of all-over longing that left me wanting to be thrown on to a bed, looked at, touched. I now yearned to be flown across the desert by the Ralph Fiennes of *The English Patient*. Sex with him in that vast, empty landscape had become my ideal of embodied freedom. But these imaginings evoked the hands and eyes of clothed, grown-up men and I felt nothing but squeamish horror about the unwillingly imagined naked bodies of the boys I encountered in daily life. My most authentic desire at this stage was for an older girl at school, who had now gone on to university: I could long more graphically for soft skin, for breast touching breast. We kissed, and perhaps this could have led to a full erotic awakening, but she disappeared, leaving me to seek out the second pair of inexpert male hands.

This time I was at least half in love with the boy in question and it should have been more promising. However, because I was now keen to impress him, I was too anxious to admit my own inexperience. The result was an abortive encounter in his college room. The foreplay I recall as minimal. A condom was produced. I kept my hands primly on his shoulders and he attempted to penetrate me, only to find that I was determinedly clenched. Eventually he gave up, discarded the condom and went off in search of a kitchen or bathroom. From the corridor, I heard him say 'it didn't work' to a male friend who had enquired about our progress. For me, this was the humiliation of failure. After that, I avoided him and focused on my A levels: here at least were tests I knew I could pass.

Van de Velde helpfully instructs his would-be lovers that 'local (genital) stimulation, to the accompaniment of kisses and words of love, with a crescendo of emotion, whose most effective instrument is the *exchange of manipulation*, continues

and accelerates itself till the male member, or *phallos*, is introduced into the vagina'. I have no idea if my suitor attempted
such subtle manoeuvrings but it seems quite possible that
I played my part in resisting them if he did. Certainly, I
experienced nothing like arousal, and still had no idea of what
anything resembling an orgasm might feel like. When actually
confronted by a boy, I seem to have been incapable of feeling
my way into my body and its wants, and I was disturbed by
the otherness of his body. I think that even with this sensitive,
poetry-writing undergraduate, my desire to have his penis
inside me was primarily a desire to ascend another rung in the
ladder towards adulthood. I enjoyed wearing pretty dresses for
him and wanted to be admired, but there was a coyness to it: I
was frightened of igniting his desire, unable to see any connection between his erection and the imagined, more consuming
longing of Ralph Fiennes or Mr Rochester.

It took a third boy, gentler and slightly more experienced,
to engage in an 'exchange of manipulation' sufficient to arouse
me enough for the male member to be introduced. By now
I had left home for university so these encounters took place
in my college room, surrounded by Victorian furniture and
pre-Raphaelite prints. My childhood was over and adult life
seemed triumphantly to have begun. After our first exploratory encounter on his bed, I went back to my own room
and masturbated, amazed by the possibilities of my body that
had been revealed. But though I had gentle clitoral orgasms
with the boy in question for the next few months, it would
be a few years before I could experience a 'crescendo of emotion' that in any way approximated the feeling of freedom
or before I could enjoy the otherness of the male body and
experience my own arousal as a response to the desire I was
evoking in a lover.

If one of the central conundrums in *The Golden Notebook* is that even liberated heterosexual women are dependent on men to arouse desire, then this is a contradiction it took me many years to understand and a contradiction destined to trouble us more as we become more insistently egalitarian. Van de Velde's ideal lover is not a man with much interest in equality. He understands sexual bliss and sees it as his role to initiate his wife into the art of lovemaking, expecting it to be some time before she plays an equal role. Their pleasure is going to be partly the result of this disjunction. In a passage that might not be out of place if found in *The Golden Notebook*, Van de Velde asserts that 'what both man and woman, driven by obscure primitive urges, wish to feel in the sexual act, is the essential force of *maleness*, which expresses itself in a sort of violent and absolute *possession* of the woman'.

This is not the lesson taken away by Martha and her lovers, though Van de Velde's book circulates around the Sports Club. Lessing observes in *Martha Quest* that 'at least two generations of rebels have gone armed to the combat with books on sex to give them the assurance they did not feel'. For both Martha and the men around her, 'making love when and how they pleased was positively a flag of independence in itself', yet they find that by determining to make it a straightforward and equal act they fail to make the potentially frightening journey into the unknown that might make it freeing. I think this was part of the problem for me. In taking charge of my own sexual education, I failed to feel anything like the more unconscious, passive desire that I was feeling in response to books and films.

Why did both Lessing and I expect sex to offer instant and ecstatic freedom – that 'drenching, saturating moment of illumination'? It must be partly because politically the notion of liberation is connected in Western societies to sexual freedom, and has been since Doris Tayler was succumbing to the toothy embraces of the Sports Club boys. This is freedom as that restless striving away from restraint she described so well; as a move away from the confines of childhood into liberated womanhood. But both she and I expected sex to involve the second sense of freedom as well. For her, the orgasm as mutual epiphany was meant to be existentially as well as politically freeing. For me, the feeling of being swept into male longing was meant to involve an escape from the mind into the expectant body that would feel like roaming freely through the imagined desert.

II

'A damned wedding ring'

Marriage and pregnancy

For Lessing, sex was followed, even more swiftly than it was for me, by marriage. She seems to have known at the time that this marriage was unlikely to make her feel free. Certainly, this is how she portrays it for Martha Quest, who is conjugally tied at the same age as her creator. Asked a few months later why she decided to get married, Martha replies that it was because of the impending war. Drugged by dance music and by the strange allure of the bloodbath about to ensue, she lost all sense of personal volition, convinced that it could not matter one way or another what she decided to do. In her autobiography, Lessing describes this as a 'numbness, a kind of chloroform', resembling the feeling of being eaten by a lion. But this wasn't the only reason. Marriage offered a form of escape; it was a chance to leave her parents and the farm behind for good. She was also probably more motivated than she would later admit by love.

At twenty-nine, Frank Wisdom was ten years older than her; an English civil servant and Sports Club stalwart who seemed to share both Doris's exaltation in her body and her progressive opinions. He was prepared as she was for good-natured and egalitarian sex and a good-natured and egalitarian marriage. Together they read copies of the *New Statesman* and complained about racial discrimination ('the colour bar'). Their wedding in April 1939 was delightfully drunken and informal; they even took some of their friends on their honeymoon.

Frank didn't succeed in making Doris feel any less constrained than she had felt in her parents' house. Talking and having sex with Frank, only part of her mind was engaged. She had now made explicit her long-standing secret assumption that she was going to be a writer and the thought itself offered a form of liberation, bringing both the promise of a new kind of self-realisation and the chance to escape inwardly from the narrow assumptions of her world. But Frank, although he ostensibly supported her literary ambitions, could not understand her writerly self; there was a part of her that she later described as being kept 'in cold storage' for a man capable of knowing her better. So too – and perhaps most tellingly – Frank took her away from the bush.

In *Martha Quest*, it's driving home with Douglas to the farm that Martha appreciates for the first time the particular quality of limitlessness she has found in the veld. The narrator observes that 'this frank embrace between the lifting breast of the land, the deep blue warmth of the sky, is what exiles from Africa dream of' and that it's possible to sicken for it even if you still live in Africa. In the city, Martha has forgotten the 'infinite exchange of earth and sky'. So it's now, married and trapped in another life that doesn't fit her, that she starts to miss it.

Perhaps marriage could have been freer for her than it was. Perhaps she just chose the wrong man. But the problem with looking to marriage as a state in which you will feel free is that, if the experience of freedom is essentially an embodied one, the body is trapped by a marriage in which there's the expectation of pregnancy. And when Doris Wisdom married, she didn't have any choice about this. The contraceptive possibilities on offer were still extremely limited so they stopped sex from being freeing.

In *A Proper Marriage* (1954), Martha feels 'caged and trapped' with Douglas because her body is no longer her own. As they battle together with installing her diaphragm and washing her vagina out afterwards, she finds that her husband has somehow earned the right to question her about her periods. Once when he interrogates her, she looks outside and sees the big wheel in the town revolving 'like a damned wedding ring'.

For both Martha and her creator, the threat of pregnancy is the threat of entrapment. Looking at her pregnant friend Alice, Martha feels caged on her behalf. Sensing the bonds tightening, she deliberately shakes them off and exults in 'the thought that she was free. Free!' At the same time, she envies Alice the 'private world of sensation' that pregnancy brings, curious as to whether there's a new possibility of freedom to be found in no longer caring about the world outside her body.

When Doris Wisdom discovered shortly after marrying that she was pregnant, she immediately sought an abortion. The world was too dangerous to bring children into and she was terrified of being subsumed by motherhood. In the summer of 1939, she travelled alone by train to the dirty consulting room of a young Johannesburg doctor who sang and danced drunkenly as she waited for her operation. A woman took her into the kitchen to warn her that the doctor had been struck off the Medical Register for wielding his scalpel when inebriated. Doris returned home where her regular doctor informed her that the foetus was already four and a half months old. She spent the next month sitting on the sofa, feeling the child quickening inside her stomach, filled with contempt for the British government as it played for time by appeasing Hitler. On the day that war was declared, she and Frank were having lunch with friends on a farm just outside Salisbury. She responded with anger that also contained an element of exaltation; this was the disaster she had been preparing for all her life.

Lessing later claimed that the experiences of pregnancy and childbirth in the Martha Quest novels were autobiographical. When I read them now, I found I was reading those scenes as a form of memoir. When Martha realises that she is pregnant, she becomes consumed by the tension she has felt in looking at Alice. She enjoys the new feeling of inwardness, absorbed in monitoring the development of the creature inside her. But she remains an anxious observer of herself, determined that she – 'the free spirit' – should not be implicated. And she resents the gradual thickening of her body. In this state, the foetus itself becomes an 'imprisoned thing moving inside her flesh', though she assures it that she will do all she can to ensure its freedom, promising it that 'no pressure would deform it, freedom would be its gift'.

Martha has started to use the word 'freedom' explicitly here. Perhaps Doris Wisdom herself had started to by now as well. Either way, whether consciously or unconsciously, the answer to constriction is the freedom of the veld, reencountered as a bodily sensation. Keen to escape the limits of their houses, Martha and Alice go for a drive in the rain. At the edge of the city they come to a field, where they emerge from the car and strip naked, launching their pregnant bodies into the saturated grass. Alice vanishes with a shout of exultation and Martha runs through the mud, screaming in triumph as her hair becomes a 'sodden mat' over her eyes and the rain drenches her shoulders and breasts in 'a myriad hard, stinging needles'. She jumps into a pothole where she stands knee deep in the thick, red clay of the veld.

Alone under the thunder, she encounters a frog, who sits staring at her, and a snake sliding down over the pulpy mud. She touches the 'crouching infant' in her womb, who now seems to have taken its place in nature, beside the creatures from the bush. This is the moment of Martha's spiritual return to the veld: the moment when, writing in a London suburb where she was yearning increasingly urgently for the sight, sound and smell of the bush in the rain, Lessing allowed myth country to infuse the actuality of Martha's adult life. Afterwards, though Martha and Alice are embarrassed about the mud on their skin, Martha feels relieved by this moment of escape. 'There was no doubt they were both free and comfortable in their minds, their bodies felt relaxed and tired.'

I was twenty-five when my husband proposed; he was thirty-five. We were in a garden full of follies, away for a weekend to celebrate our fourth anniversary. It was raining and I had a bad cold of the kind that left me in a sea of fog and made it tiring to support my own weight. I leaned against him on a bridge and he kissed me. 'Will you marry me?' he asked. It took a while for the question to filter through and when it did I worried that I didn't have the energy to rise to the occasion. I couldn't tell if this was an actual proposal and half hoped it was the kind of speculative conversation couples have in bed: 'when we are married'; 'when we have children'; 'when we are old'.

'Are you serious?' I asked. He was.

'One day,' I said, buying time, fearing the future as it swept into view.

It turned out that he had speculatively bought a ring. Here indeed was seriousness. I was touched by the image of him in the shop, choosing stones, guessing the width of my finger, both because of its vulnerability and because of the change of mind it represented. He'd lived with another woman for ten years and refused to get married. Now something had shifted; he had come to believe, he said, in romantic love. It was moving to think that I'd led so resolutely rational a man to succumb to the romance of marriage and I found that I wanted to be able to make a similar leap of faith myself. Always enthusiastic about organising parties, I started a conversation about where we might get married.

Looking back, it had begun to seem as absurd to me as it later did to Lessing that I should have joined my contemporaries in lining up so eagerly at the altar. Shortly after my return from Suffolk, I interrogated my husband about it, asking what had changed for him to make him so conventional. One evening, out for a rare dinner without our son, I turned a would-be romantic meal into a cross-questioning of this kind and was reassured by his hard-headedness.

He explained that he had wanted to get married because he'd thought that if we were going to live together as though we were married, it was deceptive to pretend that we were free. We should be gracious in allowing those around us to witness us relinquishing our freedom, while at the same time telling ourselves that this need not be permanent: we could always reverse it if we wished.

This was an explanation that many wives might have found problematically unromantic. It belied my memory of him declaring a newly found belief in romantic love. But I found it reassuring because it suggested that we could still communicate and that we remained united in the insistent rationality that would have shocked many of our friends; the sometimes sardonic rationality that often made Doris Lessing seem closer in outlook to me than I found many of the people I met. At the same time, it left me disappointed.

As I tried to analyse the disappointment, I decided that it must be partly because of the lack of romance it suggested ten years earlier; because I, like Lessing, longed to move through rationality into a Lawrentian state where the soul could be drenched in the darkness of passion. But more fundamentally, it was a disappointment in us as a couple, because it now seemed that we could have been having conversations of this kind for years. It made me aware of how many of my thoughts I kept to myself, not trusting him to understand them; aware that the thoughts I had found such relief in describing to my still absent dying friend had been thoughts that years earlier I might well have described to my husband. It felt as though it might be marriage itself that made this kind of intimacy so difficult.

What my husband did not know, when I accepted his invitation to wear his ring, was that I was not agreeing immediately to have his babies. Somehow we did not explicitly have that conversation. At twenty-six, I may have been ready to declare love in front of all my friends, but I was not ready to succumb to a life of nappies, poverty and exhaustion. More fundamentally, I was not ready to give up my identity and become someone else, which I saw motherhood as necessarily entailing. I assumed that he knew this. He just as reasonably assumed that in agreeing to get married, I was embarking contentedly on a path towards family life.

Sex at least was freer for my generation than for Lessing's. We had the Pill; there was no danger of accidental impregnation. After a few years of practice, I was starting to find that orgasms could indeed provide the illumination that she and I had hoped for. I had discovered that I was less egalitarian than I might have imagined, learning the pleasures of surrendering to that 'essential force of *maleness*, which expresses itself in a sort of violent and absolute *possession* of the woman' celebrated by Van de Velde.

I remember in particular a long night in my husband's flat, a year or so into the relationship, lying on the mattress on the floor he was using as a bed. The setting was appropriate for sexual abandon: a scene without the comforts of domesticity, which allowed us to be bodies encountering each other, away from the world. For the first time, I had one orgasm after another in a kind of trance, each one propelling me into a state of greater arousal. We were both surprised by it. I think that for me, this was the discovery of the importance of sex as a bodily act. I was learning that it could send you into a separate, quite other place, making your lover, confronted back in the world you have left, a person half-unknown.

I had discovered sex, but pregnancy seemed no less restrictive to me than it did to Doris Wisdom, though it no longer necessarily took women away from the working world. This meant that marriage with the expectation of pregnancy quickly came to feel constricting as well. I was sure that motherhood would change me and I wanted to wait until I was ready to change. George Eliot, Virginia Woolf, Elizabeth Bowen, Iris Murdoch: very few of the writers I admired had had children. I needed to delay motherhood until I was more confidently myself and was ready to soften, to lose the mental clarity I prided myself on. Prosaically, unless I had a permanent academic job and therefore knew that I had work to go back to, I could not see pregnancy as anything other than a trap that would stop me writing. Without a salary, it would be hard to justify the childcare I'd need in order to claim time to write. And though I would not have used this language at the time, I knew that I needed to write in order to feel free, or at least in order not to feel claustrophobic and lost.

Eventually, I would discover that pregnancy itself could feel freeing. When pregnant with my son, I was surprised by how little it changed me, mentally. This was because I was determined that it should not do so. Partly because I couldn't really believe that this swelling inside my body really constituted a burgeoning separate person, I did not imagine or celebrate the baby boy whose emergence it was supposed to herald. As my body grew and the midwives commended me on my progress, I felt nothing resembling liberation. There was pride at the new achievement. And there was frustration at the dwindling daily possibilities.

It had therefore been a revelation to discover that the brief pregnancy that ended in the miscarriage made me feel free in a way that the pregnancy with my son had not. This was an escape inwards of the kind that Lessing describes so well in her account of Alice's and Martha's pregnancies; a retreat into a form of embodiment that was experienced from within and that left me impervious to the workings of the outside world. Here was a new kind of liberation, gained through renunciation of other desires. It's a sensation that is hard to remember when you are not experiencing it: a feeling of limbs floating irrelevantly around a tiny growth that's more real and more alive than the flesh that encases it; of secret knowledge and secret love for a small imagined creature, protected by your body. Everything around you feels irrelevant and this state, created by a man, seems to have little to do with the man in question. Once again you are alone, free, contemplating your body like Doris Tayler in the bush.

III

'The wound inside my body which I didn't choose to have'

Bleeding

That summer, as the miscarriage receded into the past, I found myself ambivalent when confronting pregnant women. I envied them the inwardness that I imagined they must be feeling, wishing that it was my hand that was perched, self-satisfied, on the protruding bulge. But at the same time, I felt superior in my litheness, enjoying the speed of my movements. I appreciated my ability to suck in my stomach and stand comfortably with a glass of wine in my hand, tempting their husbands towards freedom, reminding the men that there were still women who existed alongside them in the everyday world while their wives retreated further into themselves.

And yet I continued to want more than anything to conceive a child. So I was distressed in June when, for the second month in a row, my period arrived five days after ovulation instead of the usual fourteen. I had what is known as a short luteal phase, and read that I would probably not be able to get pregnant until it was lengthened.

I asked my husband for sympathy, but he was the wrong person to go to because the news came as a blow to him as well, and at some level he blamed me for the delay, because we could have been doing all this years earlier.

'Will it be all right next time?' I asked, willing him to say yes.

'Probably not,' he said, and the possibility for mutual comfort was lost. I now felt that it was my responsibility to look after him, only as he was not a man prepared to be looked after, it was more a question of showing what seemed to be a mixture of contrition and gratitude, though it was not quite clear for what: contrition for my inadequacy? gratitude for his patience, in waiting for me and not moving on to fulfil his biological function elsewhere? Certainly I felt the urge to please him. Sex seemed inappropriate; it had started to seem distasteful to initiate it when there was blood present, reminding us that it couldn't be procreative. Instead I shopped and cooked for him. I thought of Anna Wulf, cooking that escalope in order to regain love and desire, or perhaps more in order to regain her own ability to love and desire.

Menstrual pain for me often takes the form of a hamster, eating its way forwards into my stomach, backwards into the lower part of my back. Lying in bed as I waited for it to cease its munching, I thought again of Anna Wulf, who describes her period at some length during the same twenty-page extended diary entry where she recounts cooking the escalope for Michael. Restlessly, I went back to those pages, seeking the company of Anna once again.

Lessing claimed in her autobiography that she had been unaffected by her periods, which had been light and manageable. *The Golden Notebook* seems to belie this in its disgusted insistence on the inescapability of menstrual blood. Anna discovers that her period has started when changing the sheets on her bed. Depositing the sex-stained linen in the basket, she notices blood and checks the dates in her diary. Now she feels tired and irritable, because she knows that 'these feelings accompany my period'. Wondering if she should avoid recording this day out of shame and modesty, she decides that these are inappropriate emotions for a writer and that she must describe herself installing a tampon. She becomes conscious of the drag in her lower belly and worries about exuding the 'faintly dubious, essentially stale smell of menstrual blood'.

At work, she pours jugs of warm water between her legs. She becomes irritable with her colleagues and realises that her period has made her feel 'helpless and out of control'. Returning home, she finds that her instinct to protect her daughter is more powerful than usual and knows that this is because she needs to cling to somebody herself. Then begins the laborious process of cooking for her lover, during which she imagines their evening. They will eat and smoke cigarettes; he will take her in his arms. 'When I have my period,' she observes, 'I rest on the knowledge that Michael will love me, at night; it takes away the resentment against the wound inside my body which I didn't choose to have. And then we will sleep together, all night.'

Her need for comfort is a need beyond sex of a kind that cannot any longer be assuaged by her lover. It is his failure to give this comfort that leads her finally to acknowledge to herself that he is in the process of leaving her. Anna is imprisoned by her body in this scene. She's frustrated by her sense that her emotions are created by the hormonal shifts of the menstrual cycle and frustrated by the resulting neediness.

Reading Anna's account, I became more conscious both of my own irritation – the rage I could feel hovering beneath every encounter with my husband, even as I tried to please him – and of the stale smell of darkened blood. I was using sanitary towels instead of tampons. This hadn't been a deliberate decision, but it seemed that I wanted to remain aware of myself bleeding.

There have been times when women were shunned when menstruating. Pliny complained that contact with menstrual blood turned new wine sour, while 'crops touched by it become barren, grass dies'. These sentiments usually seemed to me outrageous. I'd been disturbed to find in Van de Velde a passage that may have been partly responsible for Lessing's later disgust where he complains about the 'unwholesome and repulsive' odour of stale menstrual blood and recommends 'frequent and fastidious' changes of underclothing to women, while warning that even their breath and sweat would smell unusually unpleasant at this time. Surely sex is in fact perfectly compatible with menstruation, which only brings one more fluid to the mix? This time, however, it seemed reasonable and even desirable that I should retreat into a cave until the hamster had completed its excavation of my womb.

I found that I was wearing dark woolly clothes, though it was a warm June. Seeing grey hairs glistening in the mirror, I didn't pluck them out as I would usually do; they seemed fitting for my current state of mind. I wondered, thinking of Lessing, if this was a preview of the menopause – this feeling of anxious defiance in the absence of a sexual function. But it also enabled a return to the invisibility of adolescence. It brought back the feeling of confinement and helplessness that was so much a part of those years, because the future seemed in my failure to become pregnant to be turning into something I could not control. It also brought back memories of years when I, unlike Doris Tayler, was not always sure I wanted to be looked at.

The sanitary towels reminded me of periods from my schooldays, evoking years of spots and grease. Perhaps I needed to recover my disgust about menstruation to understand my early squeamishness about sex. It's problematic for adolescent girls that the change that makes sex more likely is so unpleasant. For me the blood and pain had so little to do with my early romantic sexual imaginings that it turned my erotic imagination away from the body into a more abstract realm. This perhaps was more true than she remembered for Doris Tayler as well, given her sustained disgust at menstrual blood. Her first period was an awkward moment that resulted in her mother triumphantly showing her first stained sanitary towel to her father, unable to provide Doris with physical privacy because she could only see her daughter's body as an extension of her own.

It seemed that for sex to be freeing we needed to transcend biology; or at least that this was the case for both Lessing and me. Sex is freer when you eliminate the possibility of conception; when you are no longer trapped by a monthly cycle that makes you anxious either because you are trying to prevent or to encourage the egg from implanting in your womb. In my case, my body generally felt freer when I eliminated periods altogether. I'd had years on the contraceptive pill where I ran on one packet to another and was never troubled by that malodorous hamster.

Yet Van de Velde does admit that there are some men – 'certainly a very small minority' – who are attracted to menstrual blood; some men and some women who are able to incorporate it into the state of arousal. The friend in whose garden I pondered my continued virginity at the age of eighteen now claimed that all female creativity stemmed from our lunar menstrual cycles and found it perplexing that I had managed to write during my years when the Pill filled me with chemicals and rid me altogether of that unwilling wound. Does freedom lie in escaping biology or in succumbing to it? In having sex or avoiding it? For me, as for Doris Wisdom, it was not enough to leave girlhood behind. Womanhood did not generously proffer the freedom it had promised.

3

'I'm setting you free'

Escape

A woman takes her daughter on to her lap, knowing that she's doing so for the last time. She feels as though this three-year-old girl is the only person really to understand her. Touching the small round knees and dimpled arms, she's pleased because the girl is too active to remain seated. For a few seconds, she holds the 'energetic and vibrant little creature' tight and then whispers in a flush of tenderness, 'You'll be perfectly free, Caroline. I'm setting you free.'

When I first decided to turn my preoccupation with Lessing into a book, I knew that the moment would come when I had to confront her leaving her children. It quickly became tiresome how many people mentioned it. Often, it was the first thing they said. 'Wasn't she a monster? Didn't she leave her children? Could you do that?'

I wanted to stand up for her, and found there were various ways of doing it. I could point to all the men who'd abandoned children along the way, and whom we didn't generally judge as monsters. Augustus John, Lucian Freud, John

Rodker, Michael Hoffman. I could point out the impossibility of the time in which she lived – a time when mothers could expect very little fulfilment from any other sphere. Sometimes I quoted Angela Carter in *The Sadeian Woman*: 'a free woman in an unfree society will be a monster.' Or I reflected that she may well have sacrificed her children for their own good. Even if he'd let her do so, she wouldn't have been able to leave her husband, take them with her and offer any kind of stability to the children as a single mother. But I found that as I gave these reasonable explanations, I was still trying to get my head round it all myself; still trying to work out how the love that I was convinced she'd felt for those children could have coincided with such ruthlessness. And I was confronting the worry that in defending her, I was somehow a monster as well.

It was now July. I was conscious of the oddness of wanting, more than anything, to become pregnant, at the same time as wanting to empathise as fully as possible with a woman who'd become pregnant easily, only to abandon the children she'd conceived. I was conscious, too, of distrusting her explanations. That scene where Martha sets Caroline free in *A Proper Marriage* is absurd, and the narrator half mocks her for it. By the time that Lessing wrote it, she was no longer sufficiently committed to communism to believe that she'd set her children free, any more than I did. Forty years later in her autobiography, Lessing wrote another version of the scene, no more convincing than the first one. Here she recalled explaining her need to leave home to her children John (aged three) and Jean (aged one and a half). She recollected assuring them that as adults they would understand why she has disappeared. 'I was going to change this ugly world, they would live in a beautiful and perfect world where there would be no race hatred, injustice and so forth'. With that 'so forth' she mocked the ideals that motivated her at the time. But she still seemed to believe the larger point, that she was somehow bound to destroy these children. She went on to report telling them that she needed to break the chain of doom that she carried with her like a defective gene. If she stayed, this would trap them as it had trapped her.

'I did not feel guilty,' Lessing insisted here. But did she feel free? Can freedom come from slamming a door and discarding the parts of your life that constrain you? Do marriage and motherhood necessarily preclude freedom and did she really think that her children were freer without their imperfect mother? Can motherhood bring the possibility of freedom in its own right? It was time to live through those intense early years of motherhood alongside her.

I

'Do I love her?'

Motherhood

Doris Wisdom gave birth to her son John in the Lady Chancellor Nursing Home during the night of 13 February 1940. When she arrived, the nurse told her that there was a problematic number of babies being born and instructed her to look after herself. Her husband, in line with most expectant fathers at this time, sidled off to drink with 'the boys'.

In the birth scene in *A Proper Marriage* (apparently an accurate portrait of this night) Martha begins her labour in the bath, her body shot through with the pain of the contractions. Clambering out, she glimpses in the mirror 'a fat,

69

bedraggled shining-faced slut with a look of frowning concentration'. She puts on make-up and combs her hair, before dragging herself up and down the corridors, listening to the women moaning through the doors. The pain abruptly changes gear. It now feels as though the baby is being wrung out of her stomach by a pair of steel hands. Beds are scarce so she is placed on a table, where she is racked by a pain 'so violent that it was no longer pain, but a condition of being'.

Emerging at last, the baby is whisked away by a nurse who insists that Martha must have 'a nice rest' before she can cradle her daughter. She finds it 'intolerable' that after nine months of companionship she is forbidden from making the acquaintance of her child. When the baby is finally brought in, she's allowed to suck on the nipple for only a few seconds before being ripped away screaming. From now on, Martha is allowed to feed Caroline only at four-hourly intervals during the day and forbidden to feed at night. After a couple of months, her milk supply dries up from lack of use.

Looking back, Lessing observed that if a committee wanted to prevent mothers from bonding with their children 'they could not do better than study the Lady Chancellor'. Her main memory of these months was the sound of her son's starved wailing. Yet this was standard behaviour for its day. It was not until the 1960s that the notion of 'attachment' as a necessary infant process was introduced. In the 1940s, mothers in Britain as well as Southern Rhodesia obediently followed the strictures of Sir F. Truby King, whose *Feeding and Care of Baby* had appeared in a posthumous revised edition in 1940. Anxious to improve the health of babies in poor areas and to turn the next generation into stoical empire builders who would ensure that Great Britain remained 'much longer great', Truby King berated mothers for their weakness.

'Obedience in infancy is the foundation of all later powers of self-control', he admonished, insisting that 'Feeding and Sleeping by the Clock' was the ultimate foundation of all-round obedience and that from these foundations truth and honour would follow. Therefore, 'fond and foolish over-indulgence, mismanagement, and "spoiling"' were as harmful to an infant as 'callous neglect or intentional cruelty'. The woman who gratified the whims of her baby was in danger of turning her child into 'a delicate, fretful, irritable, nervous, dyspeptic little tyrant who will yell and scream, day or night, if not soothed and cuddled without delay'.

Doris Wisdom's son John was an unusually athletic infant whom she would later describe as 'a hyperactive baby, and then a hyperactive child'. From the start, much like the apparently alien baby she would later portray in *The Fifth Child*, he lifted up his head, kicking his legs furiously as he fed. He struggled to pull himself up in his pram and cot and left his mother exhausted simply from holding him. She was distressed by the 'sack of bruised flesh' her body had become and depressed by her new routine. She spent long mornings in her flat alone with her child and long afternoons pushing the pram in the park. 'I remember those afternoons as the apex, the Himalayas, of tedium.'

Frank passed his evenings drinking at the club and was delighted when he was sent to a camp near Umtali to be trained as a soldier. Doris followed, moving into a cheap hotel with her husband and son. Now she spent her mornings struggling to wash nappies and bottles in the confines of a small hotel room and her afternoons pushing her son under flame trees and jacarandas. She had put him on a bottle and dieted back into her youthful body, so she was fantasising about the soldier who would escape from the camp and approach the svelte but frustrated young woman with the pram. 'We would embrace under the flame trees, kisses full of anguish because of the partings of war, the loss and the pain of war.'

Flung into the life of a matronly housewife at the age of twenty, Doris felt isolated by motherhood and trapped by the life of tea mornings and domesticity that it brought. She was desperate to write. She was becoming increasingly angry about the colour bar, which provided her with the privileged life she hated. And she was disillusioned with her husband, who no longer seemed to share her opinions and was too preoccupied by his own failures as a soldier (he was quickly dismissed from the army on account of his bad feet) to empathise with her. Increasingly, Doris was dreaming about escaping from this life. Sometimes she imagined taking flight with her husband and son to London or Paris. At other moments, she imagined fleeing alone and beginning again. Yet when John was only nine months old, she decided to have a second child.

A decade later, Lessing described Martha's uneasy yearning for another baby in *A Proper Marriage* in scenes that seem to try to make sense of her own decision. Like Doris, Martha fantasises about leaving home almost as soon as her daughter is born. Alienated by her husband, yearning for a romantic love affair and longing most of all to do something constructive with her mind, she resents the 'invisible navel string' that continues to connect her to her daughter, twanging like a harshly plucked string at every sound or movement that Caroline makes. Worrying that she is a failure, she finds that she is 'good for nothing, not even the simple natural function that every woman should achieve like breathing: being a mother'.

Yet this belies the ease with which she responds to the navel string when she accepts it. 'How lovely then to wash the little girl,' she observes, dressing Caroline in the morning, 'and see her in her fresh pretty cotton dress, the delicate pink feet balancing so surely and strongly over the floor'. Even when their interaction becomes more complicated, she sometimes finds that she is painfully conscious of love. After a miserable battle failing to persuade Caroline to eat, Martha discovers that her heart becomes 'a hot enlarged area of tenderness for the child whom she was so lamentably mishandling.'

'You bore me to extinction,' Martha complains to Caroline, 'and no doubt I bore you'. But she sees this as the inevitable fate of the generations and is proud that she at least can be honest about it, unlike her own mother. In other moments, she is fiercely protective of the woman that Caroline will become. 'For God's sake, Caroline, don't marry young, I'll stop you marrying young if I have to lock you up'. But she is aware, too, that this is just the kind of pressure that she must refrain from putting on her daughter if she wants to avoid being as interfering as Mrs Quest.

In the midst of this conundrum, Martha finds herself caught by a yearning to become pregnant again. This is an urge that begins with her physical love for Caroline:

There were moods when a slow, warm, heavy longing came up, when the very sight of Caroline filled Martha with a deep physical satisfaction at her delightful little body and charming little face; and this was at the same time a desire to hold a small baby in her arms again. If she looked at one of her friends' babies in this mood, the craving was painful and insistent, and the adventure of being pregnant filled her entirely.

She is conscious even now that the daily business of looking after a child and adjusting herself to a set of needs that are in 'sharp discord' with her own is 'not a fulfilment but a drag on herself'. But her awareness of this creates a sense of guilt that is given sanction by her longing for another child.

'Do I love her?' she asks herself, in one of these conflicted moods. The emotion of love vanishes as she examines it, leaving only the bond of responsibility. But then Caroline turns to her with a 'warm, confiding smile' and Martha's heart goes 'soft with tenderness'. Even this isn't simple because she is sure that it would be better for Caroline if she didn't love her. Love generates the desire to over-protect that was so destructive a force in Martha's own childhood, creating the risk that Caroline will eventually hate her. 'Yet the idea of her and Caroline hating each other seemed absurd.'

Martha doesn't give in to the yearning to begin the cycle of conception and birth again. She reminds herself that the phrase 'having a baby' conceals the middle-aged woman who has done nothing with her life except to 'produce two or three commonplace and tedious citizens in a world that was already too full of them'. It conceals too a continued marriage to a man she has come to see as a stranger. And so she escapes before she has time to complete the transformation.

Doris Wisdom, on the other hand, found herself back in the Lady Chancellor nursing home, bathing and shaving for the second time. On this occasion, the baby was born within half an hour of the onset of the sharper pain. Jean was a small, pretty baby, ready from the start to be held and cuddled. Doris found the early weeks easier than they had been with her son, but the new baby made John jealous and angry. Deciding that it was unfair to look after the two children together, Doris left Jean with a neighbour for a month and took John on holiday to Cape Town. When she returned, she found that Jean was dissatisfied with her, having spent a month in the embrace of another woman.

What Doris Wisdom was experiencing with John and Jean, and what we witness in those painful scenes between Martha and Caroline, is what's now known as 'maternal ambivalence'. Just a few years later, the psychoanalyst Donald Winnicott, that reassuring advocate of the 'good-enough mother', announced in an article on 'Hate in the Counter-Transference' that mothers were usually disposed to hate their children: 'The mother, however, hates her infant from the word go'. Winnicott's maternal figure is aggravated by the demands of a baby who remains maddeningly oblivious of all she has sacrificed for him – 'especially he cannot allow for her hate'. Her hatred emerges in his account as a natural component of her initially unboundaried love, and as a test of her maternal strength. She must tolerate hating her baby without doing anything about it and this tolerance is itself a feat enabled by love.

Winnicott's was a rare voice in the 1940s discussion of parenthood and most mothers found it difficult to admit to ambivalence on this scale. Already, though, at the time that Doris Wisdom was chastising herself for being a bad mother, there were plenty of literary models for ambivalent maternity. Mrs Ramsay in Virginia Woolf's *To the Lighthouse* is revered by all those around her as a maternal archetype, but even she finds it a relief when her children go to bed because for a few hours she need think of nobody else. 'She could be herself, by herself. And that was what she often felt the need of – to think; well not even to think. To be silent; to be alone.' More radically, D.H. Lawrence tells us that Mrs Morel, the possessively loving mother of *Sons and Lovers*, had dreaded her baby 'like a catastrophe' before he arrived. Even once the child has appeared she experiences his gaze 'as if a burden were on her heart'. And in a passage that seems knowingly or unknowingly to have influenced Lessing in *A Proper Marriage*, Mrs Morel is distressed to feel as though 'the navel string that had connected [the baby's] frail little body with hers had not been broken'. She experiences a wave of 'hot love' as she holds the infant close to her face and breast and she determines to love her child all the more as penance for her own unwillingness to have him.

However, it was only in the 1960s and 70s that this ambivalence became openly admissable. 'My children cause me the most exquisite suffering of which I have any experience,' wrote the poet Adrienne Rich in a journal entry included in her book *Of Woman Born*:

it is the suffering of ambivalence: the murderous alternation between bitter resentment and raw-eddied nerves, and blissful gratification and tenderness. Sometimes I seem to myself, in my feelings toward these tiny guiltless beings, a monster of selfishness and intolerance… there are times when I feel only death will free us from one another… And yet at other times I am melted with the sense of their helpless, charming and quite irresistible beauty – their ability to go on loving and trusting – their staunchness and decency and unselfconsciousness. *I love them.* But it's in the enormity and inevitability of this love that the sufferings lie.

Rich is concerned to show that this oscillation of pain and pleasure, frustration and fulfilment, is not simply the human condition but is the result of the 'patriarchy', which divides women into good or evil, fertile or barren, creating terrifying expectations for mothers. It seems true that if women like Doris Wisdom found it hard to admit that ambivalence, then it was partly the result of the expectations of those around them. But these mixed feelings cannot be eliminated by a change in rhetoric, though they may become easier to manage. The invisible navel string felt by Mrs Morel and by Martha is not simply a product of its time.

The baby in the womb and the baby as first manifested in the world are not radically different creatures; instead there is a continuum between the creature nurtured from the flesh of the mother and the toddler making its way experimentally across the room. I knew as well as Lessing did that when a person is wholly dependent on your body for its survival, when it displays few of the signs of personhood we usually encounter in those we interact with, it's hard to develop boundaries that enable you to see your child as a separate person. It's therefore difficult not to succumb to mirroring the baby's infantile rages and grief, experiencing disorientating and unfamiliar extremes of emotion unlike anything you can remember feeling before. This isn't just the result of pregnancy and breast-feeding. For men as well as women, the helplessness seems to bring out a corresponding helplessness in the adult; the need to keep the creature before you alive is felt as instinctively as the angry disbelief that it should be so difficult to look after, at times apparently irrationally refusing the food and sleep it most needs.

So what had changed over time was not so much the condition as the response to it. Where Lessing's generation found it hard to admit ambivalence, the Women's Lib generation celebrated it. 'The only thing which seems to be eternal and natural in motherhood is ambivalence', claimed Jane Lazarre in her 1976 account of mothering her son, *The Mother Knot.* Reading narratives like this one in the twenty-first century, I was bothered by how much harder it had become to acknowledge ambivalence than it had been forty years earlier.

At the turn of the new century, Rachel Cusk published *A Life's Work*, her account of the uneasy contradictions of early motherhood. This is a book that expresses as much love as fear, and that is primarily concerned to explore the way that in becoming a mother, Cusk became 'both child and parent' and became 'both more virtuous and more terrible' than she had ever felt before. Describing the phenomenon of the invisible navel string, Cusk writes that in giving birth a woman's understanding of what it is to exist changes profoundly:

> Another person has existed in her, and after their birth they live within the jurisdiction of her consciousness. When she is with them she is not herself; when she is without them she is not herself; and so it is as difficult to leave your children as it is to stay with them. To discover this is to feel that your life has become irretrievably mired in conflict, or caught in some mythic snare in which you will perpetually, vainly struggle.

This seems no more radical than the sentiments expressed in *A Proper Marriage* or indeed in *Sons and Lovers*; certainly not more than those described by Adrienne Rich or the feminists who wrote in her wake. Yet Cusk was vilified in the press after her book appeared. 'If everyone were to read this book,' one reviewer claimed, 'the propagation of the human race would virtually cease, which would be a shame.' This change in attitude seems connected to the change in attitude about freedom. Because since Lawrence and Lessing's day, freedom in its positive sense has become seen as less of a good in itself, mothers are no longer expected to express outrage at its sudden disappearance. Very few of the writers who have addressed motherhood in the twenty-first century have explored the question of freedom in particular; they do not seem to feel entitled to be free. Cusk does, finding that in caring for her daughter she comes to understand her 'former freedom'. Motherhood is 'a kind of slavery' because she is 'not free to go'; she has become constantly responsible for sustaining life.

For Cusk, unlike Doris Wisdom, this isn't the whole story. She is surprised and relieved to find that there are new kinds of freedom revealed by motherhood. The first – not unlike the freedom of renunciation that can be found in pregnancy – is freedom from herself: 'from complexity and choice and from the reams of unscripted time upon which I used to write my days, bearing the burden of their authorship'. Even this is a constricting thought, however. She is conscious that in feeling this she is betraying her sex; betraying the women who have fought for just this right to autonomy that she now discards with relief. And she finds that the state of motherhood provides among other things a 'demotion, a displacement, an opportunity to give up'.

The second, more hopeful kind of freedom is one that she can share with her daughter. Partly because Cusk lives in a more egalitarian world than Doris Wisdom's, the initial state of slavery does not last as long as she fears it will. She finds that she is able to leave her daughter. Returning from days of absence, she picks her up and hugs her 'like something I had thought lost'. Now motherhood becomes the work of certain periods. There are times when she is free, with the freedom of her youth, and she is surprised to find that her daughter can become part of this freedom: 'something new that is being added, drop by daily drop, to the sum of what I am'. That strange entity, motherbaby, has untethered itself and there is a relationship between two people let loose in the house. Here Cusk is grappling with the question of what it might feel like to be both free and a mother, which is a question that neither Doris Wisdom nor Martha seem able to imagine an answer to. And finding an answer to this seems to depend on deciding just how much of yourself it is possible to give to your child.

'I would give up the unessential,' says Edna Pontellier in Kate Chopin's radical 1899 novel *The Awakening*, asking herself what she is prepared to sacrifice for her children; 'I would give my money, I would give my life for my children; but I wouldn't give myself'. It is this relinquishment of self that is the final relinquishment of freedom that is most feared by Doris Wisdom, Martha, Mrs Ramsay, Rachel Cusk. And it was this that I too feared while dreading and yearning my way into motherhood in the years and months that led to the birth of my son.

My experience of giving birth – pacing, bathing, waiting, shouting – was physically not dissimilar from Doris Wisdom's, except that like many of my contemporaries I was in the 'birthing pool' for the final stages of labour. Emotionally, though, it was very different. Unlike her, I had a husband present, and also, more unusually, a friend: that same school friend in whose garden I had once wondered when I would lose my virginity, excited and frightened by the notion that one day my body could be entered by another and not yet able to conceptualise that years later a whole new person could emerge from inside it.

That evening in the birthing centre, we were products of our time. We played music; we talked; my back was helpfully massaged; I eschewed all drugs and was commended by the midwives for doing so. But when my son appeared at last, I held him for no longer than Doris Wisdom had held hers before he was whisked away, in this case because he was having difficulties breathing. I was taken down to the theatre so that they could attend to my own torn flesh. Emerging hours later I asked, bewildered, to see my baby and was wheeled in to peer at him in his fish tank. Thus it went on the following day, with me attempting to feed as Doris Wisdom had at four-hourly intervals, frightened by the ravenous cry that I seemed unable to assuage.

Because we had moved on since the days of Truby King, the nurses suggested that I might like to continue these intervals throughout the night, though the baby was being nourished through a drip. Exhausted and in pain, I responded that it might be more helpful for all of us if I was left to sleep. Distressed, my husband asked if this was all I was prepared to sacrifice for our child. I held selfishly firm; there would be enough broken nights in the weeks that followed. I benefited from my night's sleep but I was learning that from now on to assert my own needs was to do so at someone else's expense.

Gradually, the baby in the tank became my baby, lying in the cot beside my bed. My breasts became his possessions, and sleep became easier within earshot of this snuffling creature who had miraculously dived into the bath from between my legs. His smell, which might well have been my own smell, became as contenting a drug as the oxytocin that flooded my body when the milk poured out of my breasts. Conveniently, oxytocin is the sex hormone and so in those early weeks I was in a permanently post-coital state. If this was love then it was the languorous, in-love feeling that comes from spending several days in bed with someone. I was so lazily contented that I contemplated immediately having another child.

Yet from the start, I resisted succumbing too easily to this contentment. After the first week or so, as the initial flood of oxytocin wore off, I frequently resented being woken in the night, especially when the baby proved unwilling to go back to sleep. Pushing his cradle up and down on its wheels, I felt bemused that my life should have narrowed to this moment in the dark, manically engaged in a repetitive task that would have had no meaning in my former life. I was determined that enough of me should survive this experience that the personality I'd always defined myself by should endure. Though I didn't express it in these terms, I was anxiously protecting my own freedom. This meant that from the time the baby was two weeks old, I made sure that I could leave my husband with a bottle of milk and go out for occasional evenings, even if I was too tired to enjoy them. And when I was with my son, I learnt to pacify him by rocking his chair with my foot so that I could read or talk to friends while I was with him. Meeting childless friends for lunch, I did all I could to keep him quiet, determined that they should find me no different.

Urgently, I plunged myself into long Russian novels, needing to immerse myself in other worlds. When the baby was two months old, I wrote a review one morning before taking him to lunch with some other motherbabies, secretly proud that in those quiet hours of writing I had disentangled my consciousness from my son's in a way the women around me seemed to find less necessary.

Is it wrong for writers to claim a special privilege when it comes to maternal ambivalence? Writers at least are able to work in the interstices of looking after a child; frustrated lawyers or nurses have no way to slip back into their old lives for a couple of hours at a time. But if writers have no special claim when it comes to frustration, they are in the trade of ambivalence, and so might be more attentive to it. Rachel Cusk justified her book by saying that 'the experience of ambivalence that characterises the early stages of parenthood seemed to me to be kith and kin of the writer's fundamental ambivalence towards life'.

It does seem significant that so many female writers across the centuries have avoided having children. Recently, Geoff Dyer complained about writers who claim that they have to sacrifice the joys of family life for the higher vocation of writing, arguing that 'writing just passes the time and, like any kind of work, brings in money'. This may be true, but it leaves out the necessary solipsism of the writer: the fact that in disappearing into a book you have periods when your child needs to be out of mind as well as out of sight, which for many of the mothers I know would be impossible. And it leaves out the necessary disloyalty; the way that you're always observing yourself and the people you love from the outside at the same time as you are interacting with them. It was this layer of ruthless detachment that I most feared losing – the secret self that stands in clinical judgement on the world around me – rather than the time to write.

Compared to those of a young 1940s mother, the possibilities in my life were endless. I had an academic job and a writing career to return to; I had handed in a book for publication just before giving birth. I only had six months of milk and nappies before my husband was scheduled to take over, impressively taking advantage of a new law enabling men to take six months of unpaid paternity leave. Most importantly, perhaps, I had wanted this child. It had taken me a year to get pregnant, where it had taken Doris Wisdom one accidental night. I lived in an age of easy contraception and so had been able to wait till I was ten years older than she was; this had given me a chance to build a life for myself first.

Ambivalence in these circumstances did not involve suffering. If there were moments when I resented becoming part of the motherbaby entity, then they were moments in which I knew it would not last for long. But if I dwell now on my own flashes of uncertainty then it's partly because it enables me to understand Doris Wisdom's actions and also because I am unnerved by how difficult it remains to describe the doubt. The fact that we can now wait longer before having children is likely to make us better mothers. It also makes us less willing to admit our ambivalence, because we know that this is a life we have chosen and because we are surrounded by women in their thirties and forties who are struggling to conceive, or younger mothers who don't have the economic possibilities that I had to make the experience less exhausting and more pleasant. Certainly, I find it hard to write about my moments of ambivalence about the child I so much wanted; I can hear both my privilege and my ingratitude in these sentences.

When my husband went on paternity leave, the dynamics of our family changed. As my son moved into a more boisterous phase of babyhood, my husband became the favourite parent, making him laugh by energetically throwing him in the air. Gradually, I became envious of the intense nature of their bond, though I was too irritated by these noisy physical games to want to be playing them instead.

I told myself (using a phrase frequently used by Lessing) that I was in this for the long haul and that my son would eventually become someone as interested in conversational and emotional intimacy as he was in being lifted in the air; I would be ready, waiting for that moment. But the result of all this horseplay was that I tended to step aside when they were playing together, using the time to progress with domestic chores or sometimes (I write this guiltily even now) to read a book. When I was alone with my son, nothing had changed; we continued in a relationship dominated by my touching and feeding him, though the food no longer came from my breasts. Sometimes we developed shared games or jokes and I guarded them closely, not wanting them to become part of the triangular dynamics. I wondered if this all meant that I was unsuited for family life; if growing up as the only child of divorced parents had left me able to conduct intimate relationships only in pairs.

This was partly true. Later it would become one of the reasons I so insistently wanted another child; four seemed to me a far easier number than three. But in my stepping away, there was also an insistence on my own independence, mentally and physically, and this was an insistence I don't think it would occur to many men to need to make. 'I would give my life for my children; but I wouldn't give myself'. I don't think my husband would share these sentiments, or those of Martha, finding that although her inability to enjoy Caroline fills her with guilt, she cannot relax into her daughter because 'that would be a disloyalty and even a danger to herself'.

The state of fatherhood has not been much addressed in literature, partly because the loving, equally involved father is a new phenomenon. After haranguing mothers on their potential inadequacies for several hundred pages, Truby King devotes only a short paragraph to fathers. 'A child who has spent the entire day with his mother looks forward eagerly to his father's return in the evening,' Truby King informs his male readers; it is therefore 'only right that a father should make every effort to arrive home in time to spend a quiet half-hour or so with his children, prior to their bedtime.' Both Frank Wisdom and Martha's Douglas seem to have conformed to these low expectations. Fathers are absent, too, from Winnicott's less stringent account. And even today in the age of the new man, they have a secondary role in the literature on parenthood. This means that the loving, involved father has a blank page on which to create his role, unburdened by the fear of disappearing into an archetype. In my husband's case this was a strikingly creative and loving act. From the beginning, I admired this and knew that I could not have been a happy mother without his doing it, and yet when I was cooking while they played noisily together in the neighbouring room, it could feel as though it had not left enough room for me.

When my son was two, he stopped sleeping for a while. No longer used to interrupted sleep, I found that waking hourly for several consecutive nights left me too exhausted to cope with daily life. One evening, I arranged to go to a neighbour's house for a night, after my son had gone to bed. It was not unusual for me to go away, but the sight of me disappearing, armed with my duvet, for no better reason than my own mental weakness, angered my husband. In the days that followed he accused me of being unmaternal, backing up this claim with the proof that my son would rather play with him than with me.

Conscious of the disapproval emanating from him and the people I identified as sharing his views, I retreated further into a literary world in which I could experience myself – my diffident angularity, my determination that there was only so far I could be pushed away from my own needs – as normal. Though I was hurt by my husband's accusations, I remained impervious to the charge itself. It was so obvious to me when I was alone with my son that we loved each other. Despite my assertions of equality and freedom, the experience of bearing a child inside me and feeding it had created a careless, wordless bond that I now saw as inviolable; that I thought the man who was judging me could not understand, when he had started from a position of separateness, forging this relationship like any other.

It still seems unclear to me at what point the word 'love' – that word we use casually to cover such a wide variety of relationships – becomes appropriate for the bond between a parent and child. Lessing was right to make Martha question it. When my son was still in the special care unit, a couple of days after his birth, my husband and I escaped the hospital briefly, going for a walk in the central London squares in which I'm accustomed to spending my lunchtimes as an academic, feeling that it was surreal to encounter these familiar places in such an unfamiliar state of mind. Brought together by the vulnerability of the previous few days, we talked about what it was we felt for the baby sleeping in his plastic tank. We agreed that it was hard to call it love: it seemed more a recognition of preciousness. I asked whom he would save at that moment if he could only save one of us from a burning building. He said that it would be me. I was me, irreplaceable; the baby had as yet no uniqueness and could be, it seemed, recreated. I agreed that I would save my husband before my son.

This has now changed beyond doubt. It probably changed after only a few weeks or months. There would be no question for me now as to whom I would save and I am certain too that no new man would be able to induce a kind of love that would make it possible for me to save his life before my son's. I know without asking that this is true for my husband as well. And I am sure with a new child I would be able to see the person in the baby more quickly now that I know how it works; now that I have experienced the silent, passive creature turning into my child.

Yet I cannot say at what point this love developed. Sometimes it seems that the word 'love' could only really have become applicable once it had become reciprocal; once my son had the language (of gesture if not words) to express the happiness and the pain of love. I remember the first time he called me 'Mummy' as a transformative moment – a moment in which in some fundamental sense I became a mother, able unselfconsciously to use the phrase 'my son'. And as he became more of a social being, I found that I could be startled into a particularly heightened form of joy by his pleasure in giving me presents, singing me songs, making me imaginary cups of tea. I was moved by the matter-of-factness with which he made his small plastic figures fall over, in order that they should ask their mothers to kiss them better, straightforwardly enacting our love. But to see these encounters, more characteristic of adult relationships, as the times in which love exists most strongly is to expect this new kind of feeling to follow the lines that love follows between adults. And that is only half the story.

II

'My baby, if you are interested, is entirely admirable'

Trying again

It was time for me to leave my son again, albeit briefly. There were letters in Lessing's archive at the University of East

Anglia in Norfolk that I thought would help me to understand her ambivalence, letters written to her lover, the RAF
serviceman John Whitehorn, and to their mutual friend Coll
MacDonald before and after the birth of her third child.
Though the miscarriage had receded into the past and I had
regained control of my life as a woman with one child, I was
starting to feel claustrophobic in the city again and so was
grateful for the chance to escape to the wide skies and endless
beaches of East Anglia.

On the morning of my departure, I spent a fruitless half
hour arguing with my son, who was angry because he was
unable to wind up a plastic car.

'Let me do it,' he insisted, and then shook with rage when
he couldn't. I told him to go and calm down in his bedroom,
but he refused. Eventually I picked him up and carried him
upstairs, shouting. We were both furious with frustration,
but the act of carrying him nonetheless served as a kind of
embrace. I could smell him, and in that moment I felt my
love for him as a physical sensation. This is where parental
love differs from the love felt between adults. In no other relationship have I encountered anything like this easy coexist-
ence of contradictory emotions: a rage that brings with it the
urge to lash out violently, coinciding with a feeling of envel-
oping love that brings a hunger to touch. Indeed, it's at these
moments of fury that the love can be felt most strongly, drawing attention to itself because of the jagged contrast between
the feelings that are present.

Deposited in his bedroom, he cried for a couple of minutes
longer and then called for me to come back.

'I'm a bit sad,' he offered, and I asked if he wanted a cuddle. He sat on my lap, both of us contented, and I stored this

moment up for the days that would follow. On the way to nursery, I reminded him that I was going away.

'But I'll miss you,' he said, and it was all the more wrenching because it was a new phrase to enter his vocabulary. 'I want to come with you on holiday.'

As I left the nursery, with tears in my eyes, I ceased once again to empathise with Doris Wisdom. Children of that age have no sense of time; John and Jean would not have been able to understand that she was not coming back. The surge of tenderness I'd felt hugging him during and after our quarrel was recognisably similar to the moments of hunger Martha feels for Caroline: the pleasure in his skin, the feeling of animal recognition at the smell of his hair. I knew that I would be as incapable as Doris Wisdom was of being a full-time mother for years at a time; that I too would go mad with boredom and would start responding to the tantrums with irrational rage of my own. But how could you feel that anxious tenderness towards someone and be prepared to leave him behind? How could you live in the same city as your absent children without feeling agonising grief?

By the time I arrived in Norfolk, excited by the views of grass and sky from the train window, I had re-centred into a part of myself that is not a mother. My son was pushed comfortably into a corner of my mind as I read through my notes about Lessing and looked forward to the walks and dinners I would have with local friends during my trip. When I thought back to the morning, I was relieved to be away from the endless arguments that emerge out of the frustration of a small child. And I was pleased to have created a parental relationship where absences could be sustained. I did not claim to be offering him his freedom through my departure. But the possibility that we could exist away from each other did seem a necessary freedom for both of us. Going away was a method by which I could be less unfree; by which the frightening, joyful ties of love could be kept from strangling us like that uncut umbilical cord.

Hiring a car to escape to the sea when the archive shut, I was drawn into talking about children with the girl behind the desk. We both had three-year-old sons. I found it reassuring to be normal, to be able to present a version of myself that was similar to her. But then when she asked where I was driving the car, I could feel her wondering why I was having this holiday without my son. I could see the oddness of taking off on my own away from my child, though it had come to seem so reasonable to me. Whether or not it was there, I could sense disapproval emanating from her. There is such a taboo in mothers abandoning their children that it's there in every departure, even if it's only for a few days. And I was conscious of the absurdity of leaving my child to go and read and think about motherhood; of going off to read about pregnancy while removing myself from the place in which it was possible to become pregnant. But this was what I was there to do. So I took my seat in the archive, opened the folder of 111 messily typed letters and was transported easily to Southern Rhodesia in 1945.

When Doris Wisdom left Frank, she had ceased to believe in marriage as an institution. She left him to recreate the nuclear family she'd found so restrictive, marrying a neighbour who became a second mother to the children. Doris was now allowed to see John and Jean only very intermittently, meeting them for formal picnics with Frank or occasionally taking them away for the weekend. Although these could be horribly painful encounters, she still didn't regret leaving the marriage. Nonetheless, within a year she had married again.

In retrospect, she presented her marriage to the Russian-born German communist Gottfried Lessing in 1943 as a marriage of convenience. As a refugee, he had recently been interned as an 'enemy alien' and now she could save him from subsequent danger with her own British passport. Certainly, he does not seem to have attracted her much initially, though he had the excessive good looks of a silent film star. She respected his intelligence and commitment but was put off by his lack of humour or warmth. And he alarmed her with his determination to repress all unnecessary emotion and his refrain of 'and now let us analyse the situation'.

Nonetheless, he at least was in love. Shortly after leaving her children, Doris had become dangerously ill. She spent several weeks in a febrile fog, dreaming of staircases falling apart under her and ravines appearing before her. Gottfried took on the responsibility of nursing her, bringing her ice creams and cakes, and by the time that she recovered a mutual claim had been established. The relationship that developed was unsatisfying for her: the attempts at sex as perfunctory as the attempts at emotional connection. But it was partly because she didn't want to give him up that she agreed to marry him. From the start, they didn't insist on fidelity. Lessing fell in love not only with John Whitehorn but with his two RAF colleagues and fellow Cambridge undergraduates, Coll MacDonald and Leonard Smith (known as Smithie).

When the war ended in 1945, Doris and Gottfried planned to move to Europe. He wanted to go to the Soviet sector of Berlin and she wanted to go to London. However, before they could go anywhere, they decided to wait for Doris's father to die, and most importantly for Gottfried to acquire British citizenship. These were difficult, frustrating months, in which she still managed to draft the novel that would become

The Grass is Singing, a lyrical celebration of the landscape she was about to leave. While waiting, she made the odd move of getting pregnant with a third child.

Why did Doris Lessing have a third child just at the point of escaping Southern Rhodesia, only four years after abandoning two other children? This was becoming a question I needed to find an answer to, and I hoped to find it in the archive. But I quickly discovered that she gave conflicting explanations. In her autobiography, she wrote that she and Gottfried had already recognised their incompatibility and decided to divorce, but they both thought that it was a good moment to have a baby, as neither would have time to do this later. She didn't comment here on the oddness of this sudden matter-of-fact need for motherhood, given that she'd not found her other two children very conducive to her life as a communist or a writer, and that it's not ideal to conceive a child with a man you have already decided to divorce. She was only twenty-six when she became pregnant. She'd be able to conceive a child for many years yet. She was in love with John Whitehorn and was likely to have a new life either with him or with another man, with whom it might be more sensible to have children.

In the letters to Whitehorn that I was reading, there was another explanation. She told him that it was an accident. She said that she felt conflicted because she was having the child with the wrong man but that there was nonetheless an 'extraordinary satisfaction' in it 'because I miss my two very much as you know, and I won't feel so lost without them'. At this stage, she was sure that it was a girl, and had already mentally named her Catherine. It's quite possible that she claimed it was an accident here in order to protect the feelings of her lover, but it was also the explanation she gave in letters to Coll

MacDonald, adding that it was the result of 'experimenting idiotically with a new-fangled method of contraception, like idiots'. She informed MacDonald, to whom she always presented herself and her life more light-heartedly than she did to Whitehorn, that though Gottfried was 'very pleased', she was 'not a bit pleased, but am behaving as though it is the one thing I want most'. In sharp contrast to the explanation in the autobiography, she stated here that she and Gottfried had already decided to stay together, despite months of fighting and mutual promiscuity, and so this represented a logical step given that Gottfried wanted a child. They were, she said, planning to move to Berlin together.

The question remained: why did she decide to have this child? There's an element of choice, even in careless contraception. This time, she could have sought an abortion if she really wanted one. So on some level, she did decide to have another child, four years after taking the decisive step of abandoning her two existing children. Reading her letters to Whitehorn, I found that I was returning to the question of whether Lessing had gained freedom from slamming the door on her first marriage. The answer seemed to be that she didn't. It had provided a negative kind of freedom, removing one source of constraint. But it hadn't provided a positive experience of freedom and in fact missing her children had become its own source of constriction. She wished to see them more often than she did and was upset that she was prevented from doing so by her husband. I was coming to see that the problem with seeking freedom is that it constantly eludes your grasp, and so the markers of freedom endlessly change. Nonetheless, it seemed that if you were someone who craved freedom by temperament, this didn't stop you looking for it. Now she was seeking, among other things, the freedom to love.

Over the next few months she informed both Whitehorn and MacDonald about the physical and emotional progress of her pregnancy. 'I now begin to spread ungracefully in front,' she wrote in a letter to both of them in May, 'and to show a gently maternal air to perspicacious observers'. She was busy writing, campaigning for the elections and pursuing a new love affair, but she was still excited to feel Catherine coming to life inside her stomach – 'an unmistakeable and rather thrilling feeling, like a bird caught in the hand. I believe women are always supposed not to like it, but I do. Primitive again. Sorry.'

That July she told MacDonald that after months of arguing, she and Gottfried had finally agreed that they would separate as soon as possible. She became more ambivalent about the pregnancy as a result, and was plagued by 'a vivid picture of the tedium of napkins, breast feeding, looking like the Parthenon'. The only positive feeling she had towards Catherine was 'one of profound pity that she has to go through all the strain of being a human being', but she was sure that once she was born she would be 'visited by more normal feelings, such as thinking what a beautiful baby she is'.

The baby grew and the mind adapted, aided by the hormones flooding her system. By the end of September, waiting for the birth that was now imminent, she told John excitedly that she was suddenly 'thrilled to bits about Catherine'. She was sitting for hours thinking about the wonderful strangeness of having a baby: 'like taking a ticket in a lottery where you know you are going to get a prize, but don't know how much'.

A week later the baby was born. This was her third labour in the Lady Chancellor nursing home and once again there were hours of pacing in considerable pain. By midnight she was insisting that 'never under any circumstances would I sleep with anyone, the risk being too great for the pleasure'. An hour later, she was praying for death. At five minutes past two the baby appeared and at half past two she was shown her new child, a boy, immediately 'convinced it's the most enchanting child ever conceived'. She told John Whitehorn that though she was aware that 'perhaps one could not strictly call him beautiful', she remained 'suffused with the appropriate maternal feelings'.

After four days of 'purring like a cat', there was a day of weeping. But the despair was short-lived. Because this is the only birth where records remain of how she felt at the time, it's hard to compare it to the others. Nonetheless both the autobiography and the letters to Whitehorn suggest that this was her most contented period of early motherhood. 'My baby, if you are interested, is entirely admirable,' she told MacDonald and Whitehorn. This time she'd had the courage to ignore Truby King and was feeding on demand; the result was that both mother and baby were well slept. She was troubled by her novel, which was struggling to find a publisher, and by her father's illness: 'it is difficult to believe that the human body can bear so much and still keep alive'. But she remained delighted by Peter who, unlike John as a baby, was 'very cuddlesome and affectionate and always laughing'.

Waiting to travel to England, lacking in possibilities for romantic love, Doris Lessing allowed her baby to assuage her need for affection and companionship in a way she had never done before. At the end of September 1947, her father died. 'A stinking carcass, that's how we end', she observed to

John Whitehorn, finding that she had moments of envying her parents' miserable but mutually dependent marriage. She would grieve for her father for the next fifty years, attempting to make her sense of his disappointment bearable. Now she sought solace in her child. 'He wakes up like a little bird all coy and confiding,' she told her absent and unfaithful lover. He was more peaceful than her previous children had been: 'in other words, I am more peaceful than I was then, or at any rate have learned to conceal from him the fact that I am not'.

This contentment was manifested in the photographs from the time that she included in her letters to Whitehorn, which now slipped out from the folders in the Norwich archives. In April 1947 she enclosed a photograph of herself holding the enticingly chubby ten-month-old Peter above her head. Both mother and baby are smiling here and he reaches out his arms towards her. I felt relieved, looking at it. She seemed to have released herself from the grip of maternal ambivalence. Nonetheless, when her uterus dropped a year after Peter's birth, she acquiesced to her doctor's suggestion that he should tie her fallopian tubes at the same time as performing reparative surgery. 'On mature consideration I think I should get myself tied up,' she wrote to Whitehorn. 'I shouldn't have any more children. I shall regret it most passionately sometimes, that goes without saying.'

After she moved to London with her three-year-old son in 1949, all Lessing's decisions as to where and how to live were inflected by Peter and by her determination that he should be happy. She did leave him periodically, sending him to stay with friends in the country for weeks and even sometimes months at a time in his school holidays. But he remained the central presence in her life. Perhaps freedom had ceased to be so important to her. Or perhaps the need for freedom had been postponed, or, as in Cusk's account, enlarged to incorporate her child. It had turned out that there was a freedom in maternal love.

Asked about her relationship with her son in Lessing's 1962 *Play with a Tiger*, Anna (a version of the Anna in *The Golden Notebook*) states that 'he sets me free.' Her lover is surprised; how can she be free when her child brings so constraining a litany of domestic tasks?

'Don't you see?' she replies. 'He's there. I go into his room when he's asleep to take a good long look at him, because he's too old now to look at when he's awake, that's already an interference. So I look at him. He's there … He's something new. A kind of ray of light that shoots off into any direction. Or blazes up like a comet or goes off like a rocket.'

This is freedom not as an absence of constraint but as an escape from oneself enabled by love. But in Lessing's own case, the new freedom came at the price of guilt. When she insists 'I did not feel guilty' in her autobiography, she goes on to explain that if she had stayed she would have had a nervous breakdown. But she also admits here that she would live with guilt for the next decades. 'I know all about the ravages of guilt, how it feels, how it undermines and saps. I energetically fight back.' Arguably, she spent the rest of her life attempting to reconcile her guilt about the children she had left behind with her anxious love for the child who remained. This manifested itself in her writing. In London, she wrote repeatedly about ambivalent mothers and abandoned children, writing of Martha's guilt about Caroline in *A Ripple from the Storm* and more painfully writing from the perspective of the abandoned child in *The Four-Gated City* (1969). After his mother commits suicide, the five-year-old Paul spends several weeks lying curled in a chair in the kitchen sucking his thumb, unable to sleep and distrustful of the adults who surround him.

The guilt manifested itself also in Lessing's life. Already in Southern Rhodesia, she described herself to Smithie as 'always full of anxiety and uncertainty lest Peter should be wrested from me somehow, which makes me over-anxious'. These feelings seem to have resulted in a need to atone. She couldn't repair her relationships with her existing children. Both John and Jean visited her in London in early adulthood, but she was unable to re-establish an easy rapport with them. However, shortly after publishing *The Golden Notebook*, Lessing took in a troubled adolescent called Jenny Diski. Peter had written home to say that a former classmate of his was in a mental hospital, having attempted suicide. Moved on Jenny's behalf, Lessing wrote to her suggesting that she might like to come and live with her. It was an odd decision, and one that angered Peter. When Jenny arrived, it turned out that she and her apparent guardian angel did not easily get on, but were trapped in each other's lives.

Over the next few decades, Lessing's relationships with both Peter and Jenny became increasingly claustrophobic but she seems to have been unable either to extricate herself or to let any air in. According to Diski's own, undoubtedly subjective account, which she was publishing in instalments that year, Lessing and Diski disliked each other from the start but were trapped by the generosity of Lessing's gesture. Peter meanwhile resented Jenny, seeing her as taking his place in the light, and his mother compensated by turning him into a 'monstrous baby', incapable of looking after himself. It is too easy to say that in taking in Jenny

Diski and in smothering Peter, Doris Lessing was acting out of guilt on behalf of the children she had left behind. But in both cases her care does seem the result of a need to limit her own freedom – to make herself pay a price for something – rather than genuine altruism.

Martha, pregnant with her child, promises the 'imprisoned thing moving inside her flesh' that 'no pressure would deform it, freedom would be its gift'. Rachel Cusk, moving out of motherbaby dependency, hoped that her daughter would become part of her freedom. Can mothers and their children somehow free each other at the same time as they are mutually restricting? It had not worked for Lessing, but, returning home from Norwich, I persisted in hoping that it might work for me.

4

'It was like a rebirth'

Communism

When Doris Wisdom slammed the door on her children in 1943, she was flinging open the door to communism. The liberty she now envisaged was both personal and political. She was embarking on a new life as a revolutionary and freeing the world from its chains of war and inequality. The current war had proved that capitalism was doomed to destroy itself. As the Russians doggedly fought off the Germans at Stalingrad, she was at the vanguard of the revolution that would enable Britain and Southern Rhodesia to remodel themselves in the image of their 'gallant ally' in the east.

Why did the Soviet Union proffer liberation? At its best, Stalin's regime openly denied freedom of expression and freedom of political choice. At its worst, it had turned the entire citizenship into prisoners during the years of terror in the late 1930s and then signed a pact with Hitler. Circumstances might have resulted in new allegiances but the coincidence of interests was likely to be short-lived.

That summer, when I told people I was writing about Lessing, I found that her communism was mentioned almost as often as her decision to abandon her children. A few people admired her for it. After all, it was inseparable from her courageous stand against apartheid. But more often she was dismissed for her gullibility in supporting the Soviet Union for as long as she did. It wasn't until after the Hungarian uprising that she reluctantly left the Party, and it would be several more years before she gave up on the communist project altogether. This was a view that she herself encouraged, describing herself and her cohort in her autobiography as in the grip of 'mass social psychopathology'. But reading about the fervour of her early communist years, I found it hard to disapprove of her revolutionary energy. Even as I came to doubt the necessity for leaving her children and to find freedom less compelling as an ideal, I envied her sense that she was part of the current of her time; that her life mattered to the world and that the world mattered to her. Communism may not have fulfilled its promise of liberation, but she seemed to have found a form of freedom through the act of political commitment. In the world around me, political passion had started to feel more possible and more necessary than it had in my twenties. I was becoming more curious about what exactly this had felt like for her.

I

'Her eyes had been opened and her ears made to hear'

The believer

At the beginning, it was a kind of fairy story: love at first sight. On an otherwise ordinary day in 1942, the twenty-two-year-old Doris Wisdom was stopped in Salisbury by a young, left-wing campaigner called Dorothy Schwartz. Dorothy told her that there was a new group of socialists forming in her midst and that they thought it was time to meet her. The Left Book Club participants had been 'left behind by history' and exposed as reactionaries; the lies propagated about the Soviet Union by the government had been contradicted by Russian heroism in the war; the new climate required an objective assessment of the local situation.

Doris was flattered. Here was a group of intelligent people who thought that she had the makings of a revolutionary. Up until now, she'd felt isolated in her sickened disapproval of the colour bar and in her determination to read her way across British, French and Russian literature. Suddenly she was in contact with a circle of people who passionately shared her views and interests. Most importantly, they freed her from the narrowness of her life, suggesting that the individual had the power to change the world.

When she complained about her routine of coffee mornings and sundowners, they advised matter-of-factly that she should leave her family. Within ten or fifteen years, the whole world would be communist anyway; the family would be rejected as a bourgeois fallacy. It was much better for her children that she should leave them and play her part in creating a new free world for them to live in, rid of race prejudice, exploitation of labour and oppression of women.

In *A Proper Marriage* there's a definite moment when Martha decides to abandon her scepticism and embrace the ideas of her new friends. Beforehand she yearns 'to fling herself into the struggle' and become one of the army of revolutionaries. Then, with one 'sudden movement of her whole being', she discards cynicism:

It was as if her eyes had been opened and her ears made to hear; it was like a rebirth. For the first time in her life she had been offered an ideal to live for.

This brings a feeling of rage as well as hope. Lessing observes that if Martha were handed a gun at this moment, she would have no hesitation in destroying the people who have lied to her.

Despite this fervour, Martha remains critical about some aspects of communist life. She finds it comical that they refer to 'the Party' as though there can be no other and is sceptical about the language she is required to use ('social democratic treachery', 'lackeys of the ruling class'). As an incipient writer, she especially minds that interest in emotions is dismissed as Freudian and 'reactionary'. But she's convinced that the only way to save the world is through revolution and that she needs to subjugate her own desires for the sake of the greater good. And it's apparent to her that the communists are particularly necessary in Africa because they are the only people who tell the truth about the situation of the blacks.

Doris's new circle was comprised chiefly of British RAF servicemen. There were also a couple of other locals like Dorothy Schwartz. And there was her soon-to-be husband Gottfried Lessing, who had been converted to communism during a period of exile in London in the late 1930s and was the most knowledgeable among them about Marxist theory and communist practice. Initially, there was some debate about whether they should be attempting to form an actual Communist Party. Gottfried thought that it was inappropriate to do so before they had educated the working classes – both black and white – and created the conditions for revolution. The others were too impatient to wait: they wanted to be communists now. Outvoted, Gottfried agreed, and they formed a

Party. But the CP in South Africa refused to credit them with official Party status so they constituted an amateur outpost, campaigning through other organisations that had sprung up since Russia became a wartime ally: Medical Aid for Russia, Friends of the Soviet Union (set up to tell 'the truth' about 'the socialist sixth of the world').

Later, Lessing claimed that her conversion to communism was primarily motivated by social frustration and loneliness. Certainly, these were important factors, but Marxist theory had its own appeal. She wrote frequently in the 1940s that reading about 'dialectics' (by which presumably she meant reading Marx and Engels) had enabled her to make sense of the world and its contradictions. 'I remember reading all sorts of philosophy', she wrote in 1945, 'none of which satisfied me in the least, because life just wasn't like that, but when I read explanations of dialectics, then I thought 'ah, at last'.' And, with its promise of a new kind of equal freedom, communism answered a personal need.

In her daily life as a communist, Doris Wisdom was busier than she had ever been before. While in her marital home, she balanced motherhood with the demands of her work for the Party. In her autobiography, she describes cycling across Salisbury to deliver some leaflets with Jean in her basket, aware of the uneasiness of the child in front of her. After leaving Frank, she found a job in a lawyer's office, which finished at four in the afternoon. She was then occupied until two in the morning with study groups and campaigns. Early on, her cohort decided to infiltrate every other political group in town and found it easy to be elected on to most committees.

There was still time for love and sex. Indeed, reading about her life in this period it can seem as if it was dominated by amatory matters. In the scene where she delivered leaflets on her bicycle, she describes the luxuriant pleasure she took in the brevity of her skirt and the shapeliness of her brown legs rotating on the pedals. She was well aware that her unusual success in selling the communist newspaper in the military camps was the result of her looks and her attractive intensity. And when she gave a speech to an important Labour Party meeting, she made sure to wear a dress with a noticeable slit to distract her audience from the less palatable aspects of her argument.

But love affairs were relegated to the interstices of her days, because her focus was on her political work. Though Doris and Gottfried Lessing were not well suited as a couple, they were able to inspire the rest of the group with their combined energy. In *A Ripple from the Storm*, Gottfried's alter ego Anton tells Martha and her group that a communist is someone who is 'utterly, totally, dedicated to the cause of freeing humanity', sacrificing himself for the cause. Together, Doris and Gottfried made great progress in Salisbury in galvanising support for Russia and creating a context for conversations about native reform. However, their work entailed endless compromises, most notably with the Labour Party, and it was the least revolutionary aspects of their campaigning that were the most successful. When some of the military members of their cohort were posted away, the group lost its focus and became dominated by in-fighting. What was more, Doris Lessing herself found it harder not to allow doubt to intrude, partly because of the increasing availability of literature that was critical about the situation in Russia.

In the final year of the war, their group entered a new phase, dominated by the three young RAF men from Cambridge who had joined them: John Whitehorn, Coll MacDonald and Leonard Smith. Of the three, Smithie was the serious communist – although John Whitehorn was part of their group, he would not have described himself as a communist at all – but even Smithie lacked the determination of the Lessings. Once he was posted abroad at the end of 1944, he started sending Doris Lessing disturbing books and articles.

In the course of fifteen months between 1937 and 1938 there had been 1.5 million people arrested in the Soviet Union, almost half of whom were killed. It still seems remarkable that this can have been occluded in Lessing's circle for almost a decade after the war, and that those who did have an idea of the numbers were still able to see all these victims as genuine counter-revolutionaries. Yet this was indeed the case. In 1938, reviewing a book about the trial of the senior communists convicted of treason, the British communist John Strachey declared that, having read the transcripts of the trials, he was convinced by 'the authenticity of the confessions of the accused'. Similarly, Beatrice and Sidney Webb stated in their popular and compendious *Soviet Communism: A New Civilisation* (updated in 1941) that it had been proven that those tried for treason 'had begun to intrigue with the German Army against the new social order of the Soviet Union'.

It was a shock, then, for Lessing to receive a copy of the Hungarian ex-communist Arthur Koestler's *The Yogi and the Commissar* shortly after it was published in 1945, and a copy of Victor Kravchenko's *I Chose Freedom*, the memoirs of a former Soviet official who had defected to the US, when it came out the following year. Starting from the premise that the greatest danger of the Soviet Union was the way that it could immunise people to the 'smoothness of transition to successive degrees of unfreedom', Koestler asked how millions of people in the West had managed to swallow the 'constant purges, the monotonously recurrent ex-communication of the popular leaders of yesteryear'. His book provided a fact-fuelled indictment of the Soviet Union that made clear its extensive violation of its own constitution. He pointed out that the right to strike had been abolished in Russia, that inheritance had been made legal, that there was vast inequality of wages, that divorce and abortion were more difficult than they were in the West and that, most worryingly, about 10 per cent of the Soviet population was 'statistically missing' according to the current Soviet censuses.

This was bad, but Kravchenko's account was more luridly frightening, with its tales of his repeated interrogations by the secret police. A high-ranking engineer, Kravchenko had moved rapidly between favour and disfavour until in 1945 he was considered a loyal enough citizen to be posted to the US. At this point, he forsook his wife and embarked on a dangerous hidden life in America, all in order to tell the truth about the Soviet Union. 'The magnitude of the horror has never been grasped by the outside world', he stated, describing the arrests, 'perhaps it is too vast ever to be grasped. Russia is a battlefield strewn with corpses, blotched with gigantic enclosures where millions of wretched "war prisoners" toiled, suffered and died'.

After reading these books, Lessing went back to the texts she knew: the Webbs, Marx, Stalin's own speeches and an adulatory biography of Stalin by J.T. Murphy. Here was the line on the Soviet Union she had propounded at meetings throughout the war. Kravchenko claimed that the people in the Soviet Union were denied 'elementary liberties'. But the *History of the Communist Party of the Soviet Union* (widely available in its 1939 English translation) assured its readers that 'in order to strengthen Socialist society, the Constitution guarantees freedom of speech, press, assembly and meeting'. This might not be true in practice, but Beatrice and Sidney Webb had explicitly addressed the charge that communism removed personal freedom, attempting to organise the 'good life' for the masses while infringing 'the individual liberty on which the good life absolutely depends'. They challenged this, suggesting that the freedom vaunted by the West was the freedom of the rich. Freedom in socialism was constituted by the 'maximising of opportunity, to act according to individual desire', shifting the emphasis from the freedom of one person to the aggregate freedoms of the entire community. 'It is true that liberty is precious – so precious that it must be rationed', Lenin had once said.

It was a challenge to reconcile Koestler and Kravchenko with the Webbs and Murphy. Lessing wrote that she and her comrades felt 'as if our brains were being turned inside out'. If what Koestler wrote was true, then nothing they believed could be true. After reading *The Yogi and the Commissar*, she reported to Whitehorn feeling 'very shattered' by the book and described the resulting crisis:

> Darling John, having never fallen in love with
> communism how can you know what it feels like to
> have your beloved besmirched. Read Koestler till one
> this morning and thought about it till five am so feel
> a trifle battered… Behold me at the age of 23… One
> sees the world as at last finished with all the cruelty and
> bloodshed and on the verge of a general development
> towards Utopia which will be ushered in by all the
> inevitable revolutions that will take place 'after the war'.
> One lives cheerfully on the edge of millennium. This is

very satisfying. One attains to an astonishingly detailed knowledge of Soviet Russia which one thinks of with a kind of religious ecstasy.

She had read books about Russia and had come to accept the tightening of divorce and abortion laws as well as the trials, terror and hero worship as the 'shortcomings of a transitionary period'. She had learnt to regard the Communist Party not as an adored parent but as 'imperfect, narrow and often stupid', though nonetheless essential for the achievement of socialism. Now she could see that the communist mistakes had laid the way open for fascism in Germany and that all the old guard of Lenin's CP had gone.

This complete disillusion was brief. A few weeks later she told Smithie that though the book had shocked her for a fortnight, she had become convinced both that the CP could not have consciously gone on to the wrong road – it must have happened unconsciously – and that Koestler was a biased reporter. He had not mentioned the (apparent) racial equality in the Soviet Union, which 'in a world that is sick and poisoned with race hatred' mattered a great deal. She couldn't believe that the standards of living for ordinary people were as bad as he suggested. At this point, she took refuge in thinking that the Trotskyists expected too much; this was a battle against impossible odds and the Soviet Union could still be defeated at any moment. 'Far from being on the edge of millennium we are just crawling out of the slime and what right have we to talk about ends and means, when war itself is a means, which even Koestler would justify'.

Over the course of the next two years she became more despairing again, especially when she read Kravchenko in the summer of 1947, and had to confront the possibility that there was a 'reign of terror worse than anything else Hitler thought of'. She was furious with Gottfried who maintained that in spite of its many horrors the Soviet Union was 'progressive objectively although in fact it is reactionary'. In the end she told Smithie that she was losing hope, because none of the available choices seemed satisfactory:

> We are in the middle of a life and death struggle between communism and capitalism so our choice is to collaborate with the life-haters and the nigger-haters and the rest of the people who will destroy the world if they get the chance or to fight for the communist ideal although we loathe the methods. Or we can sit down, fold our hands, bandage our wounds and say I am too good for this wicked world and pretend that we are neutral.

Her solution was to remain publicly loyal to a party she had increasingly little faith in. By the time that she moved to London in 1949, she defined herself foremost as a writer and had lost most of her illusions about Soviet communism. Yet she took the surprising step of joining the British Communist Party in 1952 – a move she later described as 'probably the most neurotic act of my life' – at a point when very few British intellectuals were doing so. She had recently sold *The Grass is Singing* and she and Peter had moved in with the bohemian communist actress and fellow single mother Joan Rodker. She appears to have been drawn back into communist campaigning because here again the most interesting people she met were communists. There seems at this stage to have been no question of freedom.

Under the auspices of the British CP, she went to the Soviet Union for the Authors' World Peace Appeal in 1952, joining the first cohort of Western intellectuals allowed in to Russia since the war. It was the CP who funded her when she returned to Southern Rhodesia in March 1956, shortly after the new leader of the Soviet Union Nikita Kruschchev had delivered his 'secret speech' denouncing Stalin's 'intolerance, his brutality, and his abuse of power'. In Southern Rhodesia, she was declared a prohibited immigrant and denied entry to South Africa. She was conscious of being followed by the CID, and grew increasingly impatient with the Southern Rhodesian authorities. Though it may not easily proffer freedom, communism still seemed to offer a preferable alternative to Western capitalism, which had its own forms of constraint and surveillance. Returning home, she was stirred by her experiences to declare in her report of her trip that within a decade the communist countries would become 'freer, more democratic' than the West.

This quickly proved even more unlikely than she could have known. On 23 October, thousands of students marched through the streets of Budapest, calling for freedom on loudspeakers. On 4 November, Soviet tanks arrived in Hungary. The Executive Committee of the British CP issued a statement in the *Daily Worker*, justifying the actions of the Soviet troops on the grounds that they had been offered a choice between helping the Hungarian communists fight 'to prevent a return to fascism' or standing by and watching the Hungarian and Western forces of reaction 'crush the Hungarian people'. Lessing joined Eric Hobsbawm, Christopher Hill and others in signing a letter to the *Daily Worker* protesting against the Soviet invasion of Hungary. Later Lessing quoted Koestler saying that everyone who stayed in the CP had a secret explanation for what was happening. Her own was the belief that though the leadership of the Soviet Union had become corrupt, there were good communists waiting for the right moment to seize power and resume the march 'to the just society, the perfect society'. She now began to see that Stalin might have murdered all of them.

It was time to leave. This was not an easy decision and many of her friends concluded differently: John Berger and Eric Hobsbawm remained in the Party, preferring to criticise it from within. They were still convinced, as Hobsbawm put it, that they were 'combatants in an omnipresent war'. But on 23 November, a Party official announced in a bugged King Street conversation that 'Lessing is out'. The bureaucrats claimed not to mind. Cultural groups were better off with ordinary people; the *Daily Worker* had been 'much better since the readers have been writing it'. That was that: another door had slammed and another road to liberty had been abandoned. She was gone, but they hadn't wanted her anyway.

II

'Only in the community, therefore, is personal freedom possible'

Organised freedom

Reading about Lessing's love affair with communism left me both envious and shocked. I was shocked by her attempts to defend Stalin and his regime in the face of such incriminating evidence. But I envied the love affair. That moment of conversion had all the excitement, the recklessness of falling in love, combined with the extra pleasure of knowing that it was in the service of a higher ideal that connected her both to her new group of friends and to the rest of the world.

For me, this was a feeling, like the one I'd had at the weddings the previous summer, of finding my generation inadequate in comparison to hers. In the intervening decades, radical politics had become less possible, and it seemed to make us less passionate. Yet it was too late to turn back the clock. There was an inevitability, now, to the revelations of Kravchenko and Koestler: these were extremes born of extremist politics. So it had become harder to be well educated and well informed and to throw yourself whole-heartedly into anything. Extreme positions on collective, national life – and there were plenty of them – were left to those from different social backgrounds from mine and tended now to be right-wing. If I wanted to engage politically, I had a choice of identity politics, environmentalism, or resistance to the more active stances pursued by those I disagreed with.

Though this left me half-admiring her for beliefs I nonetheless considered to have been deluded, I wasn't convinced that her communist convictions had much to do with freedom. Certainly, she began by wanting to free the Southern Rhodesian blacks from their chains. But to go from anger at racial inequality to full-scale communism was a more oblique move than she sometimes suggested. And there was an incoherence when she talked about political freedom more generally. It's not surprising that she was so flummoxed by reading Koestler and Kravchenko. She doesn't seem to have thought that hard about how a system predicated on subjugating the individual to the state could be seen as freeing.

I was curious about how other communists of the time negotiated this, in an era when freedom was a much-vaunted good. I went back to Marx, and found that he was content to admit to denying individual liberty. In their 1848 *Communist Manifesto*, Marx and Engels announced their intention to abolish 'bourgeois individuality, bourgeois independence, and bourgeois freedom'.

Marx and Engels made what Isaiah Berlin would later define as a distinction between negative and positive freedom. Negative freedom was dismissed as the province of bourgeois society. Positive freedom – freedom to, as opposed to freedom from – was seen as compatible with communism. Marx and Engels stated in their 1846 *The German Ideology* that 'only in community [with others has each] individual the means of cultivating his gifts in all directions; only in the community, therefore, is personal freedom possible'. This kind of freedom was going to be constructed through class struggle and to consist of legislation limiting hours of work and child labour and providing free education and health care, curbing the freedom of the capitalists to exploit workers.

For Marx and his early followers, communism didn't necessarily preclude all negative liberties. Because they needed freedom of speech and of the press in order to propound their ideas, most militant advocates of revolutionary Marxism in the late-nineteenth and early-twentieth centuries encouraged some political freedom. This changed after the Russian revolution, because the communists now needed to maintain rather than to gain power. From year to year more negative freedoms were sacrificed. Not many communists in the 1940s talked about freedom; there were very few communists who'd have joined Lessing in proclaiming it the main virtue they were offering. But it remained a question in need of an answer, so they had to be prepared to advocate a form of positive liberty that was predicated on a lack of negative liberty. This was explicit in the Webbs' answer to the question of whether the Soviet Union denied freedom. It was also voiced by the British communist Randall Swingler in his contribution to the influential 1947 essay collection *The Communist Answer to the Challenge of Our Time*, edited by the Marxist philosopher John Lewis.

Starting from the premise that 'the liberal claim to freedom of the individual is really the claim of the privileged and leisured section of the community to the preservation of its privilege and leisure', Swingler suggested that in the post-war world the freedom of the capitalist had been exposed as 'a robbery and a fraud' and the freedom of the liberal as an illusion. In contrast to the negative liberal conception of freedom as an escape 'from the necessities and obligations of living', the Marxist idea of freedom was 'positive, creative, dynamic', enabling the 'fullest possible development of the faculties of the individual'. Man freed himself not by separating from society, but by 'integrating himself with it' and accepting the forces of nature and history.

By this point, the battle lines of the cold war had been drawn, so Swingler was using the term 'freedom' expediently, tackling the claims of the anti-communists head on. Shortly afterwards, the CIA set up the Congress for Cultural Freedom in 1950, using the banner of freedom to fight the Soviet Union. From now on, America designated the West the 'free world', making freedom an increasingly propagandist term in both the East and West. This became complicated for Lessing.

Part of the problem here is that Lessing's enthusiasm for freedom didn't take the form of a belief: it was more of an individual need. Her most powerful feeling of freedom – the one that resonated most for me – came from those moments of solitary expansion in the bush. This by its nature was individual; she couldn't have expected it to be universal. Yet when she left her children, she was seeking a collective form of freedom that seemed nonetheless to derive its urgency from those moments when she'd felt free.

I wanted to know if anyone had succeeded in bringing together the experience of individual freedom with a belief in political, collective freedom. I turned to Henry David Thoreau, whose experiments with creative solitude in nature I'd been thinking of when reading about Lessing in the bush. He was more of a philosopher than she was, so I thought he might have made more progress in balancing his inclinations and his opinions, while still forging his political theory out of his experiences as a walking body. I'd always liked Thoreau. Perhaps simply because we both enjoyed going away to write, I envied and admired his life at Walden. For two years, two months and two days in 1845, he lived in a cabin in the woodland, near Concord, Massachusetts, being almost wholly self-sufficient. He claimed that he could produce enough in forty days of work to enable him to spend the rest of the year reading, writing and, most importantly, walking.

'I wish to speak a word for Nature, for absolute freedom and wildness, as contrasted with a freedom and culture merely civil.' This is the beginning of Thoreau's wonderful 1862 essay 'Walking', written some years after the Walden experiment. Here he said that he needed to spend at least four hours a day wandering through the wildest landscapes that he could find, avoiding other people where possible, convinced that 'all good things are wild and free'. He liked walking west, into the future and the wild, rather than east, into the cultivated European past. 'My spirits infallibly rise in proportion to the outward dreariness. Give me the ocean, the desert, or the wilderness! In the desert, pure air and solitude compensate for want of moisture and fertility.'

This has become a cliché, now, but I think it would have resonated for Lessing, and it certainly resonated for me. I'd come to see that political and personal freedom were questionable goods, by definition unattainable because in seeking freedom you find that it constantly evades you. We could only hope to be freer, rather than hoping to be free, and if we had any sense of what freedom might feel like, it was predicated on our experience of the physical feeling of absolute freedom that could be found most easily in nature. I was learning that the connection between these could only be metaphorical and that it was therefore a weak bond at best. What interested me in Thoreau was that he grappled with this connection, more consciously than Lessing did. He knew where he'd felt free and he wanted to know how he could find a social or political equivalent for it.

Like Lessing, Thoreau fought hard against race prejudice. He wanted to abolish slavery in America. And like Lessing, his belief in the individual need for freedom seems to have emerged organically out of his own pleasure in the freedom of nature. But for Thoreau, in order for the freedom of wildness to become universal, the state needed to wither away. 'That government is best which governs least', he wrote in his 1849 essay 'Civil Disobedience', going on to suggest that his ideal government would 'govern not at all'. If even a few hundred people lived as he had in Walden, they would think from first principles, no longer compelled by mercenary self-interest to go along with the will of the majority. They would become right-minded enough to oppose slavery, and they would do so in the first instance by refusing to pay their taxes to the state.

This version of utopian politics was more consistent than Lessing's, simply because the rhetoric of freedom works better when you are advocating less state control rather than more of it. But Thoreau was still not very convincing in suggesting that the freedom he found at Walden could be a universal good. He forgot his own advantages. The land he was living on belonged to Ralph Waldo Emerson, who'd given it to him in exchange for some manual labour; not everyone had a similarly generous friend. He didn't attempt to combine personal freedom with marriage or fatherhood. More importantly, not everyone wanted as many hours as he had to read and walk. Thoreau is most enticing when he knows that he's unusual and is describing a unique experience, rather than when he's expecting to provide a model for others to follow.

IV

'I feel as if I've been let out of a prison'

Aftermath

In her autobiography, Lessing asks how long it takes after assuming a political faith – 'surrendering individuality in an inner act of submission to authority' – to regain emotional autonomy. It seems to have taken her until the publication of *The Golden Notebook* in 1962. She found it hard to let go of a promise of freedom that had once been strong enough to impel her to leave two children she loved. But she had lost interest in participating actively in politics and from now on she would always define herself foremost as a writer, stressing that she was too fundamentally ambivalent to commit wholeheartedly to any political party.

In February 1957, Lessing wrote a revealing letter to her friend Edward (E.P.) Thompson, who had asked her for her verdict on the events of the previous year. She told him that she had nothing to say because she had now finally escaped 'the straitjacket of what we've all been thinking and feeling for so long'. This was not a political statement. She knew full well that 'all my reactions now are because (if I may use this word I hate so much) I am an artist'. As a writer, she had 'exhausted all the experience and emotions that are useful to me as an artist in the old way of being a Communist'. She had no moral fervour left; she thought that anyone who felt responsible for the 'bloodbaths and cynicism' of the Communist Party over the past thirty years should be unable to 'feel indignant about the bloody-mindedness of capitalism'. She was still a socialist who believed in 'the necessity for revolution when the moment is opportune', but she needed to let herself 'simmer into some sort of knowledge', though she didn't yet know what it was. The 'dead aroma' of political words now made her feel sick; she felt as though she had been 'let out of a prison'; 'I want to write a lot of books'.

It was in this mood that she wrote the early sections of *The Golden Notebook*. For several months, she'd felt that she no longer knew what or how to write, perhaps largely because she could no longer believe in any form of social realism. The CP both in Britain and Russia had long eschewed the avant-garde, advocating a reactionary mode of writing that contrasted with the vaunted progressiveness of their policies. According to their credos, the workers needed to read about their own struggles and they needed to do so in a form that they could understand. It doesn't seem to be a coincidence that Lessing's decision to leave the Party was followed by an attempt to seek a new, freer form for the novel; that she now eschewed plot and splintered the narrative in an attempt to capture the experience of living and to look more deeply than she had done previously into the psychology of her central character. She had given up on seeking liberty politically but she was seeking it formally, and hoping in the process to understand her own lost dream of revolutionary freedom.

If my compulsion to read and to think about Lessing had begun with *The Golden Notebook*, then it had begun with her political commitment. When I told people I was writing about Lessing that summer, there was considerable enthusiasm amid the scepticism. This often came from women in their fifties, sixties and seventies who were remembering the first time they had read *The Golden Notebook*, and were looking back on this as a moment of political awakening. I was curious about what exactly this had consisted of. Given that communism had been widely discredited by then, it couldn't have been the communism. It was more likely that they were thinking of the feminism, but even here, they weren't recalling Lessing as a straightforward feminist foremother: they remembered the 'real men' and the veal escalope too uncomfortably for that. So what was it? As I thought more about her politics, I thought that what remained compelling wasn't in fact her devotion to any particular cause. It was more her determination to be always complicated: to question everything – not only what those around her thought, but what she herself thought. When we allowed ourselves to be disturbed or excited by this, it was a political response.

I read *The Golden Notebook* again, wanting to better understand these thoughts. It's a long novel, and I read slowly, lying on my back on the patchy grass of one London park after another. The August skies were grey and humid, and I became caught up in the novel's thick atmosphere of intelligent gloom. Despite its humour, I found it more depressing than I had on previous readings, because I was more conscious of the preceding period of energy and hope it mourned, both in Lessing's own life and in Anna's. I was frightened by the disintegration of self portrayed in the novel, unwilling to follow Lessing into fragmentation. And at the same time I was envious because I didn't even have a dream of political freedom to look back on.

The circumstances of Anna Wulf's life are closely modelled on Lessing's. She has been married to a German exile with whom she has had one child in Southern Rhodesia; she has joined the Communist Party in Britain in 1950 and left it in 1954. When the book opens in 1957, she and her friends are exhausted after spending considerable time attempting to convince people in the British CP that it's 'much better to admit that things stank in Russia than to deny it'. And she is trying to persuade her friend Molly (modelled on Joan Rodker) that it's time to admit that 'the great dream has faded and the truth is something else – that we'll never be any use'. Molly reminds her that she probably wouldn't be saying this if she wasn't currently disappointed in love.

The Golden Notebook is structured as a series of notebooks and commentaries, divided between the conventional realist narrative of 'Free women', the exploratory storytelling and reminiscence of the black, yellow and blue notebooks, the dry, often fragmented political diary entries and reportage of the red notebook and the lucidly manic stream-of-consciousness of the golden notebook. Through these multiple narratives we see Anna shifting in a kaleidoscope that shakes her sexual, emotional, political and artistic experiences into endless new patterns. In the background is the belief that it's inaccurate or even dishonest to tell a life story in only one way. This takes us back to the modernist experiments of Virginia Woolf, whom Lessing much admired, but in a more explicitly political context, because Lessing thought that the inner life could not be comprehended in isolation from its intellectual and political climate.

Lessing understood that writing books changes us; that the life is as affected by the books as the books are by the life. She thought that this was especially the case for her with *The Golden Notebook*, a novel where she was writing herself away from communism and more fundamentally away from politics, and writing herself into a kind of necessary breakdown. It's a novel of ideas that also fundamentally distrusts most of the ideas it explores. If there is a dominant concept being put forward then it's that labels (and the binaries they imply) are dangerous. 'Men. Women. Bound. Free. Good. Bad. Yes. No. Capitalism. Socialism. Sex. Love.' Because politics are inevitably littered with both labels and binaries, Anna can no longer speak a political language. She is concerned instead with living and with writing about life, though she doesn't yet know how to do so. 'I am interested only in stretching myself, in living as fully as I can.'

The novel reaches back to Anna's early years as a communist in the Mashopi hotel (modelled on the Macheke hotel where the Lessings had danced, drunk and campaigned with Whitehorn and Smithie and Coll). Looking back, she is filled with a 'terrible dry anguish' that's dangerously close to the pain of nostalgia. The story is built up in several interwoven time periods, moving forward to the flat where Anna lives alone with her daughter and occasional lodgers, attempting to live both passionately and honestly as a single woman and campaigning somewhat reluctantly on behalf of the communists. During this period of being a communist, she's unable to write because at the moment she sits down to begin, someone seems to come into the room, look over her shoulder and stop her. 'It could be a Chinese peasant. Or one of Castro's guerrilla fighters. Or an Algerian fighting in the FLN. They stand here in the room and they say, why aren't you doing something about us, instead of wasting your time scribbling?'

After the relationship with her married lover Michael finishes, Anna leaves the Communist Party and becomes gradually overwhelmed by a process of mental breakdown that ends with her lying shivering, alone and exhausted, in her flat, dreaming of the landscapes of communist myth. In her dreams, she becomes the Algerian soldier, threatened with disintegration, and she then flies away – delighting in the 'light free movement' possible in the air – to look down over China. Here she surveys a Chinese peasant woman, working communally in the fields, and longs to join her and become 'a peasant with other peasants'. This is a moment of epiphany. 'The joy of the dream was more intense than I have experienced, and it was the joy of freedom.' Descending, she walks towards the woman and enters her body; she is a young pregnant woman made old by work. She finds herself mechanically thinking progressive liberal thoughts about the background of the woman she's now inhabiting, and then becomes frightened by the terror of the dissolution that she's experiencing in entering the bodies of others. Waking, her stomach clenches and she becomes once again 'the sick Anna who had no will'.

By the end, the political is so bound up with the psychological as to lose all objective meaning. Where does this leave freedom? The answer seems to be found in the dream and its instant of joy. If freedom is possible now for Anna then it's in that moment of flight and the dissolution of self it brings. This is freedom, once again, as a physical experience – as an inner state given ecstatic outer form. But there's also the freedom of taking nothing for granted and of finding no thought too uncomfortable to verbalise. Her almost fanatical need to live in good faith has taken her away from lovers, friends and politics and has stopped her from writing books. It has also left her sure of the authenticity of the few thoughts she does still find possible to express.

I was startled when I first read that letter to E.P. Thompson where Lessing says that she has 'exhausted all the experience and emotions that are useful to me as an artist in the old way of being a Communist', because it seemed like she was giving up on politics altogether, and affirming her calling as a writer instead. More disturbingly, I wondered if she was saying that in fact she was only interested in politics in the first place for the material it could provide for her art. Both interpretations seemed unlikely, especially as she then went on to write the novel that would have the most political impact. Now I thought that in fact she was giving up on group politics, no longer able to align her views with those of a political party, but remained someone for whom almost all of life was political. By distancing herself from the group and insisting on the complicated individual voice, she was taking a political stance. Rereading *The Golden Notebook* that summer, I remained convinced that if her politics were remembered in the twenty-first century then it was for this complication, rather than for her early communist fervour.

As someone who had never been comfortable in seeing myself as straightforwardly political, I found this reassuring. I was coming to realise that if I was less political than she was in her mid-thirties, this was both because the politics of my time were less passionate and because I was less capable of joining in than she was then. This could only be partly explained by the generational difference: plenty of my contemporaries were more fervent about politics than I was, even if their politics were less radical than hers. So it was reassuring to see her losing this ability to join in as she got older, because it made me blame myself less.

Part of why I envied Lessing's passionate communist phase was because I envied her the freedom to be herself within a group that she found at that time. The great strength of Lessing's descriptions of communist life in *A Ripple from the Storm* and *The Golden Notebook* is her ability to describe group life; her understanding of the pull and the repulsion, the joy and the hatred of collectivity. I longed, as she had, to experience the communal, and there was something about doomed, idealistic socialism that seemed to make group existence particularly enjoyable. I was starting to realise that it was this, as much as the ideas themselves, that appealed to me. I had written a book about British socialists in the 1930s and had once written an unpublished novel about West German communists in the 1980s: a tiny group who hoped that the best of both Germanys could be combined into a new political system poised between East and West. These groups shared Lessing's sense of working for the greater good. And the people involved in them found a form of freedom simply in relinquishing their own desires and aligning them with the collective.

There had never been such a possibility for me in my own life. There had been causes I'd believed in. I had felt my share of anger in response to a series of governments that waged war, increased the gap between rich and poor and dismantled the welfare state. But I'd felt awkward marching or even signing collective letters. I felt as though I was play-acting if called upon to shout slogans because the voice in my head was observing critically, like Martha scrutinising herself as she slings around communist rhetoric. I worried that the specificity of any position was lost when you allowed yourself to speak collectively. And I just wasn't very good at groups.

That August, there was an ordinary incident that made me fear that my anxiety about group life was pathological, though at the same time it drew attention to the almost comical triviality of the group situations that confronted me, compared to those that Lessing found herself involved in. There was a picnic and volleyball game in a park organised by my husband's office. We had attended several of these occasions in the past and they'd been sources of contention. I had a tendency to be silent, which some of his friends interpreted as rudeness. Given that I can be extroverted in my own circle, my husband saw my introversion in these settings as a sign of haughty snobbishness: his friends were not intellectual enough for me.

I'd found these situations easier since having a child. You can take refuge in attending to the needs of the young and, in the more successful instances, in taking part in their games. But our son had the same tendency towards the kind of aloofness that can be interpreted either as shyness or disdain as I did. At children's parties, he would frequently refuse to join in the games. On this occasion, he was shy and wanted to sit on my lap. I sat with him, apart from the games or group conversations, responding politely but quietly when people came to talk to us. I was aware that we were a disappointment, that in a different mood I could have persuaded my son to show off to my husband's colleagues, and that I too could have found in myself a capacity to tell or at least to respond noisily to anecdotes.

Afterwards, we argued, differing on definitions of 'normal' behaviour. I claimed, accurately, that many of my friends would have felt and behaved as I'd done, missing once again my dying correspondent, who a few months earlier would have been poised at his computer, ready to write me a message on the naturalness of misanthropy. Silently, I blamed Lessing for this particular moment of disjunction, thinking specifically about the difference between Martha and Anna. Martha is a group person but Anna isn't, though we have to accept that Anna has been an easy participant in groups before the novel has started. This means that Martha (at least in the early novels) would be fully capable of publicly enjoying a noisy group conversation with people she doesn't feel connected to individually, where Anna would be unable to attempt it, too frightened by the bad faith it would entail.

We can't elide Lessing with either character, but her move away from communism was partly a move away from the communal more generally, guided by a sense that the social selves we assume within the group are likely to be false. By the time that she wrote *The Golden Notebook*, she seems to have believed that to take part socially in a group where you do not feel at ease is to implicate yourself in a kind of social lie.

I couldn't honestly claim a political justification for my own churlishness. I apologised as best I could, trying to explain the shyness that comes from feeling out of place: not so much shyness as insistent introversion and alienation from any public persona that I can muster, which manifests itself in a kind of numbed exhaustion where every phrase is an effort that makes me as irritated by myself as by the people around me. But I was left feeling disturbed by the situation.

These were people I had a reasonable amount in common with – as I would if I aligned myself with a political cause or group – but joining in seemed to be something that I found too difficult to do. I envied Lessing her early moment of joining in, while admiring the book in which she showed why, for her older heroine, just such an attempt to join in was impossible.

Yet at the same time, I was becoming more convinced that my commitment to the complicated individual constituted a political opinion and I was becoming more receptive to the possibility of doing something about it. In my own world, there was more and more politically to be angry about. I often felt rage now that I could see was political rage, and it was starting to feel that it might be enough to make me join in, though I didn't yet know what form this might take. At the same time, if reading Lessing had confirmed my sense that the belief in the complicated individual was a potential mode of countering the growing fear of difference I could see around me, then I worried that this would be blunted by turning it into a more collective rhetoric. For now, these thoughts didn't take me outward into the public sphere; instead they made me feel that in my own life it was more necessary to live honestly; to seek a muted, personal kind of political freedom simply by expressing uncomfortable opinions at home or in my social circle, at the risk of awkwardness or misunderstanding.

The summer was almost over. Neither communism nor politics had emerged as very freeing in themselves. But I was more acutely aware than I had been that Anna Wulf gains a form of freedom by remaining political at the same time as she abandons her more rigid political position. And there was something freeing for me in seeing that my own stance was political, and that it was political in a way that related to a writer who was admired specifically for her political commitment. I was more implicated in my time than I had allowed myself to know.

5

'I cannot imagine myself not loving several people at once in various ways'

Free Love

At the end of August there was an unexpected heatwave. I swam every other day, enjoying the feeling of tired muscles afterwards, happily conscious of my body. Wearing summer clothes, there was often the feeling that a dress or skirt could effortlessly come off; it was easy to imagine a hand or a mouth on my bare shoulder, stroking the collar bone, moving down gently to my breast. The fantasies played out indistinctly at the back of my mind. The men varied from day to day: men encountered in crowded rooms, or talked to in corridors. Half-unconsciously, I examined their hands, wondering if they were hands I'd like to touch me, but really these were fantasies about me rather than about them. Lessing wrote that it was only in middle-age that she realised how much narcissism was involved in sexual attraction.

It was time to think about free love, which was where this whole project had begun: with a sense that the monogamous love I was witnessing being celebrated at those weddings was a pale imitation of the riskier state I'd encountered in Lessing's novels. Now I found that there was one scene in particular from *Landlocked* (1965), the fourth Martha Quest novel, that kept coming back to me. It was a scene that I was longing to inhabit, though I could see the perils this would involve.

This is the most concentrated moment of happy freedom in the whole *Children of Violence* series and it takes place in the loft of a shed. Peacefully languorous, Martha lies watching the afternoon sunlight playing on her naked arm while below her, the brown head of her lover bobs up and down as he sells plants to one of his customers. His voice is warm from lovemaking; she can still feel the shape of his head through her fingers. She stretches her body in the leaf-scented warmth, conscious of happiness as she has rarely been before.

Thomas comes up the stairs towards her with his blue eyes filled with sunlight. Martha feels her stomach turning to liquid, while her shoulders, breasts and thighs ('apparently on orders from Thomas, since her body no longer owed allegiance to her') shrink, awaiting the touch of her lover. Looking at him, staring steadily and almost unbearably into his eyes, she feels as if doors are being opened one after another inside them as they gaze.

Thomas is a Polish communist whose closest friends have died in concentration camps. This affair has no future because both wish to leave the country as soon as possible: Martha to go to England and Thomas to Israel. But it's precisely this lack of future that gives the relationship its freedom. They are suspended in time as they are suspended in their loft in the garden, looking out on to the rainy sky, anointing each other's bodies with the warm drips of water that come in through the window.

Martha cannot remain free and in love. Now, when she has sex with her husband, her nerves react and she vomits. It seems that her body is incapable of principled sexual freedom. 'Her stomach, her intestines, her bladder complained that she was the wife of one man and they did not like her making love with another'. Then, more painfully, she finds herself accompanying a friend in visiting Thomas on his farm with his wife and child. She sits frozen in politeness at a long trestle table made by Thomas, eating the food prepared by his wife. After lunch, she wanders into the garden and encounters Thomas, his cheeks stained with tears, gently holding out a coaxing hand to his small daughter, who has turned away. In this moment Martha learns something she 'should know, should have known, about Thomas'. She feels that it's 'the real being' of Thomas that she can sense in this gesture of the big hand held out delicately and lovingly to the child.

What Martha is coming to understand is that she cannot love like this, driven 'back and back into regions of herself she had not known existed', without wanting the whole man. She feels overpowered by loneliness when she encounters him as an apparent stranger at his farm. And she is envious of his wife because she wants to have his children herself. Their love affair, which began as one free spirit claiming another in the name of a sexual freedom they both profess to believe in, has ended with a mutual need for possession that terrifies them both and leaves Martha less free than when she began.

Doris Lessing experimented with free love for thirty years between 1940 and 1970, only at rare moments enjoyably. These experiences found form in *The Golden Notebook*, with its brilliantly complex exploration of the way that love renders even the so-called 'free woman' less free. And then they were given a new complexion in *Landlocked*. For Martha as for Lessing, sex may be disappointing at first but it does eventually bring the physical freedom she's hoped for. However, Lessing found that the better sex became, the less free it made her, because it left her longing more needily for the presence of a particular man in her bed, and it involved her giving up her body, as Martha does, into the possession of someone else.

I

'The free woman was so much more exciting than the dull tied woman'

Lessing in love

Doris Tayler didn't embark on either of her marriages claiming any expectation of monogamy. The Sports Club world in which she moved with Frank Wisdom was cheerfully hedonistic, while the communist circle in which she lived with Gottfried Lessing followed the line of the more enlightened revolutionaries in 1920s Russia in seeing marriage and the family as outmoded institutions and sex as necessarily free. She and all of her better-read contemporaries were well versed in the theories of British pioneers of free love such as Havelock Ellis. And this was wartime, when (though it was rather less likely in Southern Rhodesia than in Europe) they could all be dead tomorrow, so they had to live as fully as possible.

When she left Frank, she was having an affair with a serviceman in the RAF. Many of her acquaintances assumed she was leaving her husband for him, but she was unperturbed when he was posted abroad a few months later. Her affairs during her next marriage were more serious, though not so consuming as to preclude her being in love with several men at once. This seems to have been the case in her liaisons with the three Cambridge RAF men.

Doris fell in love with Smithie first, but he didn't respond with sufficient ardour for them to begin an affair. Then in January 1945, she went on a trip to Machete (staying in the hotel that would become the Mashopi in *The Golden Notebook*) with Gottfried and their friends and fell, as she described it to Smithie, 'violently in love' with John Whitehorn. This was reciprocal passion and it resulted in a spontaneous sexual encounter in the veld that she saw as instrumental for initiating her into a new phase of physical love. Rewritten in *The Golden Notebook*, it became an elemental experience in which the lovers are liberated by the freedom of the African landscape. Anna and Paul run frantically hand-in-hand into the bush in the rain and fall into the wet leaves. Lit only by the moon, they lie trembling, their flesh hot while everything around them is wet and cold. Afterwards they sit entwined under the stars waiting for the sunrise. The older Anna observes that she has 'never, in all my life, been so desperately and wildly and painfully happy as I was then'.

The implications of the affair with John for Doris's marriage were complex. Gottfried responded by being extremely jealous and threatening divorce, but also by desiring her sexually more than he had ever done before. 'Owing to my unfaithfulness G now loves me more than ever', she reported to John, while complaining to Smithie that although she was 'all for adultery', she didn't like hurting people's feelings and so was disturbed by the 'distressingly monogamous tendencies' that Gottfried was developing. She was more damning when she rewrote the scene for *The Golden Notebook*, where Anna remembers 'lying there and hating him and wondering why the only time I could remember him making love to me with any conviction was when he knew I had just made love to someone else'.

Despite the definite passion, I found that there was something a little unreal about Doris's declarations of love both in her letters to John and in her descriptions of the affairs to others. Early on in the letters that I'd read in the Norwich archive, she told John that she wanted a 'stylised love affair', regretting that the haste with which they'd gone to bed precluded this. There's certainly a stylised quality to those letters, which erupt into real feeling only at moments. The most vivid of these moments occurred after the conception of Peter in January 1946, when she wrote to express her longing to have a child with him and to tell him how much she missed him. 'The essence of everything has been that I wanted your child.' It was at this point that she wrote a poem about John that earthed this longing in her memories of their charged encounter in the veld:

Through sleep I know your hands, your tongue.
I wake to find the darkness strong
With an acrid sense of leaves.

Even at this stage, though, Doris was also writing amorously to Smithie. I went to read these letters at an archive in Sussex, and was somewhat perturbed to find that much of the phrasing was almost identical to her letters to John. She seems to have grown to love Smithie more than she had earlier, possibly because his own feelings had become more passionate. 'I cannot imagine myself not loving several people at once in various ways,' she wrote to John in 1948, claiming that this was 'an emotional state common to more people than will confess it'. She told Smithie that although she sometimes considered monogamy 'an excellent institution', she was by nature promiscuous and liked 'flitting from flower to flower'. By this time all three of the RAF men had been posted abroad, and Doris had a succession of new love affairs, which she described to her three correspondents. While she was pregnant, there was a promiscuous Afrikaans painter called Gregoire Boonzaier, who took her to his house by the sea where he painted her, informed her that she was the first English girl he'd encountered who knew how to make love, and impressed her with his tactile sensuality and love of women's bodies. 'I have never met any man yet who so passionately loved the womanness of woman,' she informed Smithie. After Peter's birth, there was a producer from the radio station with whom she fell in love seriously enough that she later described herself wanting to stay in Rhodesia in the hope that he would marry her. This didn't stop her imagining her life in letters to both John and Smithie as one that would soon be spent with them.

Perhaps she downplayed the emotion she felt for any particular lover out of self-protection. Or perhaps there was simply not that much at stake. It can be hard to remember how young she was, despite being by now the twice married mother of three children: only twenty-four when she was lying in John's arms in the rainy bush and only twenty-five when Peter was conceived. These were youthful dalliances and she didn't expect any of them to last; she was waiting for what she would call her 'real life' to begin in England and she did not seriously believe that any of these men would have a part in it. She appears to have been unperturbed by hearing that her lovers were unfaithful and seems to have felt nothing like the ache of possessive love she would later describe between Martha and Thomas. This makes it harder to read *Landlocked* as auto-biography. Situationally, this relationship corresponds to Doris Lessing's relationship with the radio producer, which occurred at the same time in the same place. But emotionally, the affair described seems to correspond more to a later period of her life, in London, when love became both more and less freeing.

On moving to London, Lessing was determined to be inde-pendent and to earn a living for herself and her son while establishing herself as a writer. This was a bid for freedom. 'I was free,' she later wrote in her autobiography, 'I could at last be wholly myself. I felt myself to be self-created, self-suffi-cient.' But these were still the 1950s and it was a freedom that she expected to contain a husband. In *Landlocked*, Martha resolves in Southern Rhodesia that 'when I get to England, I'll find a man I can really be married to.'

Once she had arrived in London, Lessing became part of the cheerfully promiscuous artistic cohort gathered around Joan Rodker, but she seems to have been looking from the start for a man she could commit to more fully than any of the men she had loved in Southern Rhodesia. In *The Golden Notebook* Anna and her alter ego Ella (the heroine of the novel she is writing) set themselves up more self-consciously than Lessing herself ever did as 'free women'. However, in writing Ella's story, Anna observes that 'Ella was now free' – having gained 'the child, her self-respect, a future' through her divorce – but that she 'could not imagine this future without a man'.

Doris Lessing met the psychiatrist known in her autobi-ography as Jack at a party. They became lovers almost imme-diately and he began to spend most of his nights with her, though he was married with children and insisted on leaving early each morning to collect a clean shirt from home. Years later, Lessing asked herself which of her lovers had fulfilled her, emotionally, physically and intellectually. Jack was the only one she could say had satisfied her in all three respects. She also looked back here on her sex life in her first marriage and observed that 'the sex life of ninety-nine per cent of the world's people consists of a robust to-and-fro well described by the English word "bonking", and most people are happy with that'. By contrast, 'the more rarefied shores of sex may be explored only with someone with whom you share quite rare consonances of taste, nature and fantasy'. She explored them with Jack, and consequently came to dismiss previous manifestations of love as a deceptive blend of friendship and erotic desire. This was love as she had only imagined it before; sex as inseparable from the love it embodied.

Jack was a Czech Communist whose family, like Thomas's, had all died in the extermination camps; soon the closest friends of his youth would be executed in Stalin's notorious Slansky trial. As a result, he was fearful of exposure and, more bruised by his past than he was prepared to admit, unable to trust in the possibility of a happy future. Doris nonetheless committed herself wholly to the relationship, convinced that her certainty and strength would be enough to counteract his fear.

Shortly after Doris met Jack, her mother made the misguided step of moving to London to be near her daughter. This occasioned the crisis that sent Doris on to the couch of her Jungian psychoanalyst, Mrs Sussman (who became the model for Mother Sugar in *The Golden Notebook*). It also meant, though, that she was able to spend time away from Peter, so she and Jack went to Spain for a month with a budget of only fifty pounds. This was the most intense time they had spent together. For days on end they drove through the empty Spanish countryside, pausing to make love or quarrel in forests, ditches or olive groves. Sometimes they stopped off at inns, at other times they slept wrapped in blankets lying in fields looking up at the stars, or lay on the sand listening to the waves after eating green peppers and fish cooked by the fishermen on the beach. For years afterwards, Doris couldn't smell green peppers without feeling the heat of the sun as they drove from Salamanca to Avila to Burgos and then on to Gibraltar and Barcelona.

After they returned to London, the tensions in their relationship became more manifest. Jack was both jealous and unfaithful by temperament. Later, Doris was able to explain his infidelity by reflecting on all that he had lost. 'Such a man will be forced by a hundred powerful needs to sleep with women, have women, assert life, make life.' At the time, it was harder to be sanguine and she was hurt, too, by Jack's rejection of her son. Jack was frightened by Peter's attempts to claim him as a father, often pulling himself free of the embraces of a boy who was mourning the departure of his own father to East Germany, where Gottfried had been forced to cut off all contact with the West.

The grief of this period went into *The Golden Notebook*, where Anna finds that her love for Michael threatens her liberation as a 'free woman'. Most distressingly – and Lessing writes these scenes with brilliantly painful acuity – she is trapped in part by 'the shadow of the third': her relationship with the absent wife. At first she and her alter ego Ella have felt an emotion 'of satisfaction, of victory' over the wives of their male friends and lovers, because they are living more honestly and independently and they have the best (the most intense feelings, the most intense desire) that the men have to offer: 'the free woman was so much more exciting than the dull tied woman'. However, gradually Ella starts to envy

Muriel for her hold over this man whom she doesn't seem to need to desire her. To dislike a woman as Ella comes to dislike Muriel is not to feel free. And it's all the more difficult because she is engaged in a pointlessly childish and unfair competition with a wife who is not even joining in.

Though he himself remained married, Jack was becoming jealous of Doris Lessing's friendship with Joan Rodker, so he persuaded her to move to a flat of her own. In 1955, Doris and Peter moved into a large ugly flat in Earl's Court, letting rooms to lodgers in order to pay the rent. It quickly became clear that the move would make no difference to the decline in Doris and Jack's relationship. Later that year, Jack took her to Paris for a weekend. He had been posted abroad for six months and was flying there from France. They said goodbye at the station, where they both knew, though they didn't acknowledge it, that this was the end. Doris stood watching the departing figure of her lover with tears flooding her face; four years of hoping and planning were over. The man at the ticket window came out, lit a cigarette for her and put it into her mouth, telling her to cheer up because she would find another lover soon. She was less sure. 'With this man, it had been all or nothing,' she wrote in her autobiography; 'It was the worst. I was unhappy for a long time.'

II

'Women must be as free as men to mould their own
amatory life'

Models of freedom

We flew south in search of stronger sun. On the first day, alone in a house with a pool, I swam naked, half wanting to be distantly observed by people in the surrounding villas.

A decade earlier, I had been proud of my preparedness to be naked in public, flaunting my own daring. Though I was still irritated by prudishness – those awkwardly English manoeuvres to avoid being seen while changing on the beach – I had generally lost this ostentation, which had itself come to seem awkward in the insistence of its display. Swimming naked was now about the easy sensuality of bare skin touched by the sun or the water, which in turn made it easy to imagine being seen and touched by another person.

It struck me that the longing I'd had for the freedom of communal life could find its expression in sex; in moving outside the nuclear family and allowing ourselves to matter to each other. Indeed, it was the closure of these possibilities that had bothered me at the weddings the previous summer. Recently, looking back on that moment, I'd asked myself if I was misguided to judge my friends as I had then. Shouldn't I just respect their choices, and ask for the freedom to think differently myself? If there was a political force in celebrating complicated differences, then didn't I need to allow my friends their point of view?

'Do you want to split up all the monogamous couples you know?' asked one friend, distressed by the self-righteousness with which I recalled those weddings.

It disturbed us both that the answer was not a clear 'no'. I could see that there were happy, imaginative marriages that were as complex and more generous than Lessing's version of free love. Sometimes I imagined myself in such a marriage: the relief of coming home after a day of battling with the world and knowing you would be understood; the pleasure of touching after a period of absence and feeling yourself becoming weightless as you dissolved into each other, a mutual need assuaged. There had been moments like this in the early years with my husband and moments of understanding since then with other men that had shown me what this might be like.

But it seemed that nonetheless I wasn't willing simply to respect the choices of others. The problem wasn't so much the decision of other women to marry as the way that the rituals surrounding marriage seemed to shut out alternative modes of living. And I did still feel that if everyone shut themselves off in their nuclear units, some of the world's potential would be lost. I could see that other people might interpret the freedom of free love as simple indulgence: the uncontrolled gratification of selfish desires. But I sometimes felt that we had a kind of responsibility to open ourselves to intimacy in whatever form or constellation we found it and to live, as Anna Wulf puts it, 'as fully as I can'.

Expressed like this, my commitment to experience was almost religious: implicit was a sense that the gift of life was precious enough that we failed ourselves and the world at large when we closed ourselves off from experiences that had the potential to heighten our sense of being alive. This wasn't itself political, but it became political when I became conscious that those around me would judge me if I lived openly as Lessing did, and that this was more the case than it would have been thirty years earlier. I couldn't see this as a straightforward generational difference. There were plenty of Lessing's generation who weren't experimenting with free love; plenty of mine who were, though there was no longer the expectation that sexual experimentation would involve love. But it still seemed as though my very particular world of academics, writers and what were now termed 'creative professionals' would have had fewer assumptions of monogamy if I'd inhabited it fifty years earlier. And in being less free, I worried that we were living less fully.

I had sometimes regretted the conventionality of my own life on these grounds. In the early days of our relationship, my husband and I had talked frequently about sexual freedom. Even after we were married, we spent an entire day walking around a French citadel, discussing how some version of free love might work. Though in these conversations we acknowledged our desire for others, they were discussions that brought us closer; that resulted in a sense of our shared strength and willingness to approach life from first principles, rather than simply accepting inherited conventions. But then one day not long afterwards, my husband admitted to me that he would not want to know. He would feel too viscerally disturbed by the knowledge of another man's sperm inside me. This was, he said, a biological fear of fathering another man's child.

I didn't share these anxieties, but I had qualms of my own. As my husband became more conventional after the birth of our son, I felt apprehensive when I saw him becoming close to women I thought would fit better into his domestic imaginings. I realised that I wouldn't have wanted to know that he was having sex with such women; I would be too fearful that he'd rather be married to them than to me. So, with some misgivings, we cast dreams of open experimentation aside and were left only with the possibility for secret affairs, in which moments of joyful freedom would come at the cost of the constraints of secrecy and subterfuge; of love snatched only in the interstices of days and corners of lives.

Yet I now found that I was opening up these questions again. Why, given that there were marriages ending all around us and that all of us had friends whose childhoods had been shadowed by sparring or simply loveless parents, did my generation seem stubbornly to believe that monogamous marriage was the best approach? My parents had set a good example of divorce, remaining friends after they separated and enabling us all to spend Christmases and holidays together. But I wanted to think there was something between the constriction of marriage and the liberty of separation, given that such a separation would not be all that freeing if we went off in turn simply to replicate the situation with a new partner. There were moments when I wanted to break free and to slide into the arms of another man, not in search of a new husband but simply to experience my own agency and sexuality more strongly. Increasingly, I wanted to do this publicly, because I was irritated by the conventionality of those around me: by the assumption that 'cheating' husbands were necessarily wronging their wives; that sexuality could and should be domestically contained.

I was becoming curious about how other people had overcome these difficulties. Could adulterous sex be freeing? Could love or sex create the sensation of freedom through promiscuity? My life didn't currently offer the possibilities for experimentation that Lessing's had, so I took my usual, perhaps inadequately academic approach. Back from holiday, I tried to read my way towards an answer.

Because the fifteen-year-old Martha is reading the sex psychologist Havelock Ellis at the opening of *Martha Quest*, Ellis seemed a good place to begin, though I suspected that his theories would feel outdated. This is a suspicion that Martha shares, finding when she embarks on her sexual life that it's too late to believe in 'free love', which has the 'stale and jaded sound' of the 1920s, and committing instead to 'a determined hedonism, an accomplished athleticism'.

In fact, free love originated much earlier, in the nineteenth century. 'Yes, I am a Free Lover', stated the American pioneer

Victoria Woodhull (the first woman to run for the presidency) in 1871, claiming that she had 'an inalienable, constitutional and natural right to love whom I may, to love as long or as short a period as I can'. Lessing's heroine Olive Schreiner was part of the Fellowship of the New Life in Britain, founded in 1883 to promote pacifism, vegetarianism and sexual freedom. By the end of the century this movement also incorporated the philosopher Bertrand Russell, the suffragette Emmeline Pankhurst, the writers H.G. Wells, Bernard Shaw and Edward Carpenter, and Havelock Ellis. At this stage, sexual freedom didn't usually involve multiple partners but it tended to entail a belief in the need for female emancipation and a suspicion of traditional marriage.

As they grew older and emerged into a new century, Russell and Ellis both came to advocate a more modern form of free love. The book that the adolescent Martha Quest was reading lying under the Mawonga tree may well have been Ellis's 1910 volume on *Sex in Relation to Society*. Here Ellis decried marriage without the possibility of divorce, suggesting that to 'fix by law the number of women with whom a man shall have sexual relationships' and vice versa was 'more unreasonable than it would be to fix by law the number of children they shall produce'. He was not advocating polygamy, instead he was vehemently advocating monogamy – 'the relationship which most adequately corresponds to all the physical and spiritual facts involved' – but this was a form of monogamy that 'by no means excludes the need for sexual variation'. Ellis supported this point by approvingly quoting Adolf Gerson, who had argued in 1908 that just as civilised man could not be content with the coarse and monotonous food that satisfied the peasant, so in sexual matters civilised people, with their 'more versatile and sensitive tastes', were more apt to crave variety than the naturally monogamous peasants.

This is the elitism that seems to be inevitable in theories of freedom. Because it's almost impossible to conceive of a world in which no one is constrained, some people have to be less constrained than others. For Ellis, not only were the more civilised more disposed towards variety, men were more suited to it than women. He insisted that 'women must be as free as men to mould their own amatory life' but added that 'many' considered that amatory freedom on the part of women 'will be and ought to be' exercised within 'narrower limits' because women were more absorbed in the task of child-rearing and tended to love in a more focused and devoted manner.

Although he was rather irritating in his complacency, Ellis was not expressing views wholly inconsistent with Lessing's own. Nonetheless, there were contradictions here that he didn't address. If the women were disposed to be less free, with whom would the men seek their variety? Would a handful of unusually liberated women service large numbers of men? A more egalitarian theory of free love was propounded twenty years later by Bertrand Russell in his 1929 *Marriage and Morals*. Claiming that the political emancipation of women needed to be followed by their social emancipation, Russell emphasised the need to accept that sex was pleasing to well-brought-up women and to encourage nakedness and frank sexual discussion among the young.

Struck as Van de Velde had been by the prevalence of divorce among the better educated classes, Russell joined the Dutch doctor in advocating better education in the art of love: men needed to continue to woo women after marriage, while women needed to open themselves to the possibility of physical pleasure. More controversially, he also suggested that marriage might be easier if people accepted that 'familiarity dulls the edge of passion' and that in order to prolong the happy companionship of a long marriage, it was important that there should be 'no interference with mutual freedom'. Husbands and wives were warned not to regard themselves as 'each other's policemen'; instead they needed to accept the value of love, even when adulterous, because 'to fear love is to fear life, and those who fear life are already three parts dead'.

Five years later, the writer Irene Clephane picked up on Russell's argument in her *Towards Sex Freedom*, claiming that it was now 'more and more widely realised that there is fundamentally little difference in the working of the sex urge in men and women' and that both enjoyed a rebirth of the 'erotic urge' in their later thirties and forties. Like Russell, she could see the benefit of a long marriage and suggested that men and women need only rid themselves of jealousy – 'an utterly wasteful emotion' – and allow adultery to be a 'saving influence' in their marriage.

This was the intellectual climate in which Doris Tayler married Frank Wisdom. By the time of her marriage to Gottfried Lessing, she was also immersed in communist theories of free love. For me, this was the most surprising aspect of this research. The communists I read about here were advocating a form of freedom that you certainly don't find in Stalinism. In 1918, on the tide of the revolution, the highest legislative body of the new Soviet government had ratified a complete Code on Marriage, the Family and Guardianship that abolished the inferior legal status of women, eliminated religious marriage, gave children born outside marriage equal rights to those born within it and made divorce an easy formality requiring no grounds. The author of the Code, Alexander Goikhbarg, saw it as preparing the way for the time when 'the fetters of husband and wife' had become obsolete – that is, when love could be enjoyed freely. A decade later the Soviet sociologist S. Ia Vol'fson adapted one of Engels' remarks by stating that soon the family would 'be sent to a museum of antiquities so that it can rest next to the spinning wheel and the bronze axe'.

In his 1884 *The Origin of the Family*, Engels had emphasised that the notion of the paired couple had only come about because of the development of private property. With private property abolished, the conditions could be created for a return from monogamy to 'individual sex love', given that the only truly 'moral marriage' was one in which love continued.

For many communist theorists from the early revolutionary years, children were best brought up collectively by the state, leaving men and women free for work and love. Not everyone was fully open-minded. Although Lenin echoed Engels in complaining that 'petty housework' degraded women, he was anxious that free love shouldn't be promulgated too easily, disliking the concept because of its association with bourgeois promiscuity and because while it took 'two people to make love', a third person was likely to come into being as a result, giving sex a social complexion. He had an opponent in the founder of the Soviet 'Women's Department', Alexandra Kollontai, who insisted that as there was 'neither morality nor immorality' in nature, the sexual act should be recognised as 'neither shameful nor sinful... as much a manifestation of a healthy organism as the quenching of hunger or thirst'.

This revolutionary moment was short-lived. At the point that Lessing abandoned her children, the family had been reinstated as the dominant unit in Soviet Russia and the divorce and abortion reforms had been largely rescinded. However, Lessing's knowledge about Soviet Russia tended to be a decade or so out of date, so it was in the name of these earlier utopian theorists that she was acting when she claimed that the family was obsolete.

Even at her most principled, though, Lessing was less determinedly matter-of-fact than either Irene Clephane or Alexandra Kollontai, never reducing sex to the simple quenching of hunger. I found that there was something a little dusty and excessively prosaic about all these accounts, whether they were by the Fellowship of Free Life cohort or by the communists. So it was easy to see why Martha Quest dismissed free love as jaded and was drawn like her creator to the more passionate world of D.H. Lawrence.

Doris Lessing's reading of Lawrence continued into her second marriage, encouraged by John Whitehorn and Smithie, though disapproved of by Gottfried. In quick succession she read *The Rainbow, Women in Love* and *Lady Chatterley's Lover*. 'I heartily approve of all his opinions on sex', she wrote to Coll MacDonald after Smithie had sent her a banned copy of the unexpurgated *Lady Chatterley*, observing that 'its effect on me was to make me want to go to bed with John, which proves it can't be a "pure" work of art'.

Although he didn't advocate sexual variety, Lawrence celebrated nakedness and embodied life in these novels and he was as interested as Ellis and Russell in the question of whether love could be compatible with freedom. For Lawrence, this was more complicated than it was for them because he was more conscious of the emotional snares of love. He knew that it took away freedom through the drive for possession it created.

Attracted to Ursula in *Women in Love*, Rupert Birkin tells her that:

'One must throw everything away, everything – let everything go, to get the one last thing one wants.'

'What thing?' she asks, hoping he will say 'love'.

'I don't know – freedom together,' he replies.

Birkin tells Ursula that he wants an equilibrium that cannot include sex, because he's frightened that sex limits freedom by creating unsatisfied desire. This distresses Ursula. She's convinced that it's possible to be sexually in love and feel free. For a while, Birkin continues to resist love, but then he has a vision of 'the way of freedom'. This is the 'paradisal entry' into pure being, in which the individual soul 'submits to the yoke and leash of love, but never forfeits its own proud individual singleness, even while it loves and yields'. He decides to ask Ursula to marry him. Happy together at last, they vacate their jobs and homes to wander off south together. Now sex can bring freedom. Each lover constitutes 'the immemorial magnificence of mystic, palpable, real otherness' for the other. But there's still a conflict, because Ursula will always be the soft giver of herself, where Birkin remains hard and whole.

Reading *Women In Love,* Doris Lessing told Smithie that she'd spent 'futile years insisting on the absolute equality between men and women'. Lawrence had converted her to essentialism. Though she was troubled by the force of Lawrence's writing, 'which steals your soul away and unless you are on your guard, drugs your critical sense', she believed that 'no one ever knew so much about women'. She was prepared to give up on communist rationality and to accept instead his vision of sex as a dangerous act of surrender.

III

'We don't have an orgasm unless we love him. What's free about that?'

Orgasms

If there's a moment when we expect to feel the 'immemorial magnificence' of sex – when we expect to experience freedom as a physical condition of being – then it's the moment of orgasm. For Lessing, both the freedom and the potential entrapment of sex came from that moment: from the experience of distilled physical pleasure that could also for her bring a frightening consciousness of love's bonds. But she didn't have this experience with clitoral orgasms, only with vaginal orgasms, and she thought that these were only possible when she was in love.

In her autobiography, Lessing wrote that growing up, she lived in a climate where there was more emphasis on the vagina than the clitoris:

> when I masturbated in my adolescence it was the vagina
> and its amazing possibilities I learned about. The clitoris
> was only part of the whole ensemble. A clitoral orgasm
> by itself was a secondary and inferior pleasure. If I had
> been told that clitoral and vaginal orgasms would within
> a few decades become ideological enemies, or that people
> would say vaginal orgasms did not exist, I'd have thought
> it a joke.

Her experience of orgasms became Anna and Ella's in *The Golden Notebook*. For Ella here, the process of falling in love with Paul is sealed by the ease with which she has vaginal orgasms: 'she could not have experienced it if she had not loved him. It is the orgasm that is created by the man's need for a woman, and his confidence in that need.' As time goes on, he uses 'mechanical means' to give her clitoral orgasms instead, and she resents it because she sees it as motivated by 'his instinctive desire not to commit himself to her'. For Ella, a vaginal orgasm is 'emotion and nothing else', felt as 'a dissolving in a vague, dark generalised sensation like being swirled in a warm whirlpool'. Clitoral orgasms are more sharply powerful but they are 'a substitute and a fake'.

Abandoned by Paul, Ella finds that she's unable to have orgasms with new lovers. She complains to her friend Julia about the disparity between men and women and the way that this limits women's freedom:

> Free, we say, yet the truth is they get erections when they're with a woman they don't give a damn about, but we don't have an orgasm unless we love him. What's free about that?

She knows that it's only when she loves a man that she'll have orgasms again, becoming a woman whose sexuality will 'ebb and flow' in response to her male lover's. This is when, through the persona of Ella (herself a creation of Anna), Lessing makes the controversial statement about sexual dependency: 'A woman's sexuality is, so to speak, contained by a man, if he is a real man; she is, in a sense, put to sleep by him, she does not think about sex.'

I could follow Lessing in her general views of sexuality here, accepting that there was an element of unconsciousness involved in sexual pleasure that may be more important for women. I found it harder to follow her when it came to her differentiation between kinds of orgasms, though. In my own experience, Lessing is right that vaginal orgasms can occur only when the whole body is aroused and that this necessarily involves an emotional component, where clitoral orgasms can occur in a more detached state, potentially without desire. For me, even to have a vaginal orgasm from masturbation, I need to be in a state of arousal induced by thoughts of someone else's desire for me; by fantasies in which my own hands become the hands of a wanting lover. But this need not be love, in the complete sense that Doris Lessing experienced it with Jack, or Anna experiences it with Michael; it can be something much more like infatuation or simply excitement.

When vaginal orgasms do occur for me, Lessing's description of being swirled in a warm whirlpool is accurate, though I find they also have a more eviscerating quality. There's a sense that in that instant – and it's an instant of freedom – the world is being remade from somewhere deep inside me. Where I diverge from Lessing is that with this state of overwhelmed arousal comes a kind of clitoral orgasm very different from the mechanical kind that you can have without desire. I think that Lessing was unnecessarily dismissive when it came to clitoral orgasms, which may suggest simply that her own weren't very good. I find that when I'm sufficiently aroused, I reach an excited state in which the border between pleasure and pain is blurred. There's a sharpness of touch possible in this condition that creates an orgasm that's all-engulfing; there's a rush of blood, a dizzying breathlessness, and it's followed by a kind of spacey shakiness that brings a feeling of surprised, relaxed, irresponsible joy.

The history surrounding the female orgasm is, as Lessing observed in her autobiography, fraught. Scientists now seem to accept matter-of-factly that both kinds of orgasm are possible, but self-styled experts across the centuries have contradicted each other. In the sixteenth century, both orgasms were encouraged and indeed were seen as complementary components of female sexual pleasure. The Italian surgeon Renaldus Columbus was one of several writers to laud what he called 'the love or sweetness of Venus', describing how 'if you touch it you will find it rendered a little harder', while also extolling vaginal pleasure. Three hundred years later, the

Victorians were, predictably, more discouraging, and both kinds of orgasm seem to have been widely forgotten. Some doctors serviced their hysterical female clients with 'uterine massage' and even developed electric masturbation machines, but it was not uncommon in late-nineteenth-century Britain for masturbating girls to have their clitorises removed.

Sigmund Freud was instrumental in demarcating the battle lines between the vaginal and the clitoral orgasm. According to him, young girls experimented with the clitoris and then graduated in womanhood to the vagina, 'the true female organ'. Women who continued to have clitoral orgasms were both immature and masculine. This view was shared by Lawrence in *Lady Chatterley's Lover*, where Mellors complains to Constance about his wife's insistence on her clitoris: 'wriggling and shouting, she'd clutch clutch with herself down there', tearing at him with her hard 'beak'. Constance, meanwhile, is happy because the clitoral orgasms that she had to accomplish for herself with her previous lover have been replaced by the delight of vaginal orgasms, experienced simultaneously with Mellors.

This makes uncomfortable reading: why shouldn't women have orgasms if they don't manage to coincide with their lovers? Indeed, Lessing may have been one of the few female readers who hasn't found this passage irritating. It made Lawrence unpopular with a subsequent generation of feminists who decried and even denied the existence of the vaginal orgasm. In her 1970 'The Myth of the Vaginal Orgasm', Anne Koedt suggested that the whole notion of vaginal orgasm was male propaganda designed to encourage the submission of women: 'men fear that they will become sexually expendable if the clitoral organ is substituted for the vaginal as the basic pleasure for women'.

Koedt was part of a band of feminists who urged women to reclaim their clitorises, even running workshops to teach repressed middle-class women how to masturbate. They were responding to Lawrence and Freud and to a large tranche of sex manuals that downplayed the clitoris far more than Van de Velde did in his. The British National Marriage Guidance Council had published a book called *Sex Difficulties in the Wife* in 1958, stating that 'every couple' should be striving for the 'ideal' in which the wife was sufficiently stimulated by penetration not to need the excitement of the clitoris as well. In America, the gynaecologists William Masters and Virginia Johnson insisted in their influential 1966 book *Human Sexual Response* that there was no physiological difference between vaginal and clitoral orgasms and that penetration alone should be enough.

Koedt did not go unchallenged. 'One wonders just whom Miss Koedt has gone to bed with,' Germaine Greer wrote in *The Female Eunuch* a few months after the essay had appeared. Greer was in favour of bra-burning and hair-growing, but she did not want to give up on her vagina. She claimed that most men were perfectly aware of the clitoris and she thought that excessive emphasis on it echoed the previous emphasis on penetration in ignoring the rest of the body and the fact that orgasms take place as part of a much larger emotional, mental and physical encounter between lovers.

There is a strain of hysteria in all these accounts that suggests that not only for both Freud but for his female supporters and opponents there's something frightening about the female orgasm. Though I disagreed with her hierarchy of orgasms, I shared Lessing's anxiety that the orgasm is a moment of freedom that's also a moment of entrapment, because it's when we're filled with hormones that bind us to a lover from whom we may wish to remain independent. So if we follow Lessing in seeing the orgasm as at once the goal and the hazard of the free woman, then how are we to navigate this?

IV

'To make oneself passive is very different from being
a passive object'

Solutions

I was troubled by my sense that there was something glib about the arguments in favour of free love from Russell and his contemporaries. It's easy for Russell or Clephane to suggest that a marriage might be joyfully revived by a healthy bout of infidelity, but that ignores the dangerous aspect of the feelings awakened by sex. If orgasms bring the frightening possibility of dependency, then what happens if one of the lovers is unmarried, as Doris Lessing was in Jack's case, or if an adulterer falls in love too deeply and needily to return contentedly to the marital bed? A striking number of feminists had subsequently dismissed sexual freedom when it was sought in adultery. In *The Feminine Mystique*, her revolutionary 1963 indictment of women's lives in America, Betty Friedan saw infidelity as the petty escapism of Hollywood-drugged housewives who were unable to find a more creative outlet for their energies. But that was a long time ago. I wanted to know what people were finding now.

I started to talk about affairs. I might not live in a climate of free love, but among my friends there was a handful of people prepared to confide in me about extra-marital sex. There were married men and women who'd had lovers at one time or another; there were also single women who had been asked to be the 'mistresses' of men whom they might have accepted if they'd used a different, more equal word. These were not generally self-styled 'free women' or 'free men'. They were the contentedly or the discontentedly married, muddling through in the face of claustrophobia, sexual rejection, unacknowledgeable need, looking for excitement, love, vulnerability, conversation. Or they were the contentedly or the discontentedly single in search of love.

It was all very unsatisfactory, and I had found this too in my own brushes with adultery. Affairs so frequently follow the pattern of Doris and Jack, Martha and Thomas, Anna and Michael. Of course there is the pleasure: the rush of happiness at feeling known and chosen; the rediscovery of the extraordinary possibilities of your body and the subtlety with which it can respond to the body of another; the euphoria at stepping outside your life, outside your domestic responsibilities, into the freedom of the unknown. But the rush of drugged happiness is followed by the unhappiness that comes with need. The feeling of superiority that comes with providing better sex, better understanding, better conversation than the spouse, gives way to envy at the hours of unconscious domestic togetherness: the evenings reading on the sofa, the trips to the supermarket, the silent breakfasts. 'One isn't only jealous of sex', Graham Greene once wrote to his lover Catherine Walston, 'one is jealous of company and the first words on waking'. This, especially when it also involves the constraint of subterfuge and of your own or another's guilt, is far from freeing.

I wanted to think that free love could be more than this. What I minded in monogamy was that it cut you off from the sexual charge of the world. After my summer of reading, I no longer wanted to call this the communal: this gave sexual openness a collectively political quality that it didn't quite have for me. But there was still a moral charge of a kind in the belief that you have a responsibility – to yourself, to the world – at least to register sexual possibility, even if to do more than register it might be to create a vicious circle, because the new love has the potential to bring a new phase of monogamy in its turn.

A friend suggested that I should read Simone de Beauvoir's *The Second Sex,* published in 1949, just as Lessing was moving to London. Though I had enjoyed reading about Beauvoir biographically, I knew *The Second Sex* only for the famous line 'one is not born, but rather becomes a woman'. So I turned to it expecting to find an argument about gender as cultur- ally determined that would be at odds with Lessing's ambiv- alent essentialism. What I found, though, was a book that was unexpectedly open to just the contradictions that Lessing explored in *The Golden Notebook* but that also placed them in an intellectual framework necessarily lacking in Lessing's novel. Though Beauvoir began by setting women's lives in a long historical context that implied that their sexual and emotional characteristics had been formed by centuries of subjugation, she then went on to describe female girlhood, adolescence and sexual awakening in more psychoanalytic and more essentialist terms.

Beauvoir followed Freud in seeing the young girl's sexu- ality as located chiefly in her clitoris and the adult wom- an's in her vagina – a new 'erotic centre'. Beauvoir's woman becomes involved in a new 'erotic cycle' at this point, learn- ing to respond sexually throughout her body, because vagi- nal pleasure 'depends on the whole situation lived by the subject: it requires profound consent of the individual as a whole'.

Beauvoir joined Lessing in seeing the woman who takes pleasure in sex as responding to and merging with the desire of her lover (though Beauvoir was more open to the possibility that the lover could be female). Where male desire is tense – 'it can invade a body where nerves and muscles are taut' – female desire flows through the body: 'there is a surge in her that ceaselessly falls and rises'. For Beauvoir, the challenge came in succumbing to the passivity of this desire while resisting subjugation. She put forward the very enticing notion of active passivity: 'to *make* oneself object, to *make* oneself passive is very different from *being* a passive object: a woman in love is neither asleep nor a corpse.'

She also addressed the dangers to freedom implicit in allowing yourself to succumb in this way. 'Feminine arousal can reach an intensity unknown by man,' she claimed. Where male desire is violent but localised, the woman loses herself more fully because 'her whole body is desire and arousal'. Thus the woman finds the moment of separation of bodies painful and she resents the male lover who pulls away too quickly. This resonated powerfully for me; I'd often experienced grief and an exaggerated sense of rejection in the minutes or hours that followed sex. For Beauvoir, the man who retreats from intimacy at that point demonstrates that he is now a whole, independent body again, leaving his lover feeling unhomed because only moments earlier she has handed so much of herself into his keeping.

Beauvoir, unlike Lessing, had a solution to the contradiction that prevents women from being both sexually satisfied and free. She suggested that the asymmetry of male and female eroticism she described could be balanced when the woman felt both desire and respect from her lover: 'if he covets her in the flesh while recognising her freedom, she recovers her essentialness at the moment she becomes object, she remains free in the submission to which she consents.' This was a vision of happy union that Lessing and Jack didn't achieve and that might have made Lessing more contented and more free in loving so abandonedly. Beauvoir went on to describe what occurred in the ideal sexual act:

> The words 'receive' and 'give' exchange meanings, joy is gratitude, pleasure is tenderness. In a concrete and sexual form the reciprocal recognition of the self and the other is accomplished in the keenest consciousness of the other and the self. Some women say they feel the masculine sex organ in themselves as a part of their own body; some men think they *are* the woman they penetrate; these expressions are obviously inaccurate; the dimension of the *other* remains; but the fact is that alterity no longer has a hostile character; this consciousness of the union of the bodies in their separation is what makes the sexual act moving.

I liked this description because it explained so powerfully why sex mattered; why it was more than an indulgent or recreational act, and why it might therefore be too important to be confined to monogamous marriage. It made a high claim for the profundity of the kind of intimacy that is involved in exposing yourself to another person in this way, and it suggested that it was possible to be both abandoned and free. It also offered an alternative to the inequalities of Lessing's lovers, because here there was a sense of the lovers as equals, though they might sometimes experience sex differently. This was in itself freeing, because her lovers could claim responsibility for their own feelings and could trust each other as they risked journeying into the unknown together.

Beauvoir then addressed the crucial question of what kinds of relationships could incorporate sex of this kind. Here again she had more answers than Lessing, though they were not answers that were open to many of us. One option – the one favoured by Van de Velde – was the long, sexually fulfilled marriage. Lessing wrote amusedly about the limitations of marital sex to Smithie in 1947, though admittedly sex with Gottfried hadn't been very exciting even before they were married.

> What happens in marriage is that the man says 'Feel like coming into my bed darling'. One climbs in. He having read dozens of books about the way women must be 'prepared' for the sex act, makes her feel like a recalcitrant car on a cold morning. In any case he is usually far too quick, but even if he isn't, one is left feeling like a cup of tea that it is usual to drink before going to sleep... What I am saying in effect is that men should learn the art of 'wooing' their wives (hateful word) not only physically but emotionally and creating a mood. And it must be difficult to create a flirtatious mood with a woman who has just been darning your socks, putting the baby to bed and cold creaming her face.

Beauvoir was similarly dismissive, though again it's worth remembering that sex with Jean-Paul Sartre was no better than sex between the Lessings. For Beauvoir, the problem with remaining lovers after marriage was that familiarity created embarrassment: because it is hard to retain otherness, the sexual act becomes no longer 'an inter-subjective experience where one goes beyond himself, but rather a kind of mutual masturbation'.

This felt unreasonably pessimistic to me, but she was right that it becomes more difficult to lose your sense of your social self with someone with whom you are socially familiar; harder to ride on the wave of someone else's desire when that desire has lost its undertow of desperate wanting. In a way, Beauvoir was helpful in allowing us not to expect too much of ourselves. Some of my friends had been to marriage counsellors who had suggested that they should light a few candles or buy their spouse a present to enter the territory of the unknown. Beauvoir understood that otherness is an existentially complex state that cannot be artificially recreated.

So where and how should we seek that perfect 'reciprocal recognition of the self and the other' if we are not going to find it in marriage? Beauvoir shared Friedan's scepticism about adultery, and for her the problem was the 'compromises of prudence and hypocrisy' that prevented it from creating 'human and free relationships'. What she wanted was 'a pact of freedom and sincerity' in which both partners granted each other openness and freedom.

This is the relationship that Beauvoir had with Sartre, and it's not a kind of arrangement that many people have managed to enjoy. Even for them, there were moments of crisis, as when Beauvoir fell seriously in love with the Chicago writer Nelson Algren in 1947 and experienced for the first time the kind of sexual passion that she went on to describe in *The Second Sex*. In Beauvoir's 1954 novel *The Mandarins*, the portrayal of a pact of this kind is more troubled than it had been in *The Second Sex*. Her heroine Anne, a psychoanalyst living with a socialist writer who is obviously modelled on Sartre, has an affair with a writer in Chicago with a strong resemblance to Algren. Aged thirty-nine, Anne experiences for the first time in several years the actively passive abandonment that Beauvoir had described in *The Second Sex:*

> his desire transformed me. I who for so long a time
> had been without taste, without form, again possessed
> breasts, a belly, flesh; I was as nourishing as bread, as
> fragrant as earth. It was so miraculous that I didn't think
> of measuring my time or my pleasure; I know only that
> before we fell asleep I could hear the gentle chirping
> of dawn.

This love cannot last, because her lover is unwilling to remain at the edge of her life and so, feeling let down by her when she returns to her husband, he falls out of love. She is left depressed by the onset of middle age, alone, contemplating suicide because she is unsure whether she can be embodied again.

In 1984 Lessing wrote a preface to *The Mandarins* describing the excitement she and her contemporaries had felt in London when it was first translated into English in 1956. At this stage, she wrote, Beauvoir was frequently being held up by philandering men as the ideal example of a woman who had managed to overcome jealousy in order to enjoy sexual freedom. But when they all eagerly read the novel, they were disappointed to witness that Anne in fact was 'a dry and lonely woman, in a companionable marriage, resigned to early middle age'.

I was excited by Beauvoir, despite her disillusionment. But it was starting to strike me, perhaps rather belatedly, that there was something odd about this whole enterprise in which I was trying to learn about the possibilities for freedom in my own life by reading the writers of the past. I wasn't even looking back at the sixties and seventies: I was seeking a model in a book written in 1949. Why hadn't I looked around me at the radicals of the present? I had to admit to myself that I had rarely felt at home among my contemporaries. For whatever reason, my instinct when dissatisfied by the apparent conservatism of those around me was to look for alternative friends not among the living but among the dead. I could be reached most easily through the private world opened up for me by words struck on to a typewriter sixty years earlier.

When it came to free love, though, it did seem worth exploring the new possibilities that had emerged since Lessing and Beauvoir were flitting hopefully from bed to bed. Sex for every proclivity was now available through the Internet; forty-five million people were registered on Ashley Madison's 'married dating service for discreet encounters' where you could log in to view a screen full of shots of the anonymously slashed faces of men or women. You could learn their height, weight and sexual inclinations but you did not have a chance to look into their blacked-out eyes. I wasn't tempted to join in the interests of research. There was something very depressing about sites of this kind, which made me agree with Friedan. We had come a long way from the bracing freedom demanded by Clephane or Kollontai.

Of course, there were sources of a more radical kind of free love. There was the queer world, where gender was becoming increasingly fluid, and where open promiscuity was often more possible, at least when it came to gay men. But even here, the writer Maggie Nelson had recently observed (and herself partaken of) the trend towards aping the bourgeois family structure. Indeed, gay sex had become so clean-cut that I learnt that some gay men now went to countries where homosexuality was still banned in search of transgression. The possibility of gay marriage and gay parenthood fostered a very old-fashioned kind of love. Among those I talked to that September, there was a female friend who had recently been shocked to hear a gay male friend describing his parenting plans, which involved a surrogate in Thailand and an egg donor in America (two of the millions of women now reduced once again to the function of their ovaries and wombs). She was disturbed both by the casualness with which he was coopting these women into his domestic project and by the narrative in which the parenting was going to take place: he was pleased because he earned enough money to pay for the expensive eggs, while his husband made a natural homemaker.

On the edge of my circle of friends there was a handful of open marriages. The few that had survived from the 1970s (which were far exceeded by the ones that hadn't) seemed stable, but would be hard to reproduce now in my own sphere as they required the participation of a wider group of friends. These were relationships in which the marriage had coincided with a succession of additional partnerships of the kind envisaged by Ellis, Russell or Beauvoir, and they were quite different from the open marriages found among my contemporaries, in which the sexual variety tended to be more casual. For the couples I knew of in my generation, the extra-marital encounters were not love affairs in the conventional sense, but sexual interludes. Sometimes there were long nights of group or possibly successively coupled sex, in which lovers were effectively brought into the shared orbit of the central couple. I approved of these marriages in principle: this was the communal life, the freedom I'd been asking for, offering the honesty that sounded so compelling when described by Beauvoir. But there was something unpleasantly matter-of-fact about it, like the compulsory nudity in German spas, or like the revolutionary world described by Kollontai.

I read a few books about contemporary polyamory and found that there was much to admire. Certainly, I agreed with the American polyamorist Deborah Anapol that openness is preferable to secrecy, that jealousy is a sign of insecurity and, most importantly, that children are able to accept more than two parental figures in their lives. She shared Beauvoir and Russell's sense that free love was as much about love as sex, writing that 'the freedom of surrendering to love and allowing love – not just sexual passion, not just social norms and religious strictures, not just emotional reactions and unconscious conditioning – to determine the shape our intimate relationships take is the essence of polyamory'. And many of the interviewees whose stories she told sounded brave, passionate and intelligent; committed to being reliable parents and lovers while also to sustained self-exploration and to the development of a new ethical code. They seemed happier in their promiscuity than Lessing was in what was effectively (at least emotionally) her serial monogamy. But the proponents of polyamory still turned sexual relationships into something a little too academic for my liking and I found it as hard to be enthusiastic about the 'poly' conferences now springing up across America as to be attracted to the few self-styled polyamorists I encountered in my circle in London. This may simply have been a sign of my own sequesteredness; I might have been more enthusiastic if I'd been living in California. But meeting the polyamorous men of my generation whom I came across socially, I was distastefully aware of their voraciousness. And I was conscious too that this was not longing; it felt impersonal because they were looking for so little that they were firing blindly.

I could not imagine wanting sex with these men because I shared Lessing's sense that love is essentially private. In this respect, we were both in our ways rather old-fashioned. For me as for her, it was the unexpected flash of the soul that could not in the end be communal that gave sex its power and, yes, that made vaginal orgasms more likely, allowing us to expose ourselves more fully. The moments of attraction that I felt towards other people's husbands – moments of warmth, curiosity, understanding – were small moments of betrayal, and they had to be in order to matter. These are instants when you are imaginatively willing into being a world in which only the two of you exist. Here we're back to the situation of Anna in *The Golden Notebook*, finding that sex either leaves her cold, or leaves her achingly needing the man who has left her less free than she began.

And yet. The alternative was a world in which couples married as a matter of course and then went on, as several couples I knew did, to track each other's phones online, on the grounds that it was convenient and safe to do so. More than with communism, it was hard to let go of the possibility of finding freedom through sex, and of the possibility that freer sex might come from freer love. Talking about Lessing that summer, I'd been impressed that several female friends in their sixties remembered the atmosphere of the scenes between Martha and Thomas in the shed, thirty or forty years after reading *Landlocked*. The warm drips of water falling on to the naked bodies from the window; the suspension in time and space. What they were recalling was freedom vividly described. For Lessing, this may have occurred only at moments and she may have paid for it afterwards with constricting grief. But I think she'd still have agreed with Bertrand Russell that 'to fear love is to fear life, and those who fear life are already three parts dead'.

6

'It is potentially liberation and renewal as well as enslavement and existential death'

Madness

A woman opens the door to a man. She is a writer, feline, proud, conscious of her own sexual power, though also at thirty-seven conscious of herself as on the cusp of middle age. He is an American Trotskyist on the run, come to enquire about her spare room. At first glance, he looks less like a writer than a cowboy; his low-slung belt seems likely to conceal a gun.

He appraises the room, dismissing his prospective landlady's suggestion that as an American he's likely to find it too small. As she makes him coffee, he appraises her as well, amusing and riling her with the openness of his sexual inventory.

'I hope I pass.'

'Fine,' he replies, apparently oblivious of what she means, and then launches into a disquisition on communism in Britain and America and a surprisingly sensitive analysis of her situation as a woman living alone.

She knows that she should resist this man whose aggressive confidence is belied by his pallid skin and anxious eyes. But she has spent too many nights sleeping alone, waiting for a real man to take possession of her, and she is won over by his certainty about his own sexual entitlement. She falls in love as obediently and passively as she hands him the keys to her flat. It feels as though the loneliness of the past two years is over.

A man climbs the badly lit stairs of a house in west London and knocks on a glass-fronted door. He's down on his luck and on the lookout for an older woman who will provide him with shelter and protection from the world. When the door opens, he knows he's found his Woman.

She's small and high-bosomed. Dressed in slacks and a pale silk blouse, with the top buttons sexily undone. She has one of those faces that's both beautiful and ugly. Widely spaced brown eyes, high cheekbones and a thin mouth that sets upwards in a constant smile. He kisses her and throws her down on the couch. He reaches inside her blouse, approving the lack of brassiere. She unzips his trousers and reaches a dainty, nicotine-stained hand inside.

'I've been hurt by men,' she says, world-weary but tender; 'Please don't hurt me any more.'

'Relax, baby,' he replies, not listening to what she's saying. 'We're going to make great music together.'

Outside, the lorries thunder past. Inside he kisses her neck, eyes and mouth. The sex is silent until he makes her come. She screams a little and then he follows. He's struck by her smell, which excites and repels him. The thick, acrid, sexual smell of an older woman.

He watches her, but her eyes remain closed, scrunched up like a newborn baby's. He's pleased with her, but he's not going to fall in love. He's fucked his way around America and plans to do the same in London. A man needs his freedom to move from bed to bed and it's a woman's revolutionary duty to understand. This doesn't mean that he doesn't need her. He needs her desperately. He's hoping she'll help him conquer his fears and teach him to write. Lying there, he feels colder than he's ever been.

I had embarked on a new academic year and Lessing had embarked on a new relationship. Clancy Sigal. Even the name sounded like something out of a hard-boiled American novel. This was Lessing's only serious love affair with a writer, and it was therefore the only one of her relationships where the man had the chance to write about it as well. It's impossible now to know whose version of their decisive first encounter in May 1957 is more accurate. Both of them reinvented it repeatedly in subsequent years, in fiction and in memoir. What does seem clear is that this was a moment of shared madness; a moment when, lying beside him and warming his shivering body with her own flesh, she was agreeing to share the burden of his anxiety, though she couldn't yet know the torment this would entail. For the next five years, the quest for both of them was to attain freedom through madness and it was a quest they pursued jointly, even when apart.

My obsession with Lessing now expanded to incorporate Clancy. I had access to his archive. Folder after folder of scanned diaries and letters started to arrive in my inbox from Texas. My days were lived in the peculiar world created by his irregular, often childish handwriting. What I was witnessing was a man descending into madness, and I was coming to understand what it might feel like to share that madness with him. I was drawn compulsively back to those hundred-page pdfs, though I had lost any clear sense of what I was going to learn there.

It was easy to trace the outlines of Doris and Clancy's life together. Externally, it quickly started to resemble a 1950s marriage. She cooked, he philandered; she was emotionally needy while he was detached. They undertook relatively stereotypical parental roles in relation to her son. His sexual desire, such as it was, seems to have been prompted less by her body or mind than by her culinary skills. I found him describing her breakfasts, lunches and dinners in detail on four separate occasions, luxuriating in retrospect in the large rafts of toasted French bread smeared with Devon butter and home-made gooseberry jam, pausing to note gratefully that she never asked him to wash up. He also described how their best sex took place just before or after meals, often in the kitchen. 'Something about Doris cooking – her hair in disarray, pots and pans all over the place – pressed my button'. Clancy seems consistently to have had more interest in her food than her books, even announcing on one occasion that 'compared to her writing, cooking was her real genius'.

However, the conversation was markedly different from that of a typical 1950s home. They came together over a shared disillusionment with left-wing politics that both nonetheless continued to see as fundamental to their identity. And beneath the domestic contentment there was that undercurrent of madness. Clancy was in a state of acute anxiety, suffering from recurring cramps, stomach aches, headaches and dizziness. He was sure that he wanted to write but at thirty-one had still not written a publishable book. And his sense of identity was so precarious that he kept a sign saying 'Clancy Sigal' on his bedside table to remind himself of who he was. Lessing was quickly drawn into his anguish, doing all she could to analyse his symptoms and explain him to himself. 'Except for the FBI, nobody had ever been so interested in me,' Clancy's alter ego announces in his autobiographical novel *The Secret Defector*, grateful for the attention and for the writerly unblocking it enables. But in the process Doris herself could not remain unscathed. He was introducing her to madness as he introduced her to jazz.

Doris's stomach tightened like a fist and she found herself lying in bed, unable to move. She returned to her psycho-analyst, Mrs Sussman, who explained to her that these were Clancy's symptoms rather than hers. In *The Golden Notebook*, Anna wakes up feeling as she never has before; her neck is tense and stiff and she has to force herself to breathe. She goes into the room of her lover, Saul Green, and discovers that he's cold to the touch. She has caught his anxiety across the walls of their rooms.

'We're both mad,' Anna tells Saul. 'We're inside a cocoon of madness.'

'You!' he responds sullenly. 'You're the sanest bloody woman I've ever known.'

'Not at the moment.'

As Doris succumbed to Clancy's madness she found, like Anna, that it was harder to remain sanguine. She was exhausted by his abrupt transitions from one personality to another. His archive in Texas had some of her letters as well, and it was a relief to find here that she retained some objective sense of the harmful nature of the relationship. There was a letter here to Joan Rodker where she complained that he was six different men and she never knew which personality was going to emerge: the demanding lover, the cheap Lothario, the anxious adolescent or the considerate friend. She was wondering about writing a novel called 'I had a Lover who was a Teen-Age Werewolf'. She told Joan that she'd joined him in slipping from one role to the other and had started to initiate terrible rows.

Although Doris and Clancy both recognised this mutually destructive aspect of the relationship early on, neither had the strength to end it. Clancy made no secret of his continued promiscuity and lied clumsily about it afterwards, irritated that Doris should attempt to deny him his freedom. On her side, Doris remained mindful that her own stance as a 'free woman' should make her tolerate the behaviour of a 'free man'. But it was especially hard because even when Clancy did share her bed, he quickly seemed to lose any desire for her. 'You've never enjoyed me,' she complained in 1959, and it rang true for him. 'I do not look forward to sleeping with her – and yet there is no doubt I love her,' he responded in his diary, consumed by the young girls he saw in the street, his heart and neck wrenched in every direction by the sight of a waist, a bosom or an ankle.

'Rage, pain, tumult, quarrels, lies, cross-martyrdoms, infidelities – God knows we earned our way through the dry hellgate,' Clancy wrote, looking back. When it got too bad, he stayed out on the streets for days at a time. Often, he boarded a train to the north, where he wandered aimlessly from one village to another. 'My cock an antenna, my frazzled nerves a weathervane, I redrew Britain's map to fit an imagination fed on American preoccupations'. He fled in this way on the day that Doris heard that her mother had died. Unable to stay and endure her rage and grief, he headed straight to Euston station, needing to forget both himself and her.

And yet both experienced this shared psychosis as creatively fertile. As Clancy's anxiety rippled and swelled, it unblocked both of them and left them writing, urgently and freely, about the madness they were experiencing. From the start this was a textual relationship, and this is what made it so easy for me to reinhabit it, sixty years later. They wrote to each other at the same time as they talked. Clancy discovered early on that Doris was reading his diary so he started using it to write to her, turning his diary entries into pleas for understanding and sympathy. 'Nothing I say can convince her that I haven't touched another woman in many months, and damn few even at the beginning,' he protested in 1958, before threatening that 'I think at this point I should go out and do exactly what she says I've been doing these past months'. 'Why don't people take me as I am!!' he asked, observing that 'a week ago I was ready to jump on the first boat anywhere, to America, willing to risk another breakdown, anything, rather than let Doris and I drift into a kind of lacerating despair.'

She responded by incorporating some of the phrases from these diary entries in drafts of *The Golden Notebook*, which she was writing at the time, and which now featured the character Saul Green, who is quite accurately modelled on Clancy. Meanwhile, Clancy had also started writing the accounts of his first meeting with Doris that would proliferate over subsequent decades, eventually forming the basis of *The Secret Defector*. And his trips to the north resulted in *Weekend in Dinlock*, a novel set in an English mining village, which was written at speed in an unusual burst of creative energy and dedicated to Doris.

However, if the relationship was proving fruitful for both of them, then Clancy was not always comfortable with this. He was furious to discover in 1959 that his lover had written a play about them, which was to be performed in the West End. *Play with a Tiger* is set in Doris Lessing's west London flat and portrays a woman and her lover slipping chaotically from one role to another as they helplessly destroy their love. 'When you put your hands on me, I begin to breathe,' Dave tells Anna, insisting that he needs her despite his promiscuity; 'I only breathe freely when I'm with you.' 'I get so lonely without you,' Anna informs him in return; 'I sometimes think if my skin were taken off I'd be just one enormous bruise.' But this is not enough to save them because they hate each other as well. 'Sometimes I think I've never hated anyone so much in all my life,' she announces. Glimpsed in the background is the possibility that Anna and Dave can be together and remain free in a way that neither could be with anyone else. But it seems likely that the freedom will come at the cost of madness and that the madness will eventually consume them.

Retrospectively, Clancy was to see her play as prompting the break-up of their relationship, although in fact this had begun much earlier and would conclude much later. Long before her play was performed, Doris had started to find Clancy's shifts in mood impossible to bear. She begged him to find someone else to talk to. 'I'm not your mother, your psycho-analyst, your confessor,' she wrote to him. 'I have been these things to you long past the time when I should have said no – because I've loved you very deeply'.

She sent him to a series of psychiatrists and psychoanalysts. These included her own analyst, Mrs Sussman, and her former lover, the Czech psychoanalyst known as Jack. Mrs Sussman informed him that he had the 'neurosis of a young bull'. She herself would die soon and she could not allow him to kill her. More worryingly, Jack announced that he was suffering from a psychosis and prescribed an immediate course of ECT (electroconvulsive therapy). Clancy bolted, running from the room straight home to Doris, who gave a characteristic shrug when she heard the news.

They eventually split up in 1962. In the wake of Clancy's departure, Doris turned to drink and Clancy to 'anti-psychiatry' and drugs. She found that she was trundling to the corner shop to buy small bottles of whisky and drinking them alone each night. In *The Golden Notebook* Anna lists a series of ideas for novels, all based on her relationship with Saul. One of these portrays the woman writer finding that her encounter with the younger American has left her depleted; she has no creative or emotional energy left. This was Doris Lessing's state in these months and she felt foolish for allowing it to happen. But even now, she couldn't escape him, either in her life or her writing. They still met occasionally for conversation and even sex. And more importantly – and it looked like this was where I had to follow them next – they continued independently to explore the relationship between freedom and madness, engaging in quite different ways with the theories of R.D. Laing.

I

'He rejoiced in his own madness, he was free'

Going mad

I'd read R.D. Laing's 1960 book *The Divided Self* as an undergraduate, and found it compelling returning to it now through the eyes of Lessing and Clancy (as I now called him in my mind, though Lessing remained Lessing). Here Laing pioneered a new theory of schizophrenics as understandable only in the context of the society in which they lived. He took D.W. Winnicott's notion of the 'false self' and claimed that the schizoid state involved a 'persistent scission between self and body'. Then I read his later, more psychedelic *The Politics of Experience* (1967), where he went further and argued that so-called 'normality' was merely a product of societal repression ('denial, splitting, projection, introjection and other forms of destructive action on experience') while the mental state of the schizophrenic was in fact a lucid response to this repressive society. He suggested that the schizophrenic went on a voyage into 'inner space' and that there was nothing intrinsically pathological in this experience; indeed it was the bravest journey anyone could undertake. The person who entered the inner realm went 'back and through and beyond into the experience of all mankind, of the primal man, of Adam and back into the being of animals.' Madness need not be breakdown, it could instead be break-through. 'It is potentially liberation and renewal as well as enslavement and existential death.'

Although Lessing had met Laing before Clancy did, she was never as close to him. Her interest was in the work rather than the man, and it was an interest that fuelled her fiction of the late 1960s, powering the investigation of madness in *The Four-Gated City* (1969) and *Briefing for a Descent into Hell* (1971). Clancy did not write fictionally about Laing or madness until much later, but his relationship with this charismatic, truculent Scotsman with hypnotic eyes went much further than Lessing's. In the diaries I was reading, Laing seemed to dominate his life between 1962 and 1966.

Laing's observations on the divided self collided easily with Clancy's sense of his own alienation. 'The truth is, I am a man separated from himself almost permanently', Clancy observed at this time. In his early encounters with Laing, he discovered that he had been asphyxiated by his mother's nipple as a child and that he now needed to learn 'freedom and breathing'. Fortunately, Laing had offered to instruct him in both. The lessons began with taking LSD and would culminate in a schizophrenic voyage.

Clancy and Laing met regularly in 1963 to take LSD together. Laing was one of many medical practitioners in these years to use LSD clinically. In his case, he hoped that the effects of LSD would simulate the mental experiences of the schizophrenic and would therefore offer an experience of mental freedom. As Clancy experimented more with the drug, he worried that the act of writing was inhibiting this liberation. A fundamental difference between Lessing and Clancy at this point was that Lessing saw writing as freeing her alongside madness, where Clancy saw them as at odds with each other. 'My hands ink-splattered not blood-stained', he complained.

Soon, taking LSD was not enough. Clancy needed to commit more fully to Laing and to try out schizophrenia. He did this first as a so-called 'writer in residence' at Villa 21, the centre for schizophrenia set up by the South African psychiatrist David Cooper, who thought that standard mental units failed to respond imaginatively to schizophrenic patients. Laing then urged Clancy to prepare for his own schizophrenic voyage, informing him that he was a Hero, needing to embark on a 'heroic undertaking', rebirthing himself through a sea journey as in Carl Jung's formulation of the twice-born hero. This entailed a return to America. In 1964, Clancy spent a gestational nine months wandering around his former homeland, attempting to find more freedom than he'd experienced there in the past.

These were months of loneliness and alienation but they brought the revelation that he'd been wrong to rely on Lessing. 'No woman can save a man from dread,' he wrote to Laing in a letter that was included in my cache. He returned home ready to make the final commitment to his mentor, joining Laing and fellow members of the 'Philadelphia

Association' in founding a new residential centre, Kingsley
Hall, in east London in 1965 to treat self-certified schizophrenics and explore the 'dialectics of liberation'. According
to Clancy Sigal in his later fictionalised account, the goal of
the enterprise was

> freedom, from bourgeois hypocrisy, from neurotic hang-
> ups. Above all from the need to be needed, starting with
> psychoanalysis, the basis of our association. 'Nuthin','
> averred [Laing], 'gives me more satisfaction than seein''
> some poor deluded bastid tell his shrink to fuck off.'

From the start, he was sceptical about the work Laing
and his associates were doing here. He thought that in their
unhappiness the schizophrenics were, as he later put it, 'a
poor substitute for the proletariat in which leftist intellectuals once placed their revolutionary hopes'. He came to look
on the members of the Philadelphia Association as 'a Witch's
Sabbath of crapulously mad men'. Compared to the inhabitants of Villa 21, the patients at Kingsley Hall were tediously
self-regarding and middle-class.

The moment of crisis came on the night of the Jewish fes-
tival of Rosh Hashanah. Clancy had a revelation that led him
to dance on a table, singing Hebrew songs and speaking in
tongues. Then he saw God, who issued a straightforward
instruction: 'Get your ass out of Kingsley Hall and stop being
so nuts'. Obediently, he ran back to his own flat, but the doctors followed him, beat him (he later claimed they were trying to kill him) and injected him with drugs. This was the
end of his involvement with the anti-psychiatry movement
and the end of his attempts to find freedom through madness.
Subsequently, he returned to writing about Laing almost as

frequently as he wrote about Lessing, and his judgements were just as contradictory. 'Laing was brave, articulate, a warrior – also a major bullshit artist, much too handsome, restless and an acidhead', he reflected in an article forty years later.

Clancy Sigal ultimately failed to free himself through madness with Laing. But I found that Lessing remained more optimistic about Laing's theories in her fiction. It seemed to me that although Clancy and Lessing were far less in touch in the late 1960s than they had been a few years earlier, they were engaged in strikingly similar projects. She too experimented with madness, though – with the characteristic efficiency that I admired – she simply locked herself in a room and starved herself of food and sleep for a few days. She also took mescaline, and under the influence of drugs was able to give herself a new birth, replacing the world of war into which she was born in 1919 with a new, warmer world, illuminated by the 'sun rising in a glow of firelight'.

Both of these were more experiences of enlightenment than of freedom, but she still allowed madness to be a force of freedom in her fiction of the next few years. Her ideas didn't all come from Laing. Years before she read Laing, she'd heard similar sentiments expressed by D.H. Lawrence. I went back to *Women in Love*, where I found Birkin, climbing out of the valley after Hermione has hit him and wondering if he is mad. He decides that if he is, he prefers his madness to the sanity of others:

> He rejoiced in his own madness, he was free. He did
> not want the old sanity of the world, which was become
> so repulsive. He rejoiced in the new-found world of
> madness. It was so fresh and delicate and so satisfying.

Already in the *Golden Notebook*, Lessing had investigated the creative potential of breakdown. Later she suggested that breakdown had been the central theme of the novel, with Anna and Saul breaking down 'into each other, into other people', breaking through the false patterns they had made and emerging through this process of 'self-healing' into creative plenitude. But in Lessing's final Martha Quest novel *The Four-Gated City*, she investigated Laingian principles more explicitly. Reading it a year earlier, I'd thought that this was one of Lessing's two or three most brilliant novels, partly because it explodes the whole notion of genre. Now I went back to it to think more specifically about the question of madness.

The madness in this novel is at first found only in the character of Lynda, the estranged wife of Mark, the man who Martha comes to love. She is spurned by those around her, relegated to the basement of her own home, but gradually it becomes clear to Martha that Lynda is in fact saner than her insistently rational family upstairs. Martha moves into the basement with her and participates in her madness, as Lessing had in Clancy's, coming to share 'the sight, sound, smell, the *feeling* of Lynda'.

She now discovers that mind-reading is possible and comes to the conclusion that contemporary Western society is limited by its refusal to recognise the power of the unconscious mind. The 'civilised human race' knows that 'its primitive members (for instance, Bushmen) used all kinds of senses not used by itself', but has ceased to recognise these faculties. Madness becomes a Laingian mode of accepting truth. In a society that 'will not admit what one knows to be true', it is 'through madness and its variants [that truth] must be sought after'. It's because Lynda has been mad that she is able to help Martha to seek the truth, and Martha then does this on her own in a voyage into inner space that takes the form of Lessing's brief experiment with madness. Martha hides away in a friend's empty flat for a month, renouncing food and sleep and accessing a new state of sensitivity in which she encounters her 'self-hater'. Lying on the floor, beating her head and weeping, she argues with her inner Devil at the same time as she tunes in to the thoughts of the people she knows. By the end of her time there, she feels as though she's been 'turned inside out like a glove or a dress' but that she is closer to understanding both herself and her world.

The Four-Gated City was followed by *Briefing for a Descent into Hell*, a book that addresses madness more explicitly as its central theme. By now, Lessing had taken in Jenny Diski, who had quickly ended up back in a mental hospital. One of Diski's fellow inmates became the model for the protagonist of Lessing's novel. Charles Watkins is a classics professor in a state of breakdown, who has forgotten his own identity. Incarcerated in a mental asylum, he regales those around him with tales of a distinctly Laingian schizophrenic voyage, recounting his experiences of participating in bloody rituals among the tribes in the forest, his travels on the back of the White Bird across the sea of the dead and his journey into space. Watkins divides his doctors over whether he should be subjected to ECT or to a more sympathetic talking cure. 'I am one who does not believe that other people's crises should be cut short, or blanked out with drugs, or forced sleep, or a pretence that there is no crisis,' says one of his former friends. This echoes a more explicitly political statement on the original book jacket, which broadcast that 'Doris Lessing believes that society's treatment of the mentally ill is civilisation's biggest and blackest blind spot, and that it is through the minds of the broken-down that truths we choose to shut out enter like the disguised messengers in myths and fairy tales'.

Although Lessing drew the inspiration for Watkins partly from Diski's new acquaintance, I felt confident in believing that she was also writing about Clancy once again. Her lived experience of madness came from him, and she was conscious of his own recent voyages into himself. If the imagery in this novel is Laing's, then the pain is both Clancy's and Lessing's own. The outbursts of grief could come straight from Clancy's diary, as when Watkins joins the 'dark half' of his race in crying out for sleep – 'give me pills to make me sleep, give me alcohol to make me sleep, give me sex to make me sleep' – or when he falls on the face of the earth and weeps:

> Oh, I'll never know such sorrow again. I'll never know such grief, oh, I cannot stand it, I don't wish to live, I do not want to be made aware, of what I have done and what I am and what must be, no, no, no, no, no, no…

There's an almost comic reference to the experience of shared madness when Watkins looks back on the memory of the nights where he had 'drunk blood and eaten flesh with the women under the full moon', thinking of it as a 'page in my passport for this stage of the journey'. Though Doris Lessing and Clancy Sigal had parted years earlier, he remained in the background of her writing as she was in the background of his thoughts, driving him away and tugging him back as he embarked on his abortive voyages into inner space.

Fifty years later, the forays into madness of the 1960s had lost their lustre. Here I was pleased to be part of my generation rather than hers. Indeed, I was starting to feel that we might have got it right after all. We could enjoy the rewards of sexual liberation, choosing when to have sex and when to have children. We could enjoy the plunders of communism, which had at least contributed to the end of apartheid. And when it came to psychological liberation, we might be better off without the kind of freedom she espoused.

It seemed absurd to me that schizophrenia might be seen as a source of freedom; that LSD should offer the promise of lucidity. This wasn't to say that there wasn't something enticing about aspects of the relationship between Lessing and Clancy, or about some of the more restrained theories proposed by Laing. At their best, in those days of frenzied writing, those nights of talking when anything could be said, Lessing and Clancy explored the possibility that exposure to the more dangerous enclaves of the inner world would allow them to break through the surface of things and through the boundaries that usually separate people from each other. I found this tempting. It may be what we all hope for from sex, but for them it was more extreme because the sexual merging was accompanied by a mental merging and by a voyage into fantasy.

In *The Politics of Experience* Laing writes that as children our experience begins as fantasy, but in adults fantasy tends to be

> split off from what the person regards as his mature, sane, rational, adult experience… For most of our social life, we largely gloss over this underlying phantasy level of our relationship.

The chance of recapturing the imaginative possibilities of childhood was more compelling for me than the prospect of taking LSD. I was too anxiously attached to the present con-figuration of my brain to try LSD in the interests of research, but I was curious about what a Laingian fantasy might entail. I wondered now if my desire to recall the freedom of my lonely childhood holidays by the sea was primarily a desire to return to fantasy, by retreating from my adult world. Perhaps this was Lessing's desire too and it was this that drove her experiments with madness.

While I found it hard to follow Lessing on her descent into hell, I found it easy to accept her suggestion in *The Four-Gated City* that we mind-read all the time, without naming it as mind-reading. What was most appealing in her affair with Clancy was that it turned freedom into the joint enterprise that breakdown becomes for Anna and Saul in *The Golden Notebook*. In the bush, she'd experienced freedom only in iso-lation: it was a necessarily lonely state. Now it had become a state that could be accessed mutually. In this respect, Clancy's resistance to domesticating their relationship made sense, as did Anna's defiant renunciation of marriage in *Play with a Tiger*. They were reluctant to lose the freedom of the shared fantasy, though they were aware that the porous boundaries between them created an atmosphere of danger. I thought that it might be because marriage was not a sufficiently dangerous state that it didn't allow for this kind of intimacy very often.

Nonetheless, neither the relationship nor the madness seemed to have been very freeing for either Lessing or Clancy. 'I know no joy, only terror', he observed after one encoun-ter with LSD. He was deeply unhappy during this period. 'Life is dreary, depressing, pain-ridden and unsupportable' is a typical diary entry from 1960. Reading his diaries, I found that it was hard not to feel angry with both of them. She for trusting this man, who seemed so obviously to emerge as an emotional adolescent; he for allowing the continuation of a relationship with a woman whom he knew he loved without desire.

After the affair ended, Doris Lessing told Joan Rodker that she had failed abysmally to save her lover from himself. She thought that this had happened because she had been 'so lonely when he came, and I needed so badly to have someone to love and to love me that I didn't want to think'. In scenes in *The Golden Notebook* written after the relationship had failed, she described Anna's burgeoning love for Saul Green:

> I'd forgotten what making love with a real man is like.
> And I'd forgotten what it was like to lie in the arms of
> a man one loves. I'd forgotten what it was like to be in
> love like this, so that a step on the stair makes one's heart
> beat, and the warmth of his shoulder against my palm
> is all the joy there is in life... I find myself sitting in my
> room, watching the sunlight on the floor... a calm and
> delightful ecstasy, a oneness with everything, so that
> a flower in a vase is oneself, and the slow stretch of a
> muscle is the confident energy that drives the universe.

After reading Clancy's diary, I found that this made even more painful reading than it had before. Anna knows that this happiness cannot last; that at any moment Saul could retreat once more into alienated distance. And when he does, she sees the creature in her that has been created by Saul's sexual need for her quivering and shrinking.

Here Lessing was analysing her relationship with Clancy accurately. In this novel written as their bond splintered, she forced herself to admit the imbalance of love. In all of his accounts of their first meeting, she tells him that she's been hurt by men and asks him not to hurt her. He doesn't seem to have taken this very seriously, either at the time or in subsequent retellings. In this respect he became another lover who, because he relied on her strength, could never really believe in her vulnerability, however much she told him about it. 'It's necessary to you to think of me as stronger than I am,' she wrote to him as the relationship ended, 'and for an easy reason – you needed my strength'. He was unable to see that she was occluding her own needs as she assuaged his. And he couldn't always see how hurt she was by his sexual rejection.

Coming across the passage in his archive where he describes her sexual smell, I felt furious on her behalf. He was dismissing her aged thirty-seven as a kind of ageing witch. 'Sometimes, awaking in the middle of the night,' he wrote after a temporary break-up in 1959, 'I would smell her sexuality which it seemed to me was thick with age and experience, and I sometimes would lie awake and long for the sweet light vaginal odours of the girls under 25.'

Doris Lessing was conscious of her lover's disgust. In *The Golden Notebook* Anna is hurt to discover that Saul doesn't like having sex with her, though she is ashamed that she cares more about this than about whether he likes her as a person. On one occasion, Clancy recorded in his diary that Lessing had complained that he had a horror of the female body. 'How can I explain it is a horror of her body?' he asked, cruelly. Later he described how he invented trips away from London so that he could store up sufficient 'raw sexual hunger' to have sex with her on his return.

This is the kind of sexual rejection that most women fear as they get older, and it frightened me that in her case it was not an irrational fear. It was happening to her, and she was only two years older than I was. At the end of their relationship she told Clancy that she had felt frequently that in his mind his hand was on another woman's body instead of hers; that sex had been 'an act of victory – against me, against her'.

Doris Lessing was left not so much freed by the madness of the affair as trapped by her own weakness. And she was left longing for a very unfree kind of love: longing, desperately and impossibly, to have his child. Clancy recorded two occasions in his diary when Lessing suggested that she should untie her tubes and conceive his baby. In the roles they felt most comfortable playing, she was the real woman and he was the real man and so it made sense for them to have a child together. Indeed, their relationship functioned best when Clancy was being a father figure for Peter. However, Clancy's cowboy posturing was in part a product of his neurosis and it was a role that Lessing came to loathe because it took him away from her to other women. Reading his diaries it seemed impossible that she could have hoped so much and for so long that they could be happy together. It appeared as though she must have been wilfully misreading him, and relinquishing her own freedom in the process.

Clancy Sigal was still alive, aged eighty-eight, and living in Los Angeles, so I wrote to him suggesting that I come to see him. I hoped that he would help me piece together their relationship, and also clarify how the freedoms of madness, fantasy and sex related for him. And I wanted to see California, which would give me a new kind of flat landscape to explore; the desert was a frontier landscape like the African bush – a place where 'real men' and 'real women' could perhaps be easily imagined.

His initial response was discouraging. He told me that he would 'neither impede nor help' me. If I happened to be in

LA, he might have time for coffee, but would give no interviews about Lessing. I was surprised by the scale of my disappointed panic. It was clear that I was no longer conducting research in any conventional sense: I was not, as I'd suggested to him, simply an academic writing about Lessing who was curious to meet the original behind Saul Green.

What had begun with the drive to understand my ambivalence about my world through reading Lessing and thinking about freedom had become something much more single-minded. There was a liberation to be found through pursuing Lessing's ideas about freedom, certainly, but there also seemed now a more urgent and personal liberation to be found in pursuing Lessing herself: in hunting her down as a way of giving the side of me that identified with her the space and time it needed to emerge. I wanted to see Clancy Sigal because I felt that this might happen through our encounter. Reading the material in his archive, I felt that I was in daily communication both with him and with her and it seemed possible that this might continue once we met.

I decided to risk going to LA. The Clancy I had encountered in the archive was not a man who sat at home waiting for an invitation any more than Lessing herself was. If she was failing to teach me about freedom then she was certainly teaching me about courage.

II

'Enclosed by these vivid dry colours'

California

Los Angeles was in the midst of a heatwave when I arrived, which came as a surprise after autumnal London. Experiencing that first instant flood of warmth after climbing down from the plane, I wasn't sure whether to allow myself to expand into it. In London, I'd been enjoying the containment that autumn brings, clattering down the corridors in boots that clicked, as though to emphasise my new efficiency, sheathed in wool that offered a layer of protection against the madness I was encountering in Clancy's diaries.

Clancy had agreed that I could come to see him on my first afternoon. That morning I swam in the pool outside my building, gradually adjusting to the heat and to the palm trees and hills that surrounded me, but unable fully to inhabit my own body. Half-conscious that the image came from *The Golden Notebook*, I thought that it was as though I was in London, watching a film of myself in LA.

His street was incongruous. The neat bungalows with self-satisfied front gardens seemed at odds with the Chicago streets where he had grown up, or the grimy flat he'd lived in with Lessing. His much-younger wife Janice opened the door before I'd had a chance to ring the bell: intelligent-looking, brisk, warm. A cake was produced; he was still being cooked for after all these years.

Clancy himself was smaller than I had expected, which reminded me that he was smaller than Lessing had expected as well. He was wearing a baseball cap labelled 'Secret Agent' and a T-shirt and shorts that were not the costume of an ageing Lothario; there was no low-slung belt and definitely no gun. He began by interviewing me about my book. I attempted to explain what I was doing and ended up stating rather vaguely that I was writing about the experience of looking for Doris Lessing.

'Looking for what?'
'Looking for Lessing.'
Incredulity.
'Good luck!'

'We have some of her ashes in the living room!' Janice interjected from the kitchen.

Welcome to LA.

It quickly became clear that Clancy found the notion of freedom as a structuring principle for a book about Lessing absurd. He did not think that she'd cared much about the notion of freedom or that freedom was a useful concept in the twenty-first century. I insisted that she had used the word freedom frequently enough to suggest that it mattered and, what is more, that he had used it frequently in the 1960s as well. I quoted him the passage in his novel where he described Laing and his colleagues as driven by a quest for freedom and told him that he had informed Lessing that his notion of freedom was to have sex with multiple women.

'Really?' he asked. 'I told her that? The depth of my stupidity when I first met Doris was incalculable. She was a highly intelligent, highly literate, highly sexed woman, and here was I, this lumbering, non-writing Yank, the only thing going for me was I was sexy, but I didn't treat her any differently from how I treated women in America.'

This was a good start. This was not a man who would dismiss a woman of thirty-seven on account of her ageing sexual smell. And having refused to talk about Lessing, he now seemed prepared to talk about her with remarkable candour.

Gradually, as the conversation became more relaxed, I started to notice an odd disjunction. Clancy still claimed that freedom didn't matter. 'Everyone is free,' he said. 'They're free already and so they don't need it. Women have the Pill, the right to abortion and the right to sue for sexual harassment.' But at the same time he started using the word 'freedom' more often.

Sometimes, the word was innocuous, as when he stated that the first Women's Liberation conference in 1970 had been 'totally freeing' for everyone who was there. But at other times it became central to his experience. Had he wanted to have a child with Doris? Yes, he'd wanted to impregnate her, but he did not want to start a family. 'The whole point for me was freedom.' Had he resisted falling in love? Yes, he continued to see not only family life but love itself as inherently at odds with being free. 'Men find it much easier to fuck a woman if they're turned on but not in love. The guy feels freer not to be in love. To be in love is to be enslaved. You give up an enormous amount of your freedom when you fall in love. You give up everything – you give up your soul, for Christ's sake. If you're not prepared to give up your soul you might as well not be in love.'

We were getting somewhere now. This was the contradiction that troubled Lessing: the need for freedom that was prevented by the experience of love, and the clamouring for possession it brings, combined with the simultaneous need for mental expansion that was enabled by the merging of minds. I asked if he had been tempted to give up his soul for Lessing? No, he said, and she had not given hers up either. 'She was a very self-protective dame.' Even now it seemed that he was refusing to acknowledge her need in relation to him. It was also clear that after all these years he had still not gained the fundamental curiosity about her that would have enabled him to love her at the time.

'Let me make my confession now,' he told me, appealingly. 'You're like a priest. Basically, I've never read Lessing. The fact that she was a writer was not a lot of interest to me.' He claimed that he'd never read her and still had no interest in reading her; he had more interest in reading my own books.

He did not even know that she had written novels influenced by R.D. Laing. He remembered her cooking, her sexiness (here he was somewhat rewriting the past) and the 'roaring rows' they'd had together. 'We had an absolutely great, horrendous time.'

Talking to Clancy was illuminating the differences between political and physical freedom. Politically, freedom is, as Clancy kept reminding me, historically contingent. 'Lessing and her generation responded to the time they lived in, part of which was Africa and the war. Your generation have nothing like that. What you do have is relationships unimpeded by war, by racial intolerance – you have a clear field of fire.' Related to this is personal freedom, which is more universal. The fear of restraint in marriage is only partly related to the era in which that marriage is taking place. 'It's amazing you don't come out of a wedding more unhappy than you are,' Clancy observed, after I'd told him about reading *The Golden Notebook* while going to too many weddings; 'the whole idea of a wedding and honeymoon is very destructive.' And then there's physical freedom, which at its best takes us outside history, though in any encounter with nature we are encumbered by personal and historical baggage. It turned out that for Clancy as well as Lessing, the greatest experience of freedom occurred not through politics but through place. For him the apotheosis of freedom had been those trips on trains from Euston to the north and, surprisingly, he'd experienced freedom not in the towns but on the moors.

'It was a utopia. Five quid could take you anywhere. That was freedom for me – freedom was up north – I'd get off wherever I felt like it – Crewe, Northampton, Sheffield. I'd escape London, the guilt, the successful writers who were less good-looking than me, and I'd go to the north where everyone was friendly, and walk out on to the moors. I'm not an outdoors guy but they were absolutely fantastic. For me, they were pure freedom.'

It was as unexpected to find Clancy on the moors as it was to find him in this tidy Californian bungalow. But once he had started to describe it I could picture him there, and I found that there were surprising parallels with Lessing. He could have been describing the young Doris in the African bush. He could also have been describing Lessing in the years after they parted. He didn't remember that in 1964 she had bought an isolated cottage in Dartmoor. She had visited the area to see Ted Hughes, who had lived nearby, first with Sylvia Plath and then with Assia Wevill, and she had found in the desolate Devon moors a sense of limitlessness comparable to what Clancy was experiencing in the similar landscapes of the north.

It was time for me to go. Clancy wished me luck – curious, amused – and dispatched me in a taxi to the beach. I wanted to walk around and think about what he had said. But as I sat in a beach café writing my notes while music blared above me, looking out at the mountains silhouetted spectacularly in the distance against the everblue sky, I found that it was hard to think about either Clancy or Lessing. This was the sea but the crowds were too insistent for it to be freeing; it was a landscape that had nothing to do with Lessing's veld or Clancy's unexpected Yorkshire moors. And partly because Clancy had punctuated the interview with insistent questions about my husband and son, I felt their presence somewhat accusingly beside me. I became conscious of this as a place where most people were accompanied by cavorting families and felt myself becoming awkwardly isolated through being there alone. This was not a setting in which to think about freedom or to gain any distance from the world I had left behind at home.

Before I had left for Los Angeles, my husband and I had been talking about divorce. Pent up, frustrated by not being pregnant, vaguely aware of a need for intimacy that was unfulfilled, I had turned both to nature and to the excitement of material things, and had been looking into buying a cottage in Suffolk with a close friend I sometimes went away to write with, a woman in her seventies. This had been looked on as folly by her children and my husband. Our respective finances would be absurdly stretched and, though we both did our best to forget it, she had a brain tumour – a death sentence weighing her down – so there were questions to be asked about what would happen to the house when she died. But as people around us disapproved, we became all the more sure. On my side, this was something that I could do as I waited for the pregnancy that would enable me to stop dangling and take charge of the future; an antidote to the claustrophobia I was coming to feel both in London and in my marriage, where I felt that my husband had an increasingly narrow vision of who we could be for each other. For him, it came together with his irritation that I tended to retreat with a book when he was playing with our son to create the belief that I lacked commitment to the family and was impossibly bent on my own self-centred course. He announced that he did not wish to have another child with me until I could prove him wrong.

I could see the logic of his position. We become more ourselves as we get older, but do not know quite how this will happen. I was a more straightforward person when he fell in love with me in my twenties. And I was frustrating now in being both more complicated and more self-satisfied. I felt perversely attached to the more difficult person I had become, though I could see that there was no reason why my husband should be too, except insofar as I believed that in becoming more complicated I had become a more interesting and emotionally receptive mother and lover. It was this that I was angry with him for not seeing.

Weeks of arguments and distance had come to a head the day before I left, while my son had his afternoon nap. Both tired, we lay side by side, clothed, in bed, and I said, as unemotionally as possible, while tears fell almost incidentally down my face, that he needed to decide whether he wanted to set us on a course where we could stay together or to make explicit that we were on a spiral heading towards divorce. The conversation was unusually amicable: he refrained from anger, I refrained from ostentatious crying. It left us in no more certain a position than we had started, except that I ended it more open to the possibility of loving him and more able to believe that he could still believe in the possibility of loving me. I initiated sex, which began with more affection than we had demonstrated to each other in recent weeks, until it became clear that he was reluctant to come inside me.

I needed to feel our bodies combine both for the physical release of sex and for the affirmation that we still existed as a couple. I told him, accurately, that it was not a fertile time of the month; when he insisted that there was always a risk, I suggested that he could withdraw. I did not expect him to do so and I did not know how much it mattered to me that he didn't.

The sex was as urgent a relief as I had hoped for; it was as though weeks of tension were slipping away and I could believe once again in our future together. I thought of Anna

Wulf – of her surprise that life can be transformed by that moment of sexual happiness with Saul, her account of her oneness with everything, so that 'the slow stretch of a muscle is the confident energy that drives the universe'. I could feel my husband's belief growing alongside mine as we created something – not so much a potential child as simply a shared moment of faith – together.

Then, at the last moment, he did withdraw. The grief that I felt then was a grief not for my marriage, which felt as though it was ending in that moment, but for the baby that should have been born a month later had I not miscarried that spring. Perhaps all along I had managed to ration that sadness because I'd come to accept our assertion that I'd become pregnant quickly enough that we would look back on it all as the same pregnancy. But I saw now that it was not a pain that could be rationed; that, as Laing had insisted, fantasy is as real to us as reality and so, even if the twelve-week-old foetus had turned out to be merely a lump of bloody tissue, the child that had been growing in my imagination had a life whose curtailment still needed to be acknowledged.

All along, I had seen my husband as more concerned with children than relationships, where I was more dependent on adult love. But it felt then as though I was willing to let go of the marriage except in this one respect: that there was a baby whom my womb – the Lawrentian phrase does not seem excessive – was calling out to be created by us.

Now I felt that I needed to understand more about how my need for freedom – my feeling of constraint in the marriage – could coincide with this need to be impregnated: to be confined by pregnancy and then by childbirth and then by months of milk. Perhaps it was this contradiction that had angered my husband. The need for freedom that was about to send me across the world in search of Lessing had not seemed to him conducive to the well-being of the child I wished to conceive.

There were no answers to be found on the beach, so I meandered slowly back to my apartment through the LA streets, remembering Clancy's return to LA during his gestational time in America in 1963. Staying in a rooming house under a freeway, he complained to Laing that there seemed to be no room for him anywhere in the city. 'I am lost in the labyrinth of meaninglessness; proportions are distorted, importances submerged.' He felt a 'tremendous call to go out again into the body of America'; into the landscape he had left behind when he fled in 1956. I had only a few days but I could follow him into the body of America. The next morning I took a greyhound bus to Palm Springs, a strange, luxury oasis in the middle of the desert, where I had located a man with a jeep who was prepared to drive me into the wilderness.

It may be inevitable that any trip in search of answers should fail to provide them. Certainly, it was apparent as soon as the driver arrived that this expedition was going to be bathetically catastrophic. This was not the John Wayne – the Clancy of the 1960s – I'd hoped to find here. Instead it was a parodically square-jawed, incessantly jokey man accompanied by two American tourists who were as determined as he was to keep up a continuous conversation and to drive joltily from location to location, pausing only to take pictures. I became sullen, joining in only to ask intermittently if he could stop and let me walk around on my own. He was mystified as to why I wanted to walk around in the 110°F degree heat, and he wasn't alone in this: Clancy had been similarly incredulous, warning me that the previous week, a foolhardy European tourist had died here.

'In the desert, pure air and solitude compensate for want of moisture and fertility,' Thoreau had stated so confidently. But in this dry, overheated landscape, I was encountering not the freedom I was seeking but a new form of confinement. It was partly a result of my irritation, both with the people around me and with myself. I was irritated by my own brittle misanthropy, that 'dry anguish' which it only marginally consoled me to note resembled that of Anna Wulf. And I was irritated that I had expended so much effort on crossing the world only to find that the anxieties that had preoccupied me in London felt no further away. Freedom, here, now, was something I only half wanted. The arguments with my husband had left me insecure; the image of my son was now uneasily there at the back of my mind, making me conscious that, as Lessing learnt to her cost with Clancy, we can only long for freedom from a position of security. But the claustrophobia was also induced by the landscape, which was itself less expansive than I'd anticipated.

We were on a fault line between two plates that had pushed up the sharp rocks that towered above us. I felt as though the view was too small; the sky not quite big enough. And the grey dust that surrounded me seemed more a lack than a landscape. When it rose in mounds, it looked like a cat whose fur had been removed. Surveying this inaccessible, alien setting, I started to worry that the dusty earth and the scrubby bushes were comparable to what I would find in the African bush; that even once I had made my way to Lessing's myth country, I would feel no freer than I did here.

'Here is no water but only rock,' T.S. Eliot writes in *The Waste Land*, in lines written in London about a remembered, inhospitable America, that were ringing through my head now:

Rock and no water and the sandy road
The road winding above among the mountains
Which are mountains of rock without water.

I chanted what I could remember of the poem in my mind
as a kind of talismanic protection against the noise of the
conversation and the sterility of my thoughts. And when
I returned to the hotel I looked it up and found that I was
reassured by its resonance with my afternoon. It seemed that
it was through language that I could force this landscape into
meaning. The desert in Eliot's poem contains people, frus-
tratingly preventing solitude as they had in mine:

There is not even silence in the mountains
But dry sterile thunder without rain
There is not even solitude in the mountains
But red sullen faces sneer and snarl.

Eliot's dry suffocation is broken by a 'damp gust / Bringing
rain'. When the thunder speaks it is of blood shaking the
heart, 'The awful daring of a moment's surrender'. There
was no rain for me, but as the sun lowered, the evening light
brought unexpected colours. Suddenly the mountains in the
distance turned white and blue. This was an effect I hadn't
witnessed before and it reminded me of the Umvukwes
described by Lessing, turning purple and blue as she watched.
I became more aware of beauty; aware that the winding lines
etched into the stone resembled the contours of the human
body, making the whole scene less inaccessible than it had
been earlier.

Before she meets Saul in *The Golden Notebook*, Anna Wulf
has a dream about standing on the edge of a wide yellow

desert at midday. The sun is darkened by the dust hanging in the air and she knows that she has to cross this yellow expanse of dust. On the other side of the desert are mountains: 'purple and orange and grey'. The colours are beautiful but she is confined by them, 'enclosed by these vivid dry colours'. She has no water but she has to set off across the desert alone and attempt to reach the mountains. Waking, Anna understands that if she is to cross the desert, she must 'shed burdens'.

As I swam in the hotel pool in the evening light, my husband and son finally seemed further away. It felt as though I were swimming out toward the mountains, which were still blue against the reddening sky. The desert heat is known as a Valium heat. I wasn't mad, any more than Lessing had been; the same accusation could be made at me that Saul makes at Anna – I am irritatingly sane. Yet there is a half-enjoyable madness to be found in the obsessive thought processes enabled by isolation and I was starting to experience it.

I realised that what I had learnt from the conversation with Clancy was what I had known all along in returning so often to the image of Lessing in the bush. This was that the freedom that she had sought, that he had sought, and that I was ambivalently seeking, had very little to do with the political freedom of the 1960s, whether this was the freedom of madness or of sexual liberation. Instead it remained Thoreau's 'absolute freedom and wildness': an existential state of mind.

Of course, Clancy was right that we were historically contingent. When Lessing and Clancy used the word 'freedom', they were products of a time in which the pursuit of freedom was a laudable goal. When I used it, I was chafing against the very different constraints of my own generation.

Though we may, as I'd observed before my trip, have got it right in enjoying the fruits of liberation without its excesses, this had its own costs. Now that we had fewer restrictions than their generation had done, there was less possibility to enjoy the feeling of moving beyond constraint, which itself constituted an experience of freedom. We also sought freedom less willingly in its own right, because it had revealed itself to be both selfish and unachievable. Yet, in questing for a daily life that felt more like the freedom we found in nature, Lessing, Clancy and I seemed to have much in common, despite the historical circumstances that divided us. We all wanted the freedom to escape both the self and our circumstances in order to feel more fully alive.

I had seen already that when I had complained about the reactionary tendencies of my friends and when I imagined promiscuously opening my marriage, I was not primarily objecting to marriage as a political act, though that was how I had framed it initially. Instead I was objecting to being trapped in a world in which I frequently came up against the limits of admissible thought. Now I saw that it was partly a question of the imagination, and of wanting to create a life in which reality and fantasy were separated less rigidly. Rightly or wrongly, this seemed to me more possible outside the confines of monogamous marriage. However alien Laing seemed, I was attracted by the openness to fantasy that he attributed to his idealised schizoid personality and that had sent Clancy voyaging across the powerful, inhospitable terrain I now confronted. I was asking for a world in which the external day-to-day events of our lives could more often be imbued with the intensity of 'inner space' and for a landscape empty enough to allow the mind room to expand.

7

'I was able to be freer than most because I am a writer'

Writing

Returning home, I was met unexpectedly by my husband and son at the airport. The excited shout of 'Mummy, Mummy' made me want to cry with relief, and I settled back into family life. Tacitly, it seemed that we had agreed to continue, and that the continuation allowed for the possibility of having another child. If what I sought in nature was the freedom to escape the confines of the egotistical self, then I was reminded now, spending time with my son, that motherhood offered a related pleasure. This was freedom through constraint: the freedom to love and therefore to live fully, through allowing yourself to be tied, which presented another form of escape from the ego.

Nonetheless, my experiences in California felt unfinished. The time in the desert had left me restless, in need of a lone encounter with nature, and I wanted to follow Lessing and Clancy to the moors. I was still conscious of a fundamental dissatisfaction with the daily, unchanging parameters of my life. I was optimistic that when I did finally become pregnant again, it would help, introducing movement within the stagnancy, and in the meantime I put a lot of rather frenetic energy into trying to convince a series of reluctant banks to provide a mortgage for the cottage in Suffolk. Although it was looking increasingly unlikely, I held out hope, but then the friend I was buying it with wrote to say that she was going to have to pull out, under pressure from her children. My husband was relieved; now we could move forward without the added strain of his resentment. But lacking that outlet for my energy, I became more unhappy, yearning more urgently for a freedom I could not easily define.

Frustrated by both myself and Lessing, unable to progress in understanding either of us, I decided that before pursuing Lessing and Clancy to the moors, I should follow them into psychoanalysis. I had never sat in an analyst's consulting room; never had the experience of presenting myself to an impassive observer. I wanted someone to help me learn more about why freedom mattered to me and I wanted to ask myself if I had identified with Lessing because I shared her compulsive interest in freedom or if I had become compulsively interested in freedom because I identified with Lessing.

I sent a message to an analyst I had once had a brief, enjoyable and somewhat flirtatious conversation with at a party. A week later, I sat opposite an intelligent, quizzical man in his sixties, talking about my life, asking him to reflect with me on freedom. He was only prepared to see me twice: after that, it was either full psychoanalysis or nothing. But in two sessions, he unsettled many of my assumptions and left me grief-stricken on behalf of my younger self.

By now the house purchase was back on. My friend had called in tears saying that she too felt life narrowing without it, though in her case this meant defining herself as someone with cancer who could no longer project possibilities on to an open future. I had thought that I'd talk to the analyst about the house, about Lessing, and about my marriage. I did not expect to talk much about my childhood, perhaps largely because it was too predictable a use of our time. It seemed obvious to him, however, that my desire for freedom should take us back to the constraints of my past. And as I responded to his rapid questions, I found that I returned easily to those early years, when the need for freedom was simply a need to escape.

I was reassured by the extent to which he took it for granted that my mother, forbidding me to go to friends' houses where we might be allowed out on our own, swathing me in fluorescent yellow for the walk around the corner to the school bus stop that she accompanied me on well into my teenage years, was creating a feeling of suffocation that would result in a life-long fear of entrapment. It was at least in part as a result of those years that now my desire for freedom, when challenged by others, asserted itself as an unquestionable, urgent need. When my husband objected to my going away or failed to take seriously my sense of dissatisfaction in London, he was recreating the feeling of entrapment from my childhood.

I had not expected that through the analyst's questioning, I would come to see this claustrophobia as creating the need to be looked after as well as the need to escape. He made me see both that I feared the freedom I longed for and that, if I took the need for containment seriously, freedom might be the last thing I required. Indeed, I already had a lot more freedom than friends who were considerably more at ease with their lives than I was. The confrontation with my need to be looked after was painful. I realised that the parent whose protective impulses you mistrust – whose smothering dictates you know you must evade – is unable to make you feel protected, because you are too busy escaping her care to allow her to look after you. This leaves you reliant on the other parent, but in my case my father was unwilling to stand up for my need for freedom against my mother. For his own reasons – and I had seen this more clearly, watching him trying to look after my son – he lacked confidence in the possibility of parenting. I think he was partially relieved that she gave him no room to learn to overcome this.

I had chosen this analyst partly because I was curious about my frequent attraction to older men and thought that he, as an older man of the kind I might be attracted to, would help me to explore this. I was also missing my dying male friend, whom I had come to accept that I was never going to hear from again. Letters and emails continued to go unanswered, though I was told by his friend that while the prognosis remained disastrous, daily life had resumed in a muted form. As I described this friendship and its loss, it was obvious both to me and to the psychoanalyst that I was looking for a replacement; that after months of being so easily seen and accepted, these needs had started to feel unbearable. He reminded me that he was not offering to fulfil them. 'I'm not going to write you long letters every night.'

We started to talk about other friendships I'd made with older men. I described how they often took the form of my wanting to look after the men emotionally, which they were usually receptive to. The analyst suggested that this might in fact be an indirect way of asking them to look after me, which could easily remain unrecognised by either of us; an indirect desire for protective paternal parenting. This was where my relationship with the man who was dying had been so remarkable. Though at the start he had needed some protection in confronting the knowledge that his sexual desire was unreciprocated, he had increasingly derived pleasure from being the one to look after me. Realising how unusual this had been for me, and how much I'd needed it, brought a powerful feeling of loneliness. 'You are sad,' said the analyst, 'your eyes are sad now.' He suggested, rightly if a little self-importantly, that my sadness was partly because I wouldn't be able to see him again. I spent most of the evening in tears.

It was uncanny how much my realisations about my parents paralleled Lessing's, as did the conclusions that followed. Trapped by her mother's fears, unprotected by her father, Lessing emerged as an adult with conflicting drives for freedom and protection. In an important respect, it was considerably worse for her than for me because she often didn't feel loved by her mother; she felt displaced by her younger brother, who seemed to absorb more than his share of the available love.

Where did this leave my need to have another child, or leave Lessing in the late 1950s, longing to have a child with Clancy Sigal, one of many men whom she too wished to look after and then was hurt by when they didn't look after her in turn? The analyst suggested that my desire to feel a child growing inside me, enclosed by my body, was a desire to feel myself enclosed and protected. If I accepted this, which I was not especially inclined to do, perhaps the yearning to become pregnant was a yearning to escape the irritable need for freedom. But the vision of pregnancy was itself a free one; a vision of a new kind of embodiment that is self-sufficient, unlike the embodiment created by erotic longing. This was freedom from desire, rather than the freedom to pursue my desires. I wondered if for Lessing, the urge to become pregnant with Clancy had been an urge to retreat both from freedom and from madness, exciting though the possibilities of shared madness had seemed. And when it passed, she returned to the isolation of her childhood, looking no longer for protection, seeking on the moors the peaceful inner freedom she had found in the bush. It was just as the relationship with Clancy was ending that she bought the house on Dartmoor.

Like Anna in *The Golden Notebook*, what Lessing found on Dartmoor was the freedom not of sexual or gestational embodiment but of writing. Peter was away at boarding school; lovers were now relegated to the edges of her weeks; she wanted to be alone to write. It was in part this freedom – the freedom to exist as a writer independently of family ties – that I was seeking through the Suffolk house, though there were times when I also envisaged it as a rural idyll for family life. The freedom of writing can be hard to understand, but in her autobiography, Lessing suggested that it might be the greatest freedom of all:

> I was able to be freer than most because I am a writer,
> with the psychological make-up of a writer, that sets you
> at a distance from what you are writing about. The whole
> process of writing is a setting at a distance. That is the value
> of it – to the writer, and to the people who read the results
> of this process, which takes the raw, the individual, the
> uncriticised, the unexamined, into the realm of the general.

What Lessing is describing here is an inner strength that allows you to enter emotionally dangerous territory while knowing that you will be protected. The sense that everything in the present is narratable is a form of protection from the world. It was in part this feeling that I missed in my communication with my dying friend and had hoped to find with the analyst. Lessing found it easily in her novel-writing, and it's telling that though she and Clancy went mad together, she never ended up as helpless as he was. Arguably, in the battle between the lovers, she was victorious because she stayed sane enough to write: her books were her prize.

If I was looking for a landscape empty enough to allow the mind room to expand, then this surely was as much the blank page as the desert or the moors. But why was I writing publicly about myself? The analyst found this perplexing. 'Why do you want to explode the whole notion of privacy?' he asked. I didn't yet have the answer, but I felt that this exercise was essential for making me feel free, and that this was one of the most crucial lessons I was relying on Lessing to teach me. After all, she wrote about herself with such startling honesty, both fictionally and autobiographically, throughout her life.

I

'Me, I, this feeling of me'

Dartmoor

The village of Belstone sits at the top of the moors, surrounded on every side by swathes of empty land which in the autumn become a collage of brown, green, red and yellow. The centre of the village is small: there is a stretch of houses, all facing outward towards the moor, a single pub, a bed and breakfast and a village hall. This is remote enough, but Lessing's former house is set apart on a lane away from the village, looking out on to a farm, and beyond that to the moors.

Arriving, I was struck at once by my usual feeling of release on finding myself in a place where I can gaze out at grass and sky without experiencing much habitation in the way, and by a sense that I had come to a place where Lessing was easily accessible. If, as I had said to Clancy, I was looking for Lessing, then it seemed easier to locate her here than anywhere else I had been. Walking with urgent speed out on to the moors, minutes after arriving at the bed and breakfast, I felt confident in the knowledge that she had walked along this path, looking hungrily out on to this view, and felt the world receding behind her as I did now. This was a much more contented incarnation of Lessing than I'd encountered either in London or California, happy to be somewhere so open and beautiful, no longer preoccupied by her own or her lovers' neuroses.

For once, the identification with Lessing had enabled me to stop thinking about myself, and concentrate simply on picturing her feet striding along the paths in place of mine, accompanied by the sound of the river below and observed by the silent sheep and cows. It seemed that every landscape now bore for me a resemblance with my imagined picture of the African bush. I could see it in the yellow tufty grass that led down into the valley and in the hills that stood at the edge of each view. The bush was more enticing glimpsed in these surroundings than it had been in the Californian desert.

I visited Lessing's house, and was pleased to find that it almost exactly fitted the picture of it I'd built up from the descriptions of her friend Suzette Macedo, who had stayed there with her. It's a long white cottage with an appealingly rounded thatched roof. The large rooms have small windows, except for Lessing's study on the ground floor, where she created a wall of glass so she could survey the moors as she wrote. Seeing this, I wanted to stay for weeks and write myself; it made me more sure than ever of wanting the house in Suffolk. I returned to my bed and breakfast, where I sat at a desk looking out on to the moor where I had walked the previous day, and wrote about madness: about Lessing and Clancy, about myself in the desert. In her London flat, Lessing wrote in noisy bursts, punching the keys of her typewriter hard and fast. When she paused, she'd lie down to drift briefly into sleep, or stand up to pace up and down her room. I presume that in Devon more of her pacing took place outside but that the rhythm remained the same. It was my rhythm now: writing, sleeping, writing, pacing, writing, rushing out of my increasingly stifling bed and breakfast for an hour on the moors.

At Tor Down House, Lessing was writing *Landlocked* and *The Four-Gated City*, the final Martha Quest novels. If writing *The Golden Notebook* had changed her, enabling her to write away communism and exorcise Jack and Clancy, she could now return to the more straightforwardly autobiographical heroine she had created in Martha, all those years ago. Only this time, as she celebrated embodied love in *Landlocked* and investigated the freedom of madness in *The Four-Gated City*, she was experimenting with form more pleasurably than she had in the early Martha novels. In the final book in particular, she loosened the boundaries of the realist novel, enabling Martha to voyage into 'inner space' as she reads people's minds and then eventually travels to a remote island after Europe has destroyed itself.

Perhaps the most moving section of this novel is when Lessing writes from the perspective of her own mother. In her late forties, a decade after her mother's death, she seems finally to have learnt to sympathise with Maude Tayler. As

Mrs Quest castigates and infantalises her grown-up daughter, she seems genuine in believing that she has her best interests at heart. Pictured here, she's a pathetic figure whose only real intimacy comes from her relationship with a young black servant whom she helps learn to read. Moving to London to be near her ungrateful daughter, she breaks down, retreating into a vengeful but pitiful state. The reader half shares her disbelief that all the sacrifices she has made for her daughter could have occasioned only frustration and despair.

Meanwhile, Martha must escape not only her mother but the version of herself that's modelled on her mother's anxious view of the world. When Martha undergoes her days without food or sleep and overcomes her 'self-hater' persona, she is undergoing a creative transformation in which she learns who she is when free. Though Martha never writes, this is effectively the birth of the writer, and this is how Lessing described her own experiment with drugs in her autobiography. In Lessing's case, the persona escaped was not the self-hater but 'the Hostess'; again, this was the public self that was open to anxious inspection. Lessing recalled how the hostess kept performing – 'bright, helpful, attentive, receptive to what is expected' – while the inner self had the more important, private experience of frightened revelation. This inner self was the 'observer' and was explicitly figured as a writer: 'they call it loneliness, that here is this place unsharable with anyone at all, ever, but it is all we have to fall back on. Me, I, this feeling of me. The observer, never to be touched, tasted, felt, seen, by anyone else.'

'Me, I, this feeling of me'. This is the writer, beyond social interaction, beyond duty, beyond sex – not even to be touched or tasted – exposed to loneliness as the necessary price of freedom. It's the persona that Martha is liberating in her borrowed room and that Lessing was liberating in Tor Down House.

What does it feel like to reveal this person to the world? Why had it started to feel so necessary to me to do so? The answer that I had failed to give the psychoanalyst when he asked why I was exposing myself in print, was that liberating this observer self and subduing the hostess had become a necessary component of my freedom. My restlessness that autumn had been in part an irritation with my own social persona: with the side of me who wanted to please, charm and reassure a proportion of the people I met by subtly metamorphosing into the woman they wished me to be. I had spent my twenties learning to overcome shyness by developing a confident social self. It didn't always work even when I wanted it to, and now I wanted it to work less than I ever had. At the picnic in the summer where my husband had been cross because I was silent, he was coming up against my difficulty in assuming a hostess persona in this situation. He was also coming up against my sense that silence seemed increasingly to be the most honest response to social uncertainty.

Breaking down my social self had become a necessary continuation of the process of disintegration that had begun with the miscarriage. In order to be truthful and therefore in order to be free, I had to expose, both in person and in print, the side of me that was dislikeable; to expose the observer, who could be withdrawn and arrogant, and to expose the ambivalent wife and mother, ungrateful in the face of middle-class privilege, all for the doubtful good of saying something sincere. It was not that I wanted to reject the world and retreat into solitude. I needed intimacy with friends and strangers – the relief of being seen, bodily and mentally – but needed to develop a way to do this authentically, without the risk of being confronted with the invented versions of myself that they wished to project on to me. There were times when I worried that I was sacrificing my marriage by doing this, but most of the time it didn't feel like that. Though I knew that this might not be how it would look to him, I felt like I was offering my husband a more honest version of me – a version more capable of understanding a more honest version of him. If this was just a question of my marriage, I could have written it privately, but I wasn't only writing for him. Increasingly, I felt insincere in talking to people who didn't know what I was writing. It felt oddly necessary to surrender everything – to show people the swirl of pain and uncertainty and the few triumphant offerings of clarity that I could pull from its depths – and to see where we could go from there. But first I had to conquer embarrassment and shame.

While Lessing was roaming around the African bush at the age of twelve, Virginia Woolf gave the address called 'Professions for Women' where she exhorted the female members of her audience to kill the figure she termed 'the angel in the house'. This angel was the ego ideal that had to be resisted by the writer in search of prose tough enough to tell the truth. Woolf situated her in the Victorian era, but the figure she described was not one who could be easily banished to the past: 'she was intensely sympathetic. She was immensely charming. She was utterly unselfish. She excelled in the difficult arts of family life ... And when I came to write I encountered her with the very first words.' Woolf recounted how having murdered the angel, it took years before she could be sure that her adversary was not going to splutter into life once more.

Almost a century later, Woolf had successors urging comparable acts of violence. 'Sometimes I feel ashamed of this whole episode', the artist Chris Kraus wrote to the theorist Dick Hebdige in the series of fanatical unrequited love letters collectively published in 1997 as *I Love Dick*, which I had read a couple of weeks earlier. But Kraus saw shame as necessarily surmountable because by exposing herself in print in this way she was giving herself 'the freedom of seeing from the inside out. I'm not driven anymore by other people's voices. From now on it's the world according to me'. For Kraus, this freedom came from writing autobiographically, and she viewed this as an inherently feminist act. She saw it as necessary for women to ask and live the following question: 'If women have failed to make "universal" art because we're trapped within the "personal", why not universalise the "personal" and make it the subject of the art?'

Crucially, Kraus saw this as better achieved by autobiography than fiction. And Anna Wulf displays a comparable distrust of fiction in *The Golden Notebook*, where she comes to believe that 'my doing this – turning everything into fiction – is an evasion'. There were problems here. The autobiographical novel, dismissed by Kraus as 'a thinly veiled Story of Me', had done honourable service in capturing the suffering and the individual experience of both men and women. For me there was a compulsive element in reading Lessing's Martha Quest novels or Simone de Beauvoir's *The Mandarins* that I didn't quite find in their autobiographical writing. The characters and the landscapes they inhabited were given an easily embodied, sensual existence that surely added something to our sense of the contradictions of their lives. And books of this kind are freeing to write. It can be a pleasing act of escape to imagine a visual scene and create the people to inhabit it.

Nonetheless, as I typed away and looked out at the moors, I sensed that these remarks from Kraus were statements

I needed to hear. It felt like it would have been dishonest for me to turn myself into a fictional character, to invent a new name for myself or alter the details. There was a particular kind of freedom involved in truthfulness and specificity, though this wasn't necessarily more the case for women than for men and though overtly autobiographical books were sometimes published under the label of 'novel'. Karl Ove Knausgaard had described himself embarking on the six-volume book *My Struggle* as 'flaring with shame and a burning sense of freedom'. For him the freedom of writing this book that couldn't be categorised as either an autobiography or a novel was both the liberation of abandoning the usual formal constraints of fiction, accepting the messiness of life, and the liberation of transgression, describing his own bodily and mental life in potentially embarrassing detail.

I wondered if men had less squeamishness to overcome in the bodily aspect of transgression. Philip Roth, describing masturbatory orgasms through the autobiographical persona of the hero of his 1969 novel *Portnoy's Complaint*, made himself less vulnerable, I thought, than Lessing did with Anna's account of her orgasms and menstruation in *The Golden Notebook*, partly perhaps because the protective layer of humour prevented Roth from over-burdening his reader with emotion. Much as I admired Knausgaard, describing himself imagining having sex with every woman he met, I thought that he was shaming himself less than Chris Kraus, revealing her unrequited lust in *I Love Dick*.

This was because women seemed to provoke more hostility for these acts than men, and I was starting to become conscious of what this might mean for me. I had shown drafts of a couple of my own chapters to friends, male and female, who seemed anxiously protective on my behalf. Did I really want to expose myself sexually? they asked. And was I aware that I'd look like someone who already had a relatively free and extremely advantaged life, asking in a spoilt and dissatisfied fashion for more? They worried that I was dislikeable, while admitting that in real life they liked me for precisely the honesty and self-questioning that I was exhibiting. I wondered if they'd have felt this anxious if I was a man. Bellow's dangling man didn't ask what right he had to dangle. We seem to accept the dissatisfaction of the so-called male mid-life crisis more easily than that of the woman. In both cases, I remained convinced that it was worth taking the sudden urge for freedom seriously and that we could only do so by communicating inwardness; an outward act that made privacy impossible.

So I had come to feel that it was necessary to expose my least likable, weakest self in the service of freedom. And I found, during the bursts of writing where I forgot myself and my surroundings, that it was making me feel both happy and free. Indeed, if we identify the feeling of self-forgetfulness as a feeling of freedom, then I was coming to think that this was accessed more reliably through writing than through nature or sex. This seemed to be especially the case if you knew, as Lessing and I both knew, the circumstances in which you'd write in this abandoned way. In this state, it doesn't really matter what you're writing; it's the addictive feeling of watching word after word appearing on the page with very little apparent intervention from the brain that brings the happiness. Certainly, it was compulsive for Lessing, who went unrelentingly from one book to the next, and who wrote in the midst of emotional upheaval, even when she claimed to be feeling blocked.

Yet my investigation of freedom had not yet convinced me that freedom itself was an objective good and I had come to see my drive towards freedom as partly a neurosis born of stifling parenting and formative time spent by the sea. I could see that Clancy might be right that Lessing's interest in freedom was too historically contingent to be relevant for me: a response to the war and the need it created for new sources of hope. I could see in my own case that there was something oddly unfree in investigating freedom in so methodical and hard-working a way, tackling it in one of its manifestations at a time. And I could also see that the analyst might be right that freedom wasn't the element most obviously lacking in my life and that in seeking it I risked sacrificing the love and protection that I might need more.

Despite my enjoyment of the act of writing and my theoretical confidence in the project, I had frequent doubts about what I was doing. At work, I often hid behind the notion that I was 'writing a book about Doris Lessing', though it was only partially true, lacking the courage to defend the whole enterprise to more than a few trusted friends. Now I found in Dartmoor that it was almost impossible to respond to the repeated enquiries about why I was there. Why was a woman in her mid-thirties on holiday alone, spending large parts of the day in her room in a bed and breakfast, though she had admitted to having an almost-four-year-old child whom she had left behind at home? Trapped without a car and without friends, I wondered if they thought that I might never leave. I had become the ungainly overgrown teenage daughter, eating a packed lunch in her room each day.

After three days of writing, this oddness became draining. 'They call it loneliness', Lessing wrote confidently. But I knew

already that I was considerably less strong in enduring loneliness than she had been. Mentally, I kept returning to my
visit to Lessing's house, where I had encountered a boy a few
weeks older than my son, who had talked to me excitedly
about the prospect of his fourth birthday party. The sight of
this boy had made me miss my son at home, conjuring vividly
his skin, voice and smile, and the imaginative self-absorption
that seems typical for that age, when, as R.D. Laing observed,
real people and real things are incorporated so easily into fantasy. The memory of him haunted me now, as I walked on to
the moors, more conscious than I was at first of the aloof, vast
emptiness of these unfamiliar surroundings.

I was still aware of sharing this landscape with Lessing.
The river shining in slivers in the valley below her house; the
clumps of red trees plunging down into the gorge: these were
sights I could be sure she had seen, and not merely seen, but
encountered like me, close up, alone. But the glimpse of family life had left me feeing less free and this became worse at
night in bed, where I was reading a biography of Ted Hughes,
with the moors that were his at least as much as they were
Lessing's coated in darkness outside.

I had not known before that Hughes's lover Assia Wevill
had killed their four-year-old daughter Shura at the same
time as she killed herself in 1969. Coming at the end of a
day that had left me aching for the touch of my son, this
knowledge tipped me into helpless grief in which I felt furious not just with Wevill but with Hughes's first wife Sylvia
Plath, for leaving her children asleep as she gassed herself,
and with Lessing, for abandoning those children in Southern
Rhodesia. I was angry most of all with myself for going away
in search of freedom but feeling neither free nor happy; for

embarking on a quest that had ended up simply replacing claustrophobia with loneliness.

It seemed that it was impossible to empathise with these women and their unhappiness while also retaining a sense of the helpless weakness of their children, because this was precisely what they must in those moments have forgotten. What had struck me about the boy in Lessing's house – and this was a quality that reminded me of my son – was the compliance, the eagerness to please both his mother and this stranger who had come to look at his house and ask him questions. Now I could not rid myself of the image of Shura, eagerly biddable as her mother dosed her with sleeping tablets, or John and Jean Wisdom, waving obediently as their mother informed them that she was going away and leaving them to be free.

On my final night, anxious to flee myself and my fears, I took a taxi to the nearest town to see a film about suffragettes. But there was no escape possible here either, because I found myself watching a small boy being abandoned by his parents when he's sent off to strangers for adoption, and watching his mother grieving for the son who is being taken away from her because in urgently seeking her own freedom to vote, she has earned herself the title of a bad mother. This, once again, was a reminder of the price of liberation. Here, alone for a few days amid the forbidding beauty of the autumnal moors, it should not have cost very much. But my desire to be free had been thwarted by my need both to love and be loved, and this had come to centre on the love between mother and child. I was starting to think that the version of myself who sought happiness through writing freely was someone who could not really care about anyone else. During those moments of abandoned inspiration when

I seemed to evacuate my body and mind, my child ceased to exist. The next morning, as I returned gratefully to the city, I was escaping Lessing herself alongside her moors. I could see the appeal of renunciation and I had experienced the freedom of writing. But I was unwilling to enter the dark alongside her; frightened of calling upon myself to make the sacrifices she had made.

8

'A sick sweet submersion in pain'

The Dark

As autumn turned to winter, I continued to flirt vicariously with renunciation. I was aware of my presumption in doing so. 'I'm writing about the menopause,' I said eagerly to a fifty-year-old acquaintance, who had just been telling me about her hot flushes. 'About whether there's something to be gained from the changes it brings.' I blushed under her gaze as she looked me swiftly up and down, dismissing my claim to understand her. It seemed that my supplies of oestrogen remained too high to renounce anything.

Yet the more I read about other women's experiences of it, the more I believed Lessing, who had announced in an interview in 1972 that her discovery of 'the difference between what you really are and your appearance' had been 'one of the most valuable experiences that I personally have ever had':

a whole dimension of life suddenly slides away, and
you realise that what, in fact, you've been using to get

attention, or command attention, has been what you look like, sex appeal or something like that […] It's a biological thing, yet for half your life or more, you've been imagining that this attention has been attracted by yourself. It hasn't. It's got totally and absolutely and unopposedly nothing to do with you. It really is the most salutary and fascinating experience to go through.

Here the menopause is presented as an experience of freedom: it offers the chance to engage with life on new, impersonal terms. I told myself not to believe her too easily. Was it really this easy for a woman who had defined herself so confidently as a sensual being to give up on sexuality and on a shared embodied life? What kind of loss was involved?

You can learn quite a lot about Lessing in middle-age from looking at two photographs taken in 1965 and 1969. In the first, at forty-five, she retains the features of her twenties and thirties: short curly hair framing a welcoming face; eyes and mouth resting in an assured half smile. In the second, at forty-nine, she's pulled back her hair around that tight central parting, taking on the stark look that would characterise her until her death. She sits, legs apart, in what might be described as a house dress, mouth open and hand raised as though she's in the middle of making an important point. She doesn't look prematurely aged here; if anything she looks younger than forty-nine – there's an intense, adolescent quality to her posture and expression, even to her skin. Her hair is still largely dark, though it would go grey not long afterwards. But this woman doesn't have the coiffed, assured sexuality of the photograph five years earlier. In another shot taken on the same day, the adolescence becomes more awkward. Here she sits smiling coyly, one arm touching her cheek with the uncertainty of girlhood and the other folded over her stomach with the casualness of middle-aged matronhood.

The transition here seems to have begun with *The Golden Notebook*. If writing that novel gave her the strength to turn her back on one version of both her sexual and political self, then it left open a space in which to explore who she might be about to become. Her forays into the creative potential of breakdown and madness had been unsatisfactory, and in the years that followed she began seeking alternative emotional and spiritual possibilities. She looked into the Yeatsian Golden Dawn and then turned more enthusiastically to the East, reading about Buddhism and Hinduism. Then she heard about the practice of Sufism that was being modelled by Idries Shah.

Sufism as practised by Shah seems to have made an immediate impact on her. She ordered his 1964 book *The Sufis* from America, and later wrote that the book had chimed exactly with her own tentative conclusions and discoveries. '*The Sufis* was felt by people all over the world to be what we had been waiting for – to explain obstinately non-conforming thoughts and intuitions that had puzzled us all our lives'.

At first, Sufism coincided with sex. The month after writing her review of Shah's book, Lessing went to Africa to celebrate the newly established independence of Zambia. There she met a man employed by the Anglo American Corporation, a mining company operating in Zambia's capital, Lusaka. He was fifteen years younger than her, charming, quintessentially English, and strong enough to carry her around when she fell and broke her ankle. Delighted, Lessing wrote home to Joan Rodker that she was 'improbably but deliciously' in the midst of a '*tendresse* of incredible ease and charm'. She proposed not to come home immediately, unless urgently needed by Jenny Diski, announcing proudly that she was 'very happy. I am thinner and brown and relaxed and I eat avocado pears and sit in the sun'.

But she was starting to feel the waning of her sexual powers. This was one of a succession of younger men she was attracted to, and it was beginning to render her dangerously vulnerable. Soon afterwards, she had an affair with a publisher, who turned out to be chiefly interested in her public profile. If she was losing her sex appeal, perhaps the time was coming to reject men before they had a chance to reject her. It may not be a coincidence that this period of her life coincided with her intense dislike of Women's Lib; perhaps there was an element of sexual jealousy in her hostility towards this younger generation of more easily entitled women.

Suzette Macedo, by this point one of Lessing's closest female friends, told me that she saw Lessing's decision to change her appearance as a direct response to the menopause as well as to the pain of being rejected by this lover. Lessing claimed in her autobiography that she'd been completely unaffected by her periods stopping in her early forties. But it does seem likely that she might have grieved for the end of her reproductive life and that it might have manifested itself in this way. Less than a decade earlier, she'd been suggesting to Clancy Sigal that she should untie her tubes and have his babies. Though Anna Wulf may find her periods disturbing, she also sees them as an essential part of being a woman. Macedo recalls that the change in hairstyle was accompanied by a larger change in manner that suggested not so much a dignified acceptance of maturity as an animalistic enjoyment of the childishness of age. Lessing now sat slouched, with her legs defiantly splayed where they would once have been pertly crossed, and even failed to wash for a while, allowing herself to smell.

This is the disintegration evoked in *The Summer before the Dark*, a book published just after the interview where Lessing celebrated the transformations of middle-age. At the start of the book, Kate Brown is a 'pretty, healthy, service-able woman' in her mid-forties, with reddish hair done in large soft waves around her face. She is the happily married mother of four children, who are on the verge of growing up. Quickly, there are signs of disquiet. We learn that she is seen as over-protective and needy by her husband and children. Her husband has had a long series of affairs with increasingly younger women and has lost Kate's respect as a result. Though her body remains the same shape as it was in her youth, she's conscious that its spirit has changed: 'she did not walk inside, like the fine, almost unseeable envelope of a candle flame, that emanation of attractiveness: *I am available, come and sniff and taste*.' And looking back over her life, she is starting to see that her main characteristic has been 'passivity, adaptability to others'.

Suddenly, just when her husband and children are about to disappear abroad for the summer, Kate is offered a job as a translator for a large international conference on global foods. She buys herself a new wardrobe of elegant clothes, dyes her hair a sleek dark red and goes to work in Turkey where she is picked up by a younger man, who persuades her to accompany him to Spain. This is not the rejuvenating affair she might have hoped for. Once they are on the road, Kate's lover becomes ill and she ends up having to nurse him. Just as her lover is recovering, Kate herself becomes sick. She flies to London where she spends several weeks in a hotel, consumed by a fever that sends her deep into herself and then leaves her alone, stranded far away from her life as a wife and mother, curiously free. Because she has lost weight, she looks hag-like in her baggy clothes; her hair is an uneven mess of colours.

Wanting time to understand her transformation, Kate rents a room with a young bohemian woman called Maureen. Here she learns to disassociate herself from her appearance. The revelation comes when she walks across a London building site in her baggy clothes, her shoulders hunched into premature old age. She finds that she's invisible, ignored, free to wander at will. She changes into a fitted silk dress, straightens her back and walks across the same stretch of road again, her hips swaying as she moves. Now a series of whistles accompanies her from the scaffolding. Kate realises how arbitrary and unknowing men's responses to her are. 'She was trembling with rage: it was a rage, it seemed to her, that she had been suppressing for a lifetime… it was saying again and again: this is what you have been doing for years and years and years.'

She cannot escape her life for ever. She decides that it's time to go back to her family. But though she is prepared to resume her role as Kate Brown, she is determined to keep her hair as it is: plain, greying, tied neatly behind her head: 'Her discoveries, her self-definition, what she hoped were now strengths – were concentrated here… she was saying no: no, no, no, NO – a statement which would be concentrated into hair.'

It's interesting that in describing a mid-forties transformation not unlike her own, Lessing decided to explore a character with a life so unlike hers. Kate is a conventional woman who has denied herself the freedom that Lessing had more recklessly seized. There was an element of mentally living the life that would have been hers if she'd remained married to Frank Wisdom here, ridding herself of any lingering guilt by suggesting that this quite ordinary marriage had the power to drive women mad. But there was also a more urgent need to explore the process of ageing through this quieter alter ego. Lessing denied identifying with Kate: she was merely 'watching what you see so often: a woman who has not had a job and whose children grow up and she has to come to terms with the fact that she has no function'. This seems disingenuous, given the parallels in their fundamental response to age. The freedom that Kate experiences in Maureen's flat seems comparable to the freedom that Lessing was seeking; a freedom to escape her body as perceived by others and inhabit a more interior version of herself.

The woman who uncrossed her legs and allowed herself defiantly to smell doesn't sound very free. But the adolescent-cum-middle-aged woman in the 1969 photograph does look as if she could be determinedly and newly conscious of herself; as if she knows how to move beyond rage to wisdom as she becomes able to expose what lies beneath her long-assumed charm and grace. Kate learns in the novel how to live with loneliness, coming to see the truths revealed by solitude. In an interview in 1980, Lessing insisted that 'one has to accept loneliness; it's the human condition, and no matter how many parties or churches we belong to, we cannot deny this central truth… One must take risks and not think of the loneliness that awaits us'.

Her own lesson in wresting freedom out of the loneliness of middle age seems to have been made easier by her intensified commitment to Sufism. Shortly after Lessing had reviewed Shah's book, he had formally accepted her as a disciple, grateful for the attention from a high-profile writer. The two were now in the midst of a mutually flattering but also spiritually enabling collaboration that continued until his death in 1996. In 1975 she published an article called 'If you knew Sufi' in the *Guardian*, accompanied by a large, brooding photograph of Shah and a small photograph of Lessing herself. Introducing herself as 'Shah's pupil', she explained here that the Sufi 'Way' was intended to enable Man to 'break out of the very real prison he is in'. There was a current running cosmically from elsewhere 'beyond the stars' and Man could learn to attune himself with it. Shah performed the service of a 'cosmic doctor', tending this current and helping people to feel its presence.

Clancy Sigal had dismissed Shah's allure as sexual. '[Her] new guy – she actually called him the Teacher – was an oily beauty in a white turban and knee-length Nehru jacket who claimed to be a wise man from Kabul', he wrote in *The Secret Defector*. Elsewhere, he admitted that it might not be an actual sexual liaison, complaining that it bothered him even more to suspect that she was having 'an infinitely elevated, sexless affair with this guy by way of the ancient Sufi texts'. Once I started to examine Lessing in this period, Clancy seemed to me unnecessarily uncharitable. Though there may have been physical attraction (Shah was a good-looking, slightly younger man), it does appear to have enabled a relationship that gave her the ability to look differently at the world, renouncing sex perhaps neither as willingly as she suggested nor as unconvincingly as Clancy believed.

It was easy to see both how these cosmic currents, manipulated by a kindly guru, could have made the loneliness of the menopause less difficult and how the menopause could have made her more attuned to these currents. If the menopause is often experienced as a moment of death within life – a moment of seeing the whole of life passing before you, swiftly – then it might be easier at this point to see your life as part of the wider cycle of creation. And of course there is a freedom in this; a movement into the expansiveness of the cosmic, a liberation from the petty concerns of the everyday.

I

'She has felt death in her throat'

Renunciation

Lessing wasn't alone in seeking freedom through renunciation. Since returning from Dartmoor, I had been reading, feeling somewhat disloyal for enjoying the holiday from Lessing, a lot of Iris Murdoch: a writer born in the same year as Lessing, who had experimented more briefly with communism but more enjoyably with free love and had even fainted once on a lecture platform into the lap of Clancy Sigal ('I suppose there's a consolation that you're doing it with a better class of tootsie,' Lessing remarked on hearing of the incident). I'd been a great Murdoch enthusiast in my early twenties and was now curious to discover that she sought freedom through abnegation from a younger age than Lessing. 'Real freedom is a total absence of concern about yourself,' claims Mor in Murdoch's 1957 novel *The Sandcastle.* Freedom here is experienced through living lightly; through loving without claims. Murdoch told a platonic lover in 1972 that 'to be oneself, free, whole, is partly a matter of escape from obsession, neurosis' and by implication sexual love.

Murdoch, like Lessing, was fifty-two at this point: this particular moment of escape may have been menopausal. And they were joined by a handful of other women writers in seeing the menopause as potentially liberating. I was pleased to be able to turn again to Simone de Beauvoir, this time in the company of Germaine Greer. In her account of the archetypal woman in *The Second Sex*, Simone de Beauvoir writes that when the process of ageing starts, woman feels 'touched by the very inevitability of death'. She can fight it by indulging in last-minute love affairs or having more children, but it is safer to accept age. At this point, 'relieved of her duties, she finally discovers her freedom'.

Beauvoir does not seem to have found the process of ageing freeing for herself. Anne is only thirty-nine in *The Mandarins* but she can see that the white streaks in her hair are 'no longer a curiosity, a sign: they're the beginning'. Soon the mask of her face will melt, 'laying bare the rheumy eyes of an old woman'. Aged fifty-five, Beauvoir published her autobiography, where she described how she often stopped before the mirror, 'flabbergasted, at the sight of this incredible thing that serves me as a face'.

Germaine Greer did rather better. In 1992, aged fifty-three, she published *The Change*, which was a plea for women to accept the changes of age. Here she suggested that attempts to prevent the menopause with HRT (hormone replacement therapy) were part of a male-centric conspiracy to contain the wisdom and rage of older women. 'There are positive aspects to being a frightening old woman,' Greer claimed. Like Lessing, she saw this persona as enabling a form of truth.

Greer described movingly how aged fifty she had looked ahead into what seemed like 'winter, ice, an interminable dark'. She could not envisage a way to live without love and could not see many appealing older female role models. But visiting Sicily shortly after her father had died, she decided to join the Mediterranean women in wearing black to mourn and celebrate the end of womanhood. She found this liberating and a learning process had begun.

For Greer there were two possible responses to the menopause. One was misery, a 'grey and hopeless thing' that involved staring stupefied as Beauvoir did at the ruins of your face in the mirror. The other was grief, a terrible pain that left the woman who came through it stronger and calmer, 'aware that death having brushed her with its wing has retreated to its accustomed place, and all will be well'.

Once women emerged out of this grief, Greer thought that they might be happier if they allowed themselves to give up on sex. Younger women might find it impossible to believe that when they were no longer 'tormented by desire, insecurity, jealousy and the rest of the paraphernalia of romance' they would not be 'as dead as a spent match', but in fact they could look forward to a whole new realm of experience. Beguilingly, Greer compared the difference between the clamorous feelings of the younger woman and the calmness of the apparently withdrawn older woman to the difference between the way that the sea appears to someone tossing on its surface, and the way it looks to someone who 'has plunged so deep that she has felt death in her throat'. The older woman could love deeply and tenderly because she now loved without the desire for possession.

Greer described this as a uniquely female experience. I didn't think it needed to be. There were men who felt relieved by escaping their own appetites and who came to enjoy new forms of love. In Plato's *Republic*, the elderly Cephalus recalls Sophocles telling him that he was delighted to have moved beyond sex, feeling like 'a slave who has escaped from a savage and tyrannical master'. Now that he has become old too, Cephalus agrees with him, finding that 'old age brings peace and freedom from all such things'. But what did seem to be unique was the new relation that women feel to their bodies and the new relation to beauty that this brings. Having ceased the struggle to be beautiful, Greer wrote, the older woman could appreciate the beauty around her, finding the beautiful and feeding upon it. This was her chance to realise, like Thoreau, that 'all good things are wild and free'.

For Greer, HRT was problematic because it postponed this state and the truths it revealed for a decade or two, meaning that it could be too late for women energetically to learn to inhabit it and leaving them with rage instead of wisdom. Reading Greer alongside Lessing, I started to view Lessing's decision to turn middle age into old age less disapprovingly than I had before. I had always thought that the menopause came cruelly early; that now that we lived longer, it left us with too great a proportion of our lives deprived of oestrogen. It did seem unfair that, as Greer informed her readers, at fifty a woman's secretion of sebum declined sharply until it was only half as much as that of a man the same age, leaving her skin visibly thinner and drier than his. But if this could open the door to a new form of freedom, then I could see that we needed to be young enough to go through it courageously. And I could see that after all those men, all those pregnancies, all those years of yearning, hoping, and then exhaustedly reconfiguring herself after her heart had been broken yet again, Lessing might have found it a relief to learn to live in a new way.

This made more sense to me than Sufism. Though I found some of the poems of the ancient Sufi poets wise and affecting, I was less impressed by Shah. *The Sufis* begins with a long fable that acts as a kind of founding myth. Long ago, humanity lived in an ideal place, but everyone was sent briefly to a temporary island, where they had to adapt and coarsen but were meant to busy themselves with training to return to their lost paradise. However, instead of building boats and learning to swim, most people became too easily acclimatised. Someone preached a doctrine of accepting their new life and embracing rationality. Thus life as we know it on earth began. In this new state, emotion was over-privileged; all emotion was considered to be 'deep' or 'profound'.

This was quite easy to accept, but what felt more spurious was what followed. Shah suggested that his book was about some of the swimmers and builders of ships, hoping that by illustrating their wisdom he could inculcate it in others. But he progressed through a series of jokes, anecdotes and anagrams that seemed to elucidate very little. One story was about a man attempting to borrow a donkey from his neighbour. 'It's out on loan,' he is informed, but he can hear it braying in the background. When he questions this, he is asked, 'whom do you believe, me or a donkey?' Apparently the experience of this dimension of reality helps us to avoid selfishness and the mechanism of rationalisation. I found it hard not to follow Clancy in dismissing Shah's performance as 'mainly desiccated Jewish jokes minus the fast delivery'.

Where Shah chimed helpfully with Greer was in his proposal that we might learn to love more widely and less selfishly. Though the Sufi creed was love, he suggested that sexual or familial love was only a part of this; 'a limited part beyond which, under ordinary circumstances, the average person never goes'. Beyond human love was the love that bound us to the world itself. This was the love that we might attain when we ceased to dwell in the realm of emotion. It was related to the love that Greer saw as the middle-aged woman's prize for surviving the underwater plunge into grief.

Here, in unexpected agreement, were Germaine Greer, Doris Lessing and Idries Shah, collectively formulating a renunciatory form of freedom. It was tempting. I was intrigued by the idea that we could live differently by telling ourselves that desire wasn't important. I liked the idea of experiencing beauty by looking out at the world rather than inwards. I was convinced that there could be a kind of freedom, as philosophers since Socrates and St Augustine had suggested, in escaping your own appetites. I was also enticed by the notion that we should cease to be sympathetic, cease to devote our energy to pleasing and easing other people; this was, after all, part of what had appealed to me about Lessing in the first place. But though I was two-thirds of the way through my own reproductive life, I was not yet ready to give it up.

Each month, my period came, irregularly, inconveniently, the hamster emerging to gnaw its way through my womb and remind me that once again I had failed to become pregnant. I wasn't longing for a newborn baby. Instead, the covetous greed when it came was for older children, especially for girls about the same age as my son. Watching a friend cuddling her younger child on the sofa, a four-year-old daughter, I was struck both by envy and by a fearful sense of the precariousness of this child's existence; how strange that if my friend had only had one child, the source of this particular moment of tenderness might never have been born. There was, too, a longing for another child present in much of my contact with my son. My sense that he was getting older and would soon be starting school brought as much loss as pleasure. Sometimes, as he grew into himself, I had a feeling that he was the perfect child at the perfect age and this itself was painful because it brought the recognition that I might never experience that phase of motherhood again. Every time that

I waited for my period, wondering if I was pregnant, it felt as though this loss might be averted. In four years' time, I might have another four-year-old as well as an eight-year-old.

In December, on the eve of turning thirty-six, I learnt that at thirty-five I was eligible to receive free IVF if I was prepared to share my eggs with another woman. After two years of waiting to become pregnant, the chance actively to do something about it was inviting, and I wished I had known about this earlier. In fact, it turned out that I was too late. It would take a few months to prepare for the egg transfer and at thirty-six my eggs would apparently become too decrepit to be desirable gifts.

Nonetheless the plan had been set in motion and we went along for a consultation and found ourselves talking to a benign man on the verge of retirement who impressed me with his paternal charm and impressed my husband with his scientific confidence. For me, it felt oddly comparable to visiting the psychoanalyst, except that this man seemed more keen than the analyst had done that I should have another baby, less perturbed by the contradictory quality of my desires. The diagnosis was swift and reassuring. I had polycystic ovaries, which made ovulation irregular and uncertain. They could extract the eggs, fertilise them and then test them for chromosomal abnormalities. I could be pregnant within a few months; I need never have a miscarriage again. We signed up enthusiastically.

This new plan proved good for our marriage. We could start mapping out the months together again, even if we couldn't know the outcome. And we were both relieved, I think, that it was my problem. If it had been a difficulty with sperm count, I'd have felt guilty for being the one to have kept us waiting for so long, and I'd have worried that it would affect us sexually. 'Real men' may need at least the possibility of potency, but my sense of my own femininity could survive the strange black holes that loomed into view on the screen as the doctor moved the condom-clad probe around inside me. My husband had seen our trip to the clinic as a sign of failure, but now seemed to join me in seeing the gain of a medical name for my condition as an indication of progress. And we were pleased to have a shared project, with the potential to repair some of the division created by my impulsive house-buying. I didn't mind when people suggested it might be complicated and debilitating; I didn't even mind the expense. The more effort I could put in, the less frustrated I would feel.

My confidence did not, however, last for long. This too was a slow process necessitating patience; the doctor could not understand my frantic need for speed. I had high levels of the hormone prolactin, which required blood tests, an MRI scan, and then a month of pills. After this my periods mysteriously stopped for six weeks and when I finally started to bleed, it turned out that I'd developed a mysterious cyst. They needed to put me on the contraceptive pill, of all things, to clear it up. The Pill made me feel sick and I felt furious with the world. Two years after giving up contraception, I was back on it again, reading the accompanying leaflet about how to prevent pregnancy. I wanted to go somewhere else while I waited for my cyst to heal. The house in Suffolk had now been purchased and filled with builders. Needing to make arrangements there and wanting some time to walk and write, I rented a local cottage for a few days.

Initially, the friend I'd bought the house with came to join me. We spent a joyful day dashing between industrial estates to choose a kitchen and bathroom, playing at a very different kind of shared domesticity from the ones that either of us had experienced in marriage, where small conflicts become freighted with larger difficulties. Visiting the house, we were both amazed and delighted that it existed; that these were our rooms emerging out of the dust. There was a pleasure in every view and every landscape, because we both felt that the more we could claim this countryside as ours, the further we would be from the more difficult aspects of our respective lives in London. In these moods, we were sure that I would have another child and that she would continue to defy the expectations of her doctors in remaining relatively unaffected by her brain tumour. Then she had to return home, and I was left alone.

Each afternoon I went for a walk, and I found myself gravitating to the same edge-of-the-world stony beaches and estuary I'd walked in the previous spring with my missing friend. He had died in December and, though I'd gone to the funeral, I had not been as sad after his death as I had been in the autumn, when I was so bemused by his disappearance. Sometimes, since then, I'd wondered if we knew each other as well as I'd thought we did. After all, we had never engaged in ordinary life together, and however open he'd been with me when well, he'd refused to be known at the point when he became more problematically vulnerable, lacking faith in one or both of us.

It was now, back in his landscape, that his loss hit me; that I believed again in our feelings for each other, however strange and fragile they had been, and that I was reminded how much it had meant to me to write to someone every day and know that mutual understanding was possible. I was often struck by how many of the people around me – many of them with fewer close friendships than I had – seemed not to need this. Most people seemed to be comfortable revolving their thoughts in their own minds without needing them to be overheard. Though in my over-peopled London life, I spent much of my time craving solitude in which to write, I rarely derived genuine pleasure from being alone. Now, walking along paths that I'd walked along with a man who'd loved me and was now dead, it seemed time to learn to need less from people; to find out if it was possible to have the pleasure of renunciation without entering the dark; to learn to be alone without loneliness.

On my second day, I attempted to find a particular stretch of grassy sea wall above the estuary where he had taken me in the evening of a miraculously sunny day in late March, almost exactly a year earlier. After hours of walking and talking, we had stood in the quiet evening light looking out on to an island with birds flocking above it and, wanting a pause in talking about ourselves, I had asked him to tell me the names of the birds. Today, I left the car at the place on the map that looked as if it might be where we'd have parked, but found that the landscape looked both familiar and unfamiliar. Though I couldn't remember the detail of the walk we had taken to reach that spot, the path here was definitely strange to me; I'd have remembered the rhythm of crossing so many stiles. The raised grass bank and the view were recognisable, but as I reached a bend I found that there was nothing that allowed me to know with certainty whether this was indeed the spot where we'd paused.

In front of me, the river widened; behind me, it stretched in tributaries back towards the land. I was pleased to be surrounded on every side by water once again. The current gathered quietly; the birds flocked; there was no other sound. The complete peacefulness was unexpected, as it had been a year earlier. Then, shivering as the sun went down, moved by the encounter with beauty so strange and still as to be other-worldly, I had suggested that he might put an arm around me, and, to our mutual relief, he did. It was the only moment we'd touched. In my imaginings of the final encounter that for months I'd assumed we'd have, I had made up for this, seeking in his arms the solace I still felt confident in believing we both yearned for. Now it seemed fitting that there had been so little; it made it easier to make sense of his appearance and disappearance in my life. For a moment, I gained reassurance from the Sufi creeds. Perhaps our individual emotions had indeed been merely illusory; perhaps the boundaries between life and death, between one person and another, were more porous than I believed. My grief and my clamouring needs could float off into the mist of blended water and air.

There are so many forms of intimacy, and Lessing in middle age seems to have decided to learn to do without most of them. There is the daily sharing of your most private thoughts. There's the bodily fusion that comes with intense reciprocated sexual desire. And there's the simpler daily companionship of experiences quietly shared, which she increasingly had only with Peter. As in Dartmoor, I was finding it hard to cut myself off fully from the domesticity I had left behind. Knowing what the house in Suffolk had come to symbolise for our marriage, I found it painful confronting a disappointed or hostile image of my husband in my mind. There were times when my mental picture of my son at nursery – eating his lunch, walking in an obedient crocodile to the park and possibly missing me as they walked past our house – was powerfully preoccupying. But it seemed now that I too needed to try once more to do without both shared domesticity and intimacy, to gain some of the freedom of self-sufficiency described by Lessing and Greer. Though it was tempting to call the few people I knew in the area to suggest shared walks or dinners, I resisted, needing to observe myself alone.

The next day, wanting to be within reach of other people, if not to speak to them, I went to the seaside, to wander beside sand dunes and beach huts. The sun had come out; it was a bright March day; I ate a crab sandwich on the beach. Here I found that the aching need for intimacy that I'd had for the past few days left me at last, and I could experience sensual pleasure alone again. There was the feeling of the sun on my back and of the sand enfolding slightly damp feet; the sensation of the shock of the water as I plunged my toes in and out of the sea.

I felt as though I were accompanied by Lessing and Greer, urging me to experience lone embodied pleasure. This seemed to be akin to the sensation Greer described: a kind of embodiment that's about inhabiting the body from inside (in this respect it resembles the embodiment of pregnancy) and has nothing to do with being looked at. I had found the beautiful and was feeding upon it. I was experiencing a form of weightlessness in which my anxiety about my fertility could be dismissed as a symptom of striving worldliness; a form of ethereality in which the dead seemed no more absent than the living. I thought about other times I'd wandered along the same beach, consumed by thoughts of other people, and found a pleasure in this new detachment: in passively receiving the impressions of the world.

I was conscious that turning inwards in this way involved a loss of sexuality. I couldn't imagine having an orgasm in this state; I felt too disengaged from the bodies of others. But I was contented to suspend my life as a sexual being if I could explore this new form of embodied receptivity. I felt again that Greer was right that the menopause didn't occur cruelly early. If this was what we had to look forward to at fifty, then might it not be worth trying it out earlier? I was not ready yet to join Greer and Lessing in the waves but I could edge into the sea and watch them.

II

'I can't endure this desert'

Love again

How long can we be contented alone? How real is the pleasure of abnegation? Lessing didn't live without the call of sex for as long as she might have expected to. The route to sexual reawakening was surprising. In her early sixties, she had experimented with inventing a fictional world compatible with the truths of Sufism. She had created a new form of space writing, tracing the intergalactic world of the Canopus in Argos across five complex novels. These books had come to the attention of the composer Philip Glass, who had also been questing for stories that could reveal truths beyond the constraints of realism. He had just completed a trilogy of operas: *Einstein on the Beach, Satyagraha* and *Akhnaten*. Now he wanted to write an opera based on Lessing's fourth Canopus novel, *The Making of the Representative for Planet 8*.

Glass had begun to read Lessing's novels while working on *Satyagraha* and *Akhnaten*. He had been dazzled by *The Grass is Singing* and *The Golden Notebook* and gone on to read the Martha Quest novels. He was unusual among Lessing's fans in reading the Canopus novels enthusiastically as they came out, and he thought immediately that he should make an opera out of them. In September 1983 he wrote to introduce himself, enclosing a tape of *Satyagraha*. She replied suggesting that they should meet when he was next in London. He announced that he'd be there the following week and booked his flight. The day that he arrived in London, his mother died. He arranged a flight home but suggested to Lessing that they should meet for a few hours anyway. She impressed him immediately with her unjudgemental empathy.

> 'I'm glad we could meet, but why have your plans changed?'
> 'A death in my family. I'll be taking a plane late this afternoon.'
> 'Who?'
> 'My mother.'
> 'Oh… Did you know her well?'

For the next four years they collaborated on the libretto of the opera that would premiere in Houston and London in 1988. After that they began work on an earlier Canopus novel. This was a charmed collaboration for Lessing. She had initially been sceptical about his music. 'I'll not forget how my ears balked and sulked', she wrote later, 'expecting resolutions they were not getting'. But quickly she learnt to listen to it appreciatively. In an interview in 1987 she said that they had 'never had one sentence worth of difficulty over anything, ever'. Together, they were exploring the power of the meeting point between words and music. 'Words are our trade,' she wrote after they had completed both operas, 'not merely the sense but the music of words; and in the links between sense and sound are hidden all kinds of mysteries, as poets know.'

From the start, Lessing seems to have responded passionately to the man as well as to the music. Here was another man seventeen years younger than her; intelligent and amusing, forceful but also emotionally articulate. Like her, he was defiantly self-made. Until recently, he had driven a New York taxi and worked as a plumber to fund his career as a musician. Suzette Macedo describes Lessing becoming suddenly girlish in his presence and putting renewed effort into her appearance. Especially in the first couple of years, she saw a lot of him. He stayed with her when he was in London and they worked together in a back room at the ENO (English National Opera) during the rehearsals for *Akhnaten*, which was performed in London in 1985.

Philip Glass himself at this point was happily committed to his third wife, the artist Candy Jernigan, whom he had met on an aeroplane in 1981 while still in his second marriage. Candy was fifteen years younger than him, beautiful, impulsive, and had an unusually good relationship with his children. It is hard now to know what, if any, encouragement he gave to Doris Lessing; hard to know how conscious he was of the strength of her feelings. Did she comfort him when Candy died suddenly from cancer at the age of thirty-nine in 1991? What form did this comfort take? In his autobiography, he suggests that their relationship had a mother–son quality from the start, emphasised for him by their meeting on the day of his mother's death. 'Doris was then in her midsixties,' he writes in the description of their first encounter,

> a woman with grey hair gathered in a bun. She had bright
> eyes and was lively in her movements. She did not have
> a matronly appearance, but more the look and dignity of

an academic or an intellectual, which she decidedly was. There was nothing sharp or mean about her. She could easily be anyone's favourite slightly elderly aunt or cousin.

For her part, Lessing seems to have enjoyed the sensation of rediscovering physical and emotional intensity, however fearful she was of the foolishness of middle-aged unrequited lust. The terror and joy of this period go into *Love, Again,* which she published in 1996, just before their second opera was performed.

Like *The Summer before the Dark,* this is a story about an abrupt transition from middle age to old age. Sarah is a trim and strikingly youthful sixty-five-year-old when she begins collaborating on an opera about a French nineteenth-century composer called Julie Vairon. Writing the libretto for the opera, she is seduced by Julie's music and journals into a receptive state of erotic desire. 'She was restless, and she was feverish. When had music affected her like this before?' Sarah has not been in love for twenty years but it seems at once inevitable and astonishing that during the rehearsal period she should fall in love first with a vain twenty-something-year-old actor called Bill and then with the thirty-five-year-old director, Henry. The passion now is reciprocal and Henry is a worthy object of love. There are moments of ecstasy induced simply by sitting next to him and Sarah is able to identify with Julie, who wrote in her journal that she was allowing a man to break not only her heart but her life because without love she was only half-alive: 'Write your music. Paint your pictures. But if that is what you choose, you will not be living as women live. I can't endure this non-life. I can't endure this desert.' Nonetheless, Sarah does not leave the desert altogether, even briefly. The love affair is unconsummated, partly because Henry is married and partly because both are uncomfortably aware of the absurdity of the situation.

Sarah discovers that despite all her years of acclimatising to dignified middle age, the sensations of love feel if anything more childlike than they did in her youth. It's to the passions of her childhood that she returns in her dreams, waking up drenched in 'stinging hot wetness', filled with longing so violent that she has to bite her pillow. This is not the 'glow of tender lost possibilities' she feels would be appropriate for her age but a raging desire, 'a sick sweet submersion in pain'. Her erotic self has been restored, as though 'the door had never been slammed shut'. For years, her occasional masturbatory fantasies have been voyeuristic; she has looked from a third-person perspective at the younger bodies of others. Now she has become the subject of her fantasies; her lover's 'thick red penis was inside her as far up as her throbbing heart'. In so many of her novels, Lessing had explored the disjunction between the triviality of the body and the seriousness of the feelings it expresses and provokes. How can we honour the seriousness without seeming ridiculous or simply humourless? Sarah is troubled by this disjunction as she lies masturbating first in France and then in England, the object of her fantasy lying only half-conscious of her in a room along the corridor.

She realises that though the sight of her ageing body in the mirror has become habitual and she has learnt to clothe it in the respectable garb of the elegant matron, she is unable to inhabit it from the inside; unable to remember that she doesn't have the same dazzling effect on men as she did thirty years earlier. Sarah is in love and hate with her former self.

Her longing for the young men is in part a yearning for her own lost, smooth flesh – her 'animal and glistening physicality' – while her anger with Bill, in his casual arrogance, and with Henry, in his complacency in his life as a married man, is a resentment of the entitlement of her own youth, when she was oblivious to the pain infusing the longing of the men around her.

Lessing's identification with Sarah is not complete. This is a comedy, though a bitter one, and she luxuriates in its preposterousness. Love descends on this group of players as though in a sudden cloud of rain. At one stage Sarah compares the frenzied and apparently arbitrary passions overtaking the whole cast to those in *A Midsummer's Night's Dream* and there is a sense throughout that they have all stumbled into a Shakespearean comedy, though few of them are erudite enough to know this. But if Lessing is sharply distanced from Sarah then she is also uncomfortably identified with her as she mercilessly catalogues her pain, her breasts burning and her abdomen aching with desire. And she shares Sarah's perplexed fascination for Julie's music, which bears a striking resemblance to that of Philip Glass, dominated by 'long flowing rhythms' in which occasionally a 'primitive theme' appears. 'If unemotional, why did it bring tears to the eyes?' Sarah wonders. 'Did that mean it acted on some unnamed part of the organism, such as a disembodied heart or liver?'

Cruelly, as Lessing satirises Sarah's absurdity, she forces her into reluctant old age. Sarah teaches herself painfully to identify with her newly wrinkled flesh in the mirror, aware that after she has done this she will be an old woman who has shut out love for ever. For a while she avoids music, knowing that it will affect her too strongly, and avoids reading words with any connection to love or passion. As the months pass, she finds that she has aged by ten years. Her hair has gone grey and 'she has acquired that slow cautious look of the elderly, as if afraid of what they will see around the next corner'.

I felt that there was an element of stern admonishment in this book. By making the men so much younger than Glass himself, Lessing made the age gap more extreme than it was in life, impeding readers from easily believing in either of her passions as convincing potential relationships. There was also, though, an implicit complaint about the unfairness in the divergent situations of ageing men and women. 'Most men and more women', the narrator observes, 'punish older women with derision, punish them with cruelty, when they show inappropriate signs of sexuality'. Why should this derision not be applied to men? At the same time as Sarah falls in love with Bill and Henry, her middle-aged colleague Stephen falls in love with Molly, the young actress who plays Julie. Though Molly isn't interested, he doesn't lose any dignity in admitting this publicly, and indeed is pursued by Molly's replacement Susan into bed. The discrepancy is partly the result of social conditioning but also the result of the essentialist inequality of desire that had fuelled Lessing's own youthful sexual passions. If both male and female desire gains its force from the image of the female body, the price of ageing is inevitably going to be higher for women. Though Stephen is somewhat sceptical about Susan's mind, he seems unconflicted in his happy admiration for her body. He is unassailed by Sarah's anxiety that should she end up in bed with Henry, they will both be forced to confront her awkwardness in exposing her wrinkled skin, or that she will want the light off for the first time in her life.

Reading the novel again, I found the final scene particularly painful. Lessing here seemed to be bleeding the wounds of middle age into the wounds of childhood by portraying a sexually rejected, ageing woman observing a maternally neglected young girl. Sarah, now described as an 'old woman', watches a small girl excluded from her mother's affections by a baby boy. Witnessing the scene, Sarah recalls fairly exactly the anguish of Lessing's own childhood, remembering how her yearning love for her younger brother was in conflict with her envy of his favoured place in her mother's affections. Sarah even uses Lessing's own habitual image of a door being slammed. Watching the young girl in pain when she is sharply rejected by her mother, Sarah tells her silently to 'hold on': 'Quite soon a door will slam shut inside you because what you are feeling is unendurable. The door will stand there shut all your life: if you are lucky it will never open again.' Doris Lessing had reopened the door on to intense feeling and the result had been almost unbearable. Once she had finished writing this novel, she had completed the process of ageing that she had begun prematurely twenty-five years earlier. She was now seventy-six and would never drop her sexual guard again.

Back in London, I was grateful for the ease of intimacy with my son; for his demands for a cuddle and the straightforwardness with which he said 'I missed you, Mummy' when I collected him from nursery, both of us enjoying the pleasurable pain of manageable absence.

With the need to touch came the resurgence of sex. It was an unusually hot April and as legs and arms were exposed to the sun once more, I saw sex everywhere, developing crushes on several unlikely men at once. Living with Lessing now turned out to involve sharing her lust. I looked at the photograph of Doris Lessing and Philip Glass that he includes in his memoir. The man, aged fifty-one, is large, full-lipped and nosed, with thoughtful eyes and an appealingly messy shirt and hair. The woman is still beautiful at sixty-eight, though perhaps a little matronly. She is wearing a rather fussy dress – shiny, with a flower on it – but looks svelte, with the features on her face well defined. Though her hair is as severe as always, it is complemented by her bone structure. Her body is self-contained, her hands on her lap, while he spills out of his chair, his arm touching hers.

I could feel that touch: the relief of it; the simplicity of sinking slowly into his embrace, as the photographer took picture after picture, hoping it would last for ever. Easily able to imagine falling for the man looking out at me, I felt somewhat disloyally affirmed by my confidence that he appeared the kind of man who might be attracted to me. Appraising him, I saw the falseness of my abandoning my sexual self on the beach. It was easy to do so when you could leave it in waiting; how much harder when it might never return. If at my age I were suddenly to meet Philip Glass aged fifty-one and find myself burning with unexpected lust, I could pursue him with ease, whatever self-abnegating vows of chastity I'd made the week before. Indeed, it was to the man in the photograph that I addressed myself when I wrote a letter, asking if he'd be prepared to meet me in New York, later in the spring.

The answer was no. I was disappointed, but I was not going to risk it this time. I knew, anyway, that the Philip Glass I would meet would have little in common with the man I had created out of Lessing's novel. Nonetheless, I remained curious about him, so I went to see a performance of his opera *Akhnaten* in London.

Akhnaten tells the story of the ancient Egyptian pharaoh who reconfigured his world by establishing a new monotheistic religion. At the heart of this story are Akhnaten's relationships with two women: his mother Queen Tye, with whom he is said to have had an incestuous love affair, and his wife Nefertiti. Appropriately, this was the first of Glass's operas that Lessing herself saw. While they were bringing into being the icy world of Canopus, the ENO had created the hot, sandy landscape of the Egyptian desert. Lessing sat with Glass in some of the rehearsals and was there on the opening night. So, it was partly through her eyes that I looked down expectantly at the stage at the ENO as the prelude started, curious about what I was going to see.

The prelude builds slowly, adding layer after layer of juxtaposed rhythms. There are fast arpeggios from the clarinets and violas; we're meant to imagine ourselves by the River Nile in the hot desert sun. Then the funeral of Akhnaten's father begins and his son steps forward to be robed and crowned in glorious gold. We haven't yet heard his voice but in the third scene he sings.

'Oh, one creator of all things
Oh, one maker of all existences.'

He is singing to Aten, his god. But his voice is completely unexpected. He has the high, unearthly voice of a countertenor. For Lessing, it was this voice that gave the opera its power: 'It was the countertenor in *Akhnaten* that set the piece where the distant world should be – well beyond our grasp of it. That unhuman voice, the naked heads, the cruel gods, an unhuman religion of pure love.'

Akhnaten's voice is joined by those of his mother and wife. His mother's voice is the same pitch as his; she caresses him vocally, winding up and down around his notes. His wife's voice is unexpectedly low: she's a contralto. Once she starts to sing, the scene gains depth. As it ended, I realised that I had been lured in. The repetitive music was having its effect. I felt as though I'd gone into a kind of trance; my mind had been emptied and I could respond sensually to the strange, melancholy beauty of the voices. I was partly watching this as Lessing, awed that this enchanted world was the result of one man's vision. I was there with a male friend and, conscious of the solidity of his body next to mine, I could believe that I was Lessing sitting next to Philip Glass; could feel the strangeness of visually inhabiting the imagination of the man beside you. For years she'd thought that she could cross the boundaries between minds. Now, here, in a sense, she was doing so, looking at the world of his fantasies conjured into vivid being.

In the second act, the realities of establishing a new religion are played out. Akhnaten chisels out his father's name from monuments, including his own tomb; he and his mother defile the temples with lurid excitement. Then a quieter scene begins. A man stands in the middle of the stage; this is the Scribe; and he proclaims the text of the scene.

I breathe the sweet breath
Which comes forth from thy mouth.
I behold thy beauty every day.
It is my desire
That I may be rejuvenated
With life through love
Of thee.

At first he speaks these words solemnly, calling out to his god. Then Akhnaten and Nefertiti enter the stage and the Scribe recites the text again. This time it's a love poem.

In the performance I saw, Akhnaten and Nefertiti were now naked underneath diaphanous red robes. He had developed breasts, so there was a symmetry between their bodies. They stood at opposite ends of the stage, with trains of red fabric floating behind them as they glided, so slowly that the movement was imperceptible, towards each other. Then they began to sing, reciting the poem in Egyptian, accompanied by more arpeggios on the violin. The notes were long, strong and unearthly, their voices close together. Repeatedly, she pushed into dissonance and he joined her, resolving her note, though the dissonance itself had a strangely tender beauty.

They were closer together now and they stretched out their arms. The arpeggios sped up as their singing came more urgent.

Give me thy hands,
Holding thy spirit.

Soon they were within touching distance, their fingertips only a few millimetres apart. Holding my breath as they came closer together, I was Lessing, sitting next to Glass, and I was Nefertiti, reaching out my hand to Akhnaten. My hands ached with the need to be touched and there was a moment of physical relief as they finally clasped hands onstage.

It is my desire
That I may be rejuvenated
With life through love
Of thee.

Their faces drew closer together in slow motion; I was almost painfully aware of the staggering erotic power of the moment before the kiss. Then at last, their mouths touched. Floating somewhere between my seat and the stage, I felt myself being undressed and spun round by the composer in the photograph. I felt him running his hand, decisively, from my neck down to the bottom of my spine. I ached with longing as he swirled me back towards him and my mouth opened, seeking his. Onstage the lovers parted, turning their backs on each other.

Were these the fantasies that Lessing had, I wondered, when she woke up drenched in sweat? Lessing knew, even before she saw *Akhnaten,* that imagined touch could be more powerful than actual touch; she knew the power of fantasy within embraces between lovers. And it might have struck her that the sexuality displayed here resembled the androgynous sexuality of her Canopus novels. She had abandoned sex, and made her characters androgynous as a result, but now Glass was revealing a new way of being sexual, far from 'real men' and 'real women'.

But can fantasies be pleasurable, when the version of yourself that is projected has little to do with the physical reality? If Lessing is right that the sexuality of the middle-aged woman is treated with derision, then this seems to apply as much to fantasy as to sex itself. Indeed, it may apply more to fantasy, because it's by its nature visual, while sex can be reduced to a discreet nocturnal act. That spring, I had mentioned that I was reading *Love, Again* to a prominent feminist in her seventies, a woman generally prepared to talk about the need of older women for sex. 'It's such an embarrassing book,' she said, and I sensed her queasiness in her brief shudder.

But I thought that the strength of the book – and it's one of Lessing's most powerful novels – was in just this: its suggestion that these feelings were important enough that it was worth risking embarrassment in describing them; that humiliation needn't make the feelings themselves less serious or trans-formative. If you had the courage to accept all this, then I thought the fantasies could remain pleasurable. I couldn't imagine that Lessing would have forsaken the energy that charges the pages of *Love, Again,* that embarrassing novel that I would never learn if Philip Glass had actually read.

'Write your music. Paint your pictures. But if that is what you choose, you will not be living as women live. I can't endure this non-life. I can't endure this desert.' Julie concurs with Bertrand Russell, telling us that to fear love is to fear life. But she still fears it, and rightly. She ends up dying for it. Lessing wasn't going to do this: she was protected by sense, by resilience, and by her age, and the comforts of renunciation it had already brought.

Sarah's skin glistens in *Love, Again.* The lust and excitement have flooded her with hormones that make up for her waning oestrogen. Love for her is comical, absurd, easily transferred, but though its object may be both unworthy and random, the feeling is one of being alive. Perhaps that's what I was seeing in the photograph of Lessing with Glass: a moment of rediscovered youth. Nonetheless, Lessing had a stronger sys-tem of defences in place than Sarah. The quietness of Sufism did not go away. Indeed, their commitment to Eastern phil-osophy was one of the things she and Glass had in common. Shah remained just as crucial a figure in her life, more neces-sary, presumably, than ever. She could continue to build her boat, preparing her escape from the inadequacies of ordinary human existence. 'From... the end of the fifties – there was a main current in my life, deeper than any other, my real pre-occupation… this was my real life,' she wrote in the second volume of her autobiography, published in the same year as the second Glass opera was performed.

I was no closer to renunciation, though I could see its appeal. I could see how it might make me more grateful for all that I already had and I could see how in a self-abnegatory mode, my moments of disintegration could become both redemptive and freeing. Perhaps I had to push myself further into isolation.

9

'Full of restless stars'

The Bush

Returning to Southern Rhodesia in 1956, Doris Lessing found that the African sun alone was enough to make her feel free. The moment that the plane swooped down over Ethiopia, she saw the sun rise dramatically for the first time in seven years. Cutting across the view was the rim of a dark mountain. Above it, the sky was 'big, cool, empty', flushed with delicate colour; below, the sun was hanging, a delicate white pearl about to explode. Suddenly, it swelled into red incandescence, roared over the horizon and rocketed up into the sky. Already, it was easy to believe that she could hear the birds singing far below in the swelling heat; she could feel the long grass straightening as the dewdrops dried in the warmth; she could see the workers moving into the fields to herd and hoe.

This was a sun capable of power and anger, unlike the English 'dispenser of pale candlepower', and it reminded her of her own strength. Disembarking the plane, she discovered that she had turned inwards in England, and that now she could turn outwards again. 'This was my air, my landscape, and above all, my sun'. She was once more in physical touch with her surroundings, appreciating the 'infinite exchange of earth and sky'.

That evening, she flew into Salisbury, where she saw a 'wide scatter of light over spaces of dark'. It was already clear from the air how fast the town was growing, sprawling outwards in proliferating suburbs. She drove through the darkness along avenues of subdued light, looking out at the buildings glowing under the full moon, and arrived at the rose-filled garden of her friend's suburban bungalow.

The house felt wrong. This was not what she had returned to find. Though her home in the bush had burned to the ground years earlier after her parents sold the farm, it was those walls of grey mud that had haunted her dreams for the past decade and she felt no freer in the streets of Salisbury than she did in London. So she was grateful when her hosts suggested they should drive into the bush in search of friends. In just a few minutes, they emerged into the endless emptiness of the veld and she felt at last that she was really home:

> The night was magnificent; the Southern Cross on a slant overhead; the moon a clear, small pewter; the stars all recognisable and close. The long grass stood all around, tall and giving off its dry, sweetish smell, and full of talking crickets. The flattened trees of the Highveld were low above the grass, low and a dull silver-green.

I

'They were *her* hills'

Suffolk

Lessing was thirty-six when she made that trip: the same age as me. And I too was ready for the bush. The people

I contacted in Zimbabwe warned me against it. Lessing's farm would be impossible to find, the landscape changed beyond recognition; her houses in Salisbury were just ordinary suburban dwellings in a town that bore no resemblance to the place where she'd written, danced and loved. If I went in August, the bush would be dry, so this would not be the lush, green world I'd initially imagined. But I had learnt about disappointment and would not let it put me off.

First, though, I was going to have a summer in Suffolk. That April, I had been presented with a large box of injections to administer, with the aim of developing multiple follicles. Each night, my husband inserted a long needle into my stomach and I found that I enjoyed the strange closeness of this act, in which both of us accepted my weakness. Every other day I went to be scanned and they measured and counted the developing follicles. Polycystic ovaries make you more capable of producing eggs in these conditions, so this time, at least, I was a high achiever. Gradually, a lattice of fine white lines appeared on the screen and soon there were twenty-two eggs large enough to be collected; in two weeks I had produced as many eggs as are usually produced in two years. We spent Easter hunting for chocolate eggs in a rural hotel, my injections stored inside a bag of frozen peas in their industrial freezer. 'Another one!' my son shouted excitedly and repeatedly, as he spotted the shiny foil. A few days later, there was an egg-hunt inside my womb. All twenty-two were collected and doused with sperm. Eighteen were fertilised and over the next five days I received morning calls telling me how many of this large brood had survived the night. We were left with eight, which were sent to be tested. Three passed the test, and were frozen until I was ready to receive one.

With these eggs in the freezer, we had become hopeful again. My husband even described it as a moment of secret impregnation. At last, we had made plans finally to renovate our London house, which was continuing to become rapidly less habitable. The builders were now about to start and we'd agreed that it was a good moment for me to move to the Suffolk house and find a local nursery there for my son. I had three months in which to find out if I was happier or freer looking out every day on to clear, empty skies. I would also find out how I fared when cut off from adult company for protracted periods of time, because the friend I owned it with was only going to visit intermittently and my husband was going to stay in London and come at weekends.

I spent my first weeks painting windows and buying furniture. Then I was ready to write, sitting cross-legged in an old library chair where I could survey the fields I now thought of as 'my fields' that had turned from yellow to green as the spring had progressed. Most days I went to the sea but I found that I didn't always need to; the landscape surrounding the house could be enough for me and, though there were no hills to frame the fields, they were blending in my mind with the view from Kermanshah Farm.

It was a relief to find that this idyll of lone writing and walking had turned out to be compatible with motherhood. When I sat at my desk looking out on to those fields, I was sitting next to the bed my son had recently slept in; occasionally I'd climb in among his bears and blankets for those brief between-paragraph naps that both Lessing and I found so useful. I spent the final hour of the afternoon pleasurably anticipating the moment that he'd run across the room to me when I arrived at his nursery, though once we were home I started looking forward to the particular peace that settled on the cottage when he was asleep upstairs. Reassured by his hidden presence, I sat on my own watching the sun setting over the field, the sky a sudden burst of deep blue, white and red that seemed as dramatic as anything I could imagine in Africa.

This was motherhood experienced without ambivalence, and the lack of conflict had turned out to be a source of liberation. Though it was motherhood itself that I had feared in my twenties, it had turned out that what threatened freedom was not motherhood but the tyranny of the dominant notion of family life. It was the expectations of 'the family' that Lessing had escaped when she left Frank Wisdom, and that she managed to avoid by mothering Peter in a different setting. Relaxing into motherhood, I had a sense that there was freedom simply in the unconsciousness of presence that operates in the relationship between parent and child, away from the noisier family dynamics. In some of my happiest moments, my son and I were comfortable enough to feel oblivious of each other; to be alone in each other's company. It felt as though this was the freedom of solitude without the loneliness.

Marriage too felt less constricting now that it was only part-time. What had troubled me in London, making me feel both claustrophobic and isolated, was the combination of excessive proximity and insufficient intimacy. Now I was pleased to sleep alone, moving back and forth across the double bed when I woke in the night, but I also appreciated my husband's visits. By day, I felt waves of relief every time he seemed happy in the house. At night, there was the revelation of a need forgotten until it was assuaged, as I felt the comfort of my body held against the naked flesh of another. I knew that my husband still struggled with the symbolism of the house, but hoped that he would forgive me once I became pregnant again and I could demonstrate my commitment to our shared future. On my side, I was amazed that life should turn out to be this simple; that freedom should reside in so bourgeois an acquisition as a second home.

In June it was time for the first embryo to be unfrozen and placed inside my womb. I watched on a screen as the doctor carefully sucked it up into the syringe and then released it inside my cervix. I'd been taking oestrogen and progesterone for three weeks so I already felt pregnant, my breasts sore and my moods volatile. A week later, these symptoms were validated by a positive pregnancy test: the two purple lines that I'd been waiting to see for over a year. Now I succumbed to tiredness, real or imagined, lengthening the naps. But though my body felt pregnant, I found it difficult to believe it. I liked to talk about it with my husband, planning the months ahead, pleased that this pregnancy did indeed seem further to restore our marriage, making us gentler with each other and sustaining our optimism about our future. Yet even as the weeks progressed, there was an unreality to it, I think for both of us.

Just at that moment of beginning to look contentedly inwards, I turned outwards. Politics intervened. After several months of campaigning in which the division and despair in British society had been brutally revealed, the British people voted to leave Europe. There were a few days of depression and disbelief, but then I discovered that there was a kind of excited energy to be found in taking up arms in what many of the people around me were experiencing as a civil war. For the first time in my life, I believed that I played a role in the life of my country, frantically monitoring the news and circulating the numerous desperate petitions that sprang up in a disbelieving attempt to reverse the decision. As one politician after another resigned and the country seemed to be frighteningly, sometimes comically, imploding, I found that there was a satisfaction in caring; in feeling that I was at one with the millions who thought as I did. Here at last, in the political greed and rising nationalism that had given rise to this vote, we might have the opponent awful enough to bring about a new era of passionate politics. At this unexpected moment, I was learning to understand a little more of what Lessing felt when she found that small differences could be forgotten as the individual took her place within the collective.

Then it became apparent that the suspended uncertainty was likely to go on for years. It was demoralising to feel part of so riven a nation. The rhetoric in the media had made clear that this had been in part a vote against privilege and difference; against experts and elites. It felt as though the values that I'd unconsciously inherited from Lessing's generation were under threat. Now that action of some kind seemed required, I became anxious about the inward-looking, self-conscious aspect of my life with Lessing, and about the whole enterprise of searching for freedom when the world was facing more urgent problems. It seemed distasteful to complain about the weddings of people with whom I shared opinions on these more crucial matters. I expressed some of this in an email to a friend and was partially reassured by her response: 'now, more than ever, we need to write in good faith'. I wasn't wholly convinced that this justified what I was doing, but I thought that perhaps, after all, Lessing would have done no more than that.

All this made the pregnancy feel even more illusory, until it was time for the seven-week scan and suddenly nothing mattered except the probe entering my vagina. It was unusually uncomfortable; I'd failed to empty my bladder. The doctor carefully moved the probe around, while I watched her face and my husband watched the screen. She was looking for the heart-beat that would tell us if this pregnancy was 'viable'. Instead she found nothing at all. She looked again, wondering if a sac might be developing outside instead of inside the womb, but the search was fruitless and it turned out that I couldn't have been actually pregnant for long; it was the hormones I was tak-ing that had stopped my body from miscarrying.

Afterwards, I clung to my husband, conscious of my renewed dependence on him, not wanting to go alone to col-lect my son and take him back to Suffolk. There were two days of grief and then a bored, dull pain. This was sadness not so much for a life lost as for the depletion of myself. 'You again,' I thought, confronting myself in the mirror, my hair and skin drying as a result of the sudden withdrawal from oestrogen. I hadn't always been aware of it, but I'd been liv-ing inside a version of myself that had gained lustre from housing developing life. Now I was just me, doing the things I had always done, unable to experience pleasure or joy except occasionally when they were initiated by others.

'I'm tired of being resilient', I told the friend I shared the house with. I could see where strength might lie but it was tempting to evade it, to succumb to the depression that I could feel ushering me into its cavern, to punish my body by avoiding sleep and forcing myself to exercise despite my sore breasts and stomach. My son wet his bed for the second time in the week and I interrogated him pointlessly about why he had done it. When he asked me lazily to help him put his shoes on, I accused him of being a baby. It seemed that no one was allowed to be a baby now that the remains of a non-existent embryo and a needlessly thickened womb were bleeding away from me. It was only when he was out at nursery that I regretted my own cruelty.

Then the bleeding stopped and the sun came out and I experienced the return of my old body as an unexpected gift. My skin browned and moistened; I could tighten my stomach muscles again at will. I remembered how after the last miscarriage I had reported on these moments of renewed energy to my now dead friend, walking with him across the long empty beaches of east Norfolk, and how we were both surprised by how much myself I seemed already to feel. I decided to try once more to find that spot on the estuary I associated with him.

This time I parked in the next village along and I knew from the start that I'd come to the right place. Though I couldn't say that I recognised them, the paths felt innocuous enough to be familiar. It was a hot day; the sun a brilliant blue against the luminous green of the grass, speckled with purple flowers. The landscape was noisy with birds and with the sound of a lone water skiier.

I knew what I'd see when I climbed up on to the grassy sea wall, but it still came as a surprise to be somewhere so wonderfully dreamlike – so unlike anywhere else I had been. I walked along the wall towards the island, confident that when I reached the bend I'd know that I was standing at the spot where we'd paused the previous March. When I got there, I was more moved than I'd anticipated. For once, expectation, memory and experience collided and I could feel my way back across the intervening months and stand there with a dead man. But almost immediately, I was distracted by seeing that just below me there was a stretch of gravelly sand I hadn't noticed before, dipping into the shallow water. The water itself was tempting now, in a way that it wouldn't have been that March evening, so I stepped down and paddled. It was much warmer than I'd imagined and I urgently wanted to swim.

I stood dithering. There was no one around; it would be easy to take off my clothes and wander in. But I was frightened by the current, which seemed to be gathering in circles just ahead. My sombre mission was forgotten as I wandered further down the sea wall to find a spot where the current was calmer, stopping at another bank and taking off my clothes. At first, though I plunged straight in, I found that it remained awkwardly shallow, so I was not so much swimming as slithering along mud, which I could feel sliding with enjoyable gloopiness against my breasts. I kept swimming and the depth changed. I was floating, free and happy in an absolute way in which nothing existed beyond my body and the sun and the water.

This was not a moment of renunciation. Somewhere just below the surface of my mind there was even a gentle fantasy playing out with the water skier I could still see silhouetted in the distance. But it was the first time I'd swum naked in wild waters alone, and I felt a pleasing sense of independence, enjoying even the slight fearfulness as I was swept gently out by the current. I turned back towards the shore and swam forcefully, realising that it required effort just to remain in one place. I swam harder and eventually returned to a depth where I could push my feet into the muddy ground. I stood still, with my feet buried, feeling the current pressing against me, and then waded back towards the shore. The dead had been laid to rest; grief had transmuted into a sense of wonder that I could feel so astonishingly alive.

Returning home, I thought that there was a freedom in recovering my equilibrium unaided; usually I would rely on friends at such moments, but now I was learning how to experience happiness again alone. As I sat down at my desk to write about my swim, I felt that this had become a house in which to learn to be self-sufficient. It was where I'd learn to be more like Lessing, but also to be more like the friend I owned the house with, who had lived contentedly alone for years.

She had been on my mind as I drove home from the estuary. Driving past tea shops where she and I had been together, I was conscious of the unfairness that she was spending so much less time in the house than I was. For her now there was a freedom simply in movement and so, though she showed no sign of resenting or even envying my relative mobility, I was all the more grateful for the expansive pleasure of walking and swimming. I was also grateful for the part she'd played in bringing me there, not only practically but emotionally.

She and I both knew and acknowledged the painful truth that, if I could afford it, I would continue to come to the house after she had died. Our friendship wasn't always easy, especially as it mattered to us both that we should pretend that there was less wrong with her than there really was. Her legs were growing weaker as a result of the tumour and on her previous visit she had fallen in the bathroom. When I helped pull her up, we avoided eye contact, wanting to pretend that it hadn't happened. Afterwards, we sat in the garden, surveying the plants we had chosen together and analysing the nuances of both of our shifting psychological states. As she matter-of-factly dismissed the conventional expectations and paths I was trying to evade, I was conscious that, even as I helped her up off the floor, she remained for me inspirational as someone who had managed to live both freely and responsibly. Most importantly, she had found a way to make her need for self-sufficiency triumph over her need to be looked after, and this mattered to her even now that her health was deteriorating so rapidly. After her departure, it had felt as though she was passing on her independence and freedom as Lessing was less wittingly passing on hers.

In the month that followed, bringing day after day of sun, I could feel myself falling into deepening love with the house and the surrounding landscape, much as I would fall in love with a person. 'They were *her* hills,' Mrs Gale tells herself in one of Lessing's African stories; 'that was how she felt.' This was not something I'd experienced before; this blend of admiration, familiarity, possession. It was a feeling that became almost tangible in the evening light, the sky wide and translucently blue, with the trees silhouetted against it. By the middle of August, the fields around me were full, ready to be denuded. My son went to see a combine harvester at work at nursery and told me knowledgeably about how it worked. I sat at my desk and watched one rapidly strip the now golden field in front of the house. I was reading about Zimbabwe in preparation for my visit, and as I sat looking out on to the brown earth, it became daily more easy to believe that I was gazing at the bare soil of the Rhodesian veld.

II

'The jewel of Africa'

Zimbabwe

After her trip in 1956, Lessing stayed away from the country she still thought of as home for twenty-six years. Later she described how 'night after night I wept in my sleep and woke knowing I was unjustly excluded from my own best self'. Though she could experience the infinite African skies in Zambia, she remained a prohibited immigrant who was forbidden to return to Rhodesia. Her absence was all the more painful because she knew that the country was tearing itself apart in a brutal civil war. Where once the Taylors had left the windows and doors of their house open as they slept, the whites now barricaded themselves fearfully inside their farms because the desperate men fighting for the black nationalist cause had been told that it was finally time to reclaim the land that the whites had stolen.

At last, the war came to an end. The blacks were victorious, though this success had come at the price of the destruction of much of the country they were fighting for. The Rhodesians had to submit to the majority rule that now prevailed throughout the former African colonies. In April 1980 Robert Mugabe was ushered into power in the country whose original name of Zimbabwe had been reinstated. 'You have the jewel of Africa in your hands', he was told by the rulers of Tanzania and Mozambique; 'now look after it'. The populace was optimistic, believing that he'd fulfil his promise to restore the land to the blacks and offer free education to all.

Lessing, too, was hopeful when she returned in 1982. She had been transformed overnight from a prohibited immigrant to a national celebrity; one of the few white Southern Rhodesians who was seen by the new regime as being on the right side. Changing her money at the airport bank, she was asked by the official if she was the author and welcomed in the name of Zimbabwe. She barely saw the airport: 'the smells, the colours of the earth had undone me, and my emotional balance was gone'. She walked out into the dry, scented air and wept.

She spent only a single morning in Harare, disappointed by the urban sprawl and by the people she met, who seemed hardened by the years of war. She went into the bush, driving to Marondera, where she'd camped with her family while visiting her brother at school, and found that most of the animals had vanished and that the birds had been silenced. But the landscape had not lost its beauty: 'the road still rolled high in sparkling air, and, as you reached the crest of one rise, blue distances unfolded into mountains and then chains of mountains.'

She didn't go back to the farm. It wasn't until 1988 that she had the courage to return, accompanied by Anthony Chennels from the University of Zimbabwe, who had written a thesis about the use of myth in Lessing and other African writers. Now they were re-entering her myth country together. And as they drove out of Harare on the new urban road, familiar valleys and hills came into view. In her childhood memories, this was a corrugated dirt track where the family had slid and skidded in rainy weather, often having to get out and wait for hours for a patch of water to clear.

Soon they were in Banket, where once a dusty girl with bare burned arms and legs had appeared with a .22 rifle dangling from her hand and six guineafowl under her arm. Now where there had been only a hotel, butcher, grocery and truck store, there was a whole little town. The seven miles from Banket to Kermanshah had taken an hour when they drove it in Doris's youth, and several more when she'd walked, dawdling as Martha does to savour her freedom along the way. Today it was just a few minutes' drive on the straight road through the rich, red soil before she saw the hill where she expected the low grass-thatched house to appear, 'confirming so many dreams and nightmares', but found instead a graceless grey bungalow.

The house was disappointing, the Mawonga tree had gone, but when she turned away and looked out at the view, she found all she could have hoped for. The field stumped out by her father with the aid of a team of oxen was still there. Though much of the bush next to the house had been turned into fields, further in the distance there were still the Hunyanis, the Umvukwes or Great Dyke and the Ayrshire Hills, in all their old splendour, glowing against the blue sky. This was the view that her parents had built their house to survey, and which, on rainy mornings or starry nights, had made up for all the disappointment and frustration suffered inside the house. It was more beautiful than she had allowed herself to expect and she stood in silence on the verge of tears, unable to believe in the magnificence:

> I had been brought up in this place. I lived here from the age of five until I left it forever thirteen years later. I lived *here*. No wonder this myth-country tugged and pulled… what a privilege, what a blessing.

***

The African sun filled the sky as I awoke above Zambia, still drowsy from cramped, chemically aided sleep, surprised by the swathe of red. Although I didn't notice the yellow ball appearing and rising, I caught sight of it once it had ascended above the window. It remained on my eyelids as I faded back into unconsciousness.

Harare was in the midst of an attempted revolution – the opposition uniting against the government – that seemed more significant outside the country than inside. In the city, people seemed just to ignore the small area where protestors were being fired at with tear gas, carrying on as usual. I did the same, relieved that my political courage was not going to be tested. On my first day, I went Lessing-hunting in town, aided by a helpful guide, an out-of-work ecologist able to identify every tree we saw along the way.

In the 1980s, Lessing had made a list of her addresses in Harare. It turned out that some of these no longer existed, while some had been misremembered. There was no number 145 in Livingstone Avenue, though this was where she'd recalled sitting John and Jean on the grass to learn that she was going to set them free. I was still pleased to wander around the avenues, though, and I found that what struck me most was how small an area this was. You wouldn't be able to avoid bumping into most of the people you knew on a daily basis. Livingstone Avenue was only a couple of streets away from Fife Avenue, where she'd lived with Gottfried and Peter; she'd even resided on Fife Avenue at one stage with Frank as well. After leaving her marital home, she must have expected to encounter her husband and children every time she left the house.

The apartment block at 119 Fife Avenue was still there, though it had now been turned into a Braille library, and I stood at the fence and imagined my way inside the building, half listening to flamboyant birdsong in the enormous fig trees outside, which may well have been there in Lessing's day. All these streets had become quite shabby now. This area that had been wholly white had become now almost wholly black as the remaining whites retreated to the new suburbs, and the new owners had less money for their upkeep. But this building was still as bright and clean as it would have been then, a one-storey white 1930s block with two painted green gables and a crisp green trim on the windowsills and walls. There were stone benches on the lawn at the front where I pictured her sitting feeding Peter, chatting to the neighbours as they passed.

I could imagine feeling claustrophobic here and longing like her to be somewhere messier, larger or simply more anonymous. It was hard to reconcile this building with the letters of longing she'd written to John Whitehorn at that time, or with the charged energy of *The Grass is Singing*, the novel that had come slowly into being within these neat white walls. I couldn't envisage being able to write in there at all, observed by the street and constantly interruptible, but perhaps her frustration was strong enough to enable her to write anywhere.

We went next to the Lady Chancellor Maternity Home where she had given birth to her three children, now the maternity wing of the main state hospital of Harare. It was a white curved 1930s building; the kind of optimistic, sunny architecture that you expect to encounter at the British seaside rather in the Zimbabwean suburbs. You could see how it might have been intended to reassure the Rhodesian women, longing for home as their bellies swelled. My guide had been born there too, forty years earlier, so the nurses let us loose to wander around the corridors and wards. I was surprised how unchanged it all seemed. It was easy to imagine Doris Wisdom pacing up and down the dark linoleum corridors during that long night of labour with John. Much of the signage seemed not to have been replaced in the intervening seventy years and when we peered into an empty ward, the beds were still the same white cast-iron frames that she had lain in, waiting with increasing desperation to be presented with her baby. We passed a heavily pregnant woman, who held her back in pain as she hobbled down the corridor and then sank into a chair. I felt more in touch with the woman I was here to find than I'd felt at any point that day. Though deep inside the wards some of the equipment must have changed, the body had not, and here was another tired, puffed figure, longing to release her burden.

The beds that had sparkled in Doris Wisdom's day were now rusted, the springs disappearing. These triumphant symbols of empire had been left to the blacks by whites who had newer furniture in private hospitals. I went into the patient toilets, and found that they were all filled with blood. It was a visceral reminder of childbirth; this time not of Doris Wisdom's experience of labour but of my own. This was the gushing red liquid that I had once watched emerge while peeing painfully, wondering if the blood would ever stop. But here the toilets were unflushable. There was no chance to eliminate that reminder of what you'd just gone through and women at every stage of pregnancy and maternity had to encounter each other's blood.

I started to feel uncomfortable; a white tourist looking in on a scene of segregated poverty that was once a scene of segregated privilege. I suggested that we should leave. And on the way out, as we walked along the neatly planted flowerbeds and on to the dusty earth of the pavement, I saw that the soil here was the same red clay that had reminded the pregnant Martha and Alice of the bush. When the rains that the whole region was awaiting finally came, this would become a bath of red mud. Would desperate, bloated women again be tempted to strip off their clothes and wallow in it?

We went to the sports club where Doris was first awkwardly kissed; we went past the town hall where she'd married two men. As we drove across the city and round its edges, I felt that there was something provisional about the town I was seeing. It wasn't just because of reading Lessing that I felt the presence of the bush; it was there at the edge of quite ordinary roads, long grass strewn with wild, elegant trees, some of them blossoming now because spring was just beginning. Friends at home were asking me what the African bush was like. From what I'd seen so far, the landscape itself was not radically different from some landscapes in Europe – the sunburned countryside of southern Italy or Greece. What was different here was the way that the bush seemed in some fundamental way to constitute the country. The towns were temporary edifices, liable to be taken over by the grass and trees surrounding them at any moment. I wouldn't begin to feel I was in Zimbabwe until I had headed further out into the veld.

'Twenty-three years later and the "jewel" is ruined, dishonoured, disgraced,' Lessing berated Mugabe in 2003. She had returned to Zimbabwe at regular intervals in her seventies and had found herself increasingly unable to defend the regime to her white friends. Now, in her early eighties, she wrote stringent attacks on the new government for ruining the country she loved, both in this essay on 'The Tragedy of Zimbabwe' and in her novel, *The Sweetest Dream*, which begins as an autobiographical portrait of 1960s London and ends as a devastating depiction of thwarted human effort in Zimbabwe.

In the novel, Lessing juxtaposed the corrupt leaders in the city, too isolated to care about what is happening in the villages, with a group of idealistic doctors and teachers at a small Catholic mission, attempting to run a village school and hospital. When Sylvia, a young white doctor, arrives from London and puts all her energy and money into improving the so-called hospital, she is seen by most of the blacks around her as a saint. But she makes the mistake of letting common sense prevail over legality, taking provisions from the half-built would-be state-of-the-art hospital that has been left to rot with its walls unfinished because aid money has been diverted into the hands of crooked officials. She also undertakes a dangerous appendectomy and is shunned as a witch when the patient dies. Sylvia's hospital is shut and almost all her friends and their children die of the unacknowledged AIDS epidemic that is sweeping the village. The final picture of the empty village, the library shelves bare and the medicine cabinet bereft of provisions, is a desolate one that can invite only despair.

The indictment is punchier in the essay, where Lessing reminds her readers with furious disbelief that this regime inherited a nation with functioning railways, good roads, towns that were policed and clean, land capable of growing everything and a powerful supply of electricity provided by the Kariba lake. They'd also had such widespread popular support at home and abroad that anything could have been achieved: 'never has a ruler come to power with more goodwill'. But Mugabe had been inflexible and cowardly, cutting himself off in a self-created prison, governing with rigid Marxist rules and allowing violence and corruption to proliferate among his officials.

The disappointment here was personal. Lessing had spent her twenties and thirties fighting for a new Southern Rhodesia and had spent the rest of her adult life deeply concerned about the future of the country. It also coincided with a period of private dissatisfaction. In London, though she still saw friends, went to the theatre and gave occasional talks in her public persona as an only partially benevolent witch, her home life was increasingly depressing. Peter was becoming larger, sicker and more dependent on her. Friends describe how in this period it became hard to see her without his hulking presence, and how even when silent he seemed to cast a shadow of entitled bitterness on the conversation. This was hardly freedom, though perhaps she had come to see the loneliness that freedom entailed as too high a price. At the same time, she felt increasingly burdened by the various symptoms of age.

Nonetheless, she managed determinedly to see ageing itself as offering a form of liberation. In an essay called 'Old' written at this time, she described how 'at some point along the way certain events will take place, we know: we have been warned'. Teeth, eyes, ears, skin deteriorated; these were not a surprise. Less expected was her diminishing height. But alongside this came freedom. The best discovery was 'a fresh liveliness in experiencing'. She felt as though a gauze had been dissolved and she had been given 'new eyes'; she was frequently shaken by the improbability of life as though by a fever. 'Everything is remarkable, people, living events present themselves to you with the immediacy of players in some barbarous and splendid drama that it seems we are part of.'

Lessing used her new eyes to look back once again at her childhood, this time making one final attempt to escape the ghosts of her parents by offering them a peaceful afterlife. In *Alfred and Emily* she gave her parents the lives she now felt they had deserved. This was a chance, too, for Lessing to return once again to the house and landscape of her childhood. For at least the fifth time in her writing life, she described the black linoleum floor, the Persian carpets scattered across them, the grey-brown of the mud walls decorated with bright Liberty fabrics, the copper basin and jug on the washstands and the deep orange curtains in Doris's bedroom, flaming and burning when the sun rose. But there was another ghost to lay to rest. For the first time she wrote about the destruction of the house, imagining the tiny screaming of the hornets, mice and beetles as the walls and floors burned around them. And she asked 'who would ever know that here had stood this house of dreams'.

While she was still writing this novel, Lessing received the Nobel Prize. The news did not come at a hopeful moment. Peter had been in hospital with a broken arm and Lessing had just gone to collect him, demoralised by visiting her son in the latest of a series of hospitals as he'd had heart problems for a couple of years. Arriving home, they were greeted by a mob of journalists and cameras. The footage of Lessing's response to the news of the prize has become one of the most enduring images that people have of her in the years since her death.

She climbs carefully out of a taxi, clasping the door handles with both hands as she does so. Her grey hair is in a messy bun and she wears old lady clothes: an ankle-length skirt with thick white tights and a sensible shirt and woolly waistcoat. Leaving Peter in the taxi, she grabs her carrier bag of shopping and walks up to the reporters, asking them what they're photographing.

'We're photographing you, have you heard the news?'

'No.'

'You've won the Nobel Prize for Literature,' an enthusiastic American informs her.

'Oh Christ,' she replies, with a dismissive shake of her hand. 'It's been going on now for thirty years, one can get more excited.'

Waving them off, she returns to the taxi to take her change, while Peter emerges out of it. His arm is in a sling; he carries an artichoke in one hand and a bag of onions in the other; he seems eager that some of the attention should be for him. He stands and stares while his mother goes to shut the taxi door that he's left open. And then he makes an indistinct pronouncement that ends 'somebody must have died'.

'Have you got everything?' Lessing asks, fussing over her son. 'Have you got your...' And then she turns, summoning professional dignity, to the assembled crew.

'Right. I'm sure you'd like some uplifting remarks of some kind.'

'Any kind of remarks, just tell me what this prize means to you.'

'Well, it's been going as I say for thirty years.'

'But this is a recognition of your life's work.'

'There you are, you see, you're saying it all for me.' They help her on to the pavement. Becoming warmer, she takes the arm of the English journalist who is asking her to talk to Radio 4. 'Look, you tell me what to say and I'll say it,' she says, smiling, agreeing that he can come and interview her in five minutes.

The American persists. 'Does it mean anything to win a prize?'

She turns back from her front door. 'Look. I've won all the prizes in Europe. Every bloody one. So I'm delighted to win them all. It's a royal flush.'

It's hard to know how to respond to this. It's admirable: there's a kind of courage in her defiance – in her apparent obliviousness to honours at a time when most other writers were desperately seeking them. But it's also horribly depressing: her exhaustion is palpable and there is something disturbing even here in her relationship with Peter. They make an odd couple, captured on film like this, lumbering awkwardly out of the taxi with their groceries. And it's clear that despite her own infirmity she's the one who needs to have both the practical sense and the worldliness for both of them.

Lessing was able to be stronger and wiser when it came to writing her prize acceptance speech, which was read out by her publisher in Stockholm two months later. And here, leaving behind the trivial daily struggles of her London life, she returned magisterially to the country of her childhood.

Her speech began in the present tense, setting the scene in Zimbabwe as it had been when she visited in the 1980s. 'I am standing in a doorway looking through clouds of blowing dust to where I am told there is still uncut forest.' This was a landscape she had known earlier, when it had contained the most wonderful forest she had ever seen. It had now dwindled to a desert of stumps where people had cut down the trees to use as fuel for fires. In an increasingly desperate country, they did what they could to live.

She went on to describe the impoverished situation in schools, where staff and pupils begged her urgently to send books. And she chastised her British readers for not valuing the books they had enough, complaining about the reluctant reading of the British young. This was a speech about literature; a reminder of how literature could and did matter and of the power of stories, which will 'recreate us, when we are torn, hurt, even destroyed'. But it was most of all a speech about the Africa she once loved, in which she made an act of virtual return. 'My mind is full of splendid memories of Africa which I can revive and look at whenever I want'. From wintery London, she looked about her at the endless freedom of the Rhodesian bush:

> How about those sunsets, gold and purple and orange, spreading across the sky at evening. How about butterflies and moths and bees on the aromatic bushes of the Kalahari? Or, sitting on the pale grassy banks of the Zambesi, the water dark and glossy, with all the birds of Africa darting about. Yes, elephants, giraffes, lions and the rest, there were plenty of those, but how about the sky at night, still unpolluted, black and wonderful, full of restless stars.

III

'A high, dry, empty sky'

The bush

As we drove out of Harare, the grass by the side of the road became gradually wilder and the trees bigger and more colourful. It was the season when the leaves of the Msasa tree suddenly acquire a coppery sheen and the red bean tree drips with bright red pods like the one given to me by my guide's father the previous evening when we had sat drinking sundowners on his verandah, discussing political unrest in the most tranquil surroundings imaginable. I wanted to feel free, as Lessing had, driving out of the city in 1956 or 1982, but my life in the city had been too interesting for me to feel constrained.

On the approach to Banket, my guide pointed out a large Mawonga tree, like the one whose spine left its imprint on the back of the young Doris as she read and dreamed her way through adolescence. He stopped the car so I could sit on the roots, feeling the bark against my spine. I read a few pages at random from *African Laughter* and found that I was reading about the look and feel of granite: 'It has a sparkle to it, a liveliness. If you put your hand on it on a hot day it seems to pulse.' We were on our way to the granite kopjes.

Banket surprised me by looking just like she'd described it, but unlike I'd imagined it because it was unlike any town I'd seen. Here were the boarded shop fronts laid out in a makeshift row; there was the butcher where she'd brought her guineafowl. On the other side of the road, there was a faded Rhodie tea shop, battling like Maude Tayler for English gentility with its teapots and milk jugs, and a general store that felt as though it could have been there for seventy years. I was ready now to enter myth country as we climbed the straight Mazwikadei Road, following the line of the old railway, looking for the spot on the map where the previous day Anthony Chennels had suggested that we might turn to the left in search of the hill where the Taylers had once decided to site their home.

We turned; there was bush ahead and a small farm. There was no sign of a hill, but Anthony had said that the word 'hill' was an exaggeration and that you didn't know it was a hill until you were on it. We introduced ourselves to the farmer and his family, who seemed friendly after some initial suspicion about why a pair of whites would appear from nowhere and ask to wander on their land, and my guide left me to walk off into the veld.

It was all unexpectedly quick. Suddenly I had found myself set free in the bush I had waited a year to roam in, and I was not quite sure what I felt. I walked further, encountering a woman who introduced me to her children. I gestured that I had one too, about the same size as her son, and then walked on until I could see nothing except grass and trees on each side. This wasn't the red soil that I'd found at the hospital: it was a dusty whitish brown. I couldn't see any of Lessing's hills now, but we had situated ourselves as we arrived with the Great Dyke – blue in the distance – and I knew that they were all there. I could be sure that this was bush she'd have wandered in; that some of the larger trees would have been trees she'd touched; that she might have lain reading in the spot where I now sat down on the dry grass to look around me. She loved the rainy season but she loved the dry season too. Away from the veld, Martha craves 'dryness, barrenness, stunted growth, the colours that are fed from starved roots – thin browns and greys, dull greens and sad yellows – and all under a high, dry, empty sky'.

Sitting quietly on the ground, I started to hear the sound of birds, as well as of the cows mooing in the background; I could also hear the longer grass as it waved in the breeze. I began to see that the yellowed grass that had become so dry it could ignite easily in the wind was in fact a whole range of colours. I became more attentive to the differences in the shapes of the trees, all of them extravagantly beautiful, and the shades of their bark. This was turning out to be a landscape that gave itself slowly, rewarding attention.

The children I'd seen earlier ran past me, looking back curiously to see what I was doing. They came closer and I offered them some of the pens I'd bought at the post office at Banket. They ran gleefully back to tell friends who had emerged out of the bushes, all as at home here as the young Doris. I took out one of the pens myself and started to write, describing my surroundings and asking myself if I felt free. It seemed now as though it wasn't the right question. Certainly I was happy. It felt a little absurd to have travelled across the world, looking for this, but there was also a great sense of rightness in looking out and seeing nothing but bush in every direction, as far as the most distant horizon. A small boy rushed towards me, addressing me with a stern 'good afternoon'. I gave him my last spare pen and he looked back, unsmiling, and then clutched it to his chest and ran off, shrieking with laughter. I wrote in my book that I was in danger of being swept into my own African dream.

My guide, who was turning out to be extremely good at talking to the locals we encountered, was in conversation with several men when I returned to the car. One of them lived at Kermanshah Farm, now known as 'Kimasha', the name still unwittingly tying its inhabitants to the Taylers' lost days of happiness in Persia. We were to drive him back with his shopping and he'd show us the hill.

We returned to the Mazwikadei Road and took another turning. This didn't feel any hillier than the first one but suddenly our passenger was telling us to stop and I could see that we had indeed ascended a hill without noticing. Below us the ground slipped down into valleys and in the distance there were the mountains I'd been wanting to see on three sides: Koodoo hill straight ahead with the Ayrshire hills behind it, the Great Dyke to our left, the Hunyani to our right. Koodoo hill was dark with granite and grass, but the other hills were pale blue against the horizon, the sky brighter than the landscape. Since Lessing was last here in 1988 a new house had been built: a large bungalow exactly where hers had been. We were told that this was now owned by a local councillor, who was at work in the next town along. His daughter was a girl in her twenties who spoke good English and invited me to wander around while my guide drove the man with the shopping back home.

I walked down the slope into the bush that had now reclaimed the fields that Alfred Tayler had once stumped for farming, looking out at the hills. The soil here was reassuringly red and I was almost crying with happiness. There was the sense of something falling into place. I had a very calming feeling that this was exactly where I needed to be. Sitting down again with my notebook, I wrote that I could see how spending days at a time here might make me feel free, even if this would be a protected, Western freedom that had nothing to do with the more constrained lives of the people around me. Just in being there, I felt a kind of weightlessness.

What Lessing had opened the way to was not a feeling of escape but a new sense of scale. The weddings with which I had begun this quest seemed far away now, though the wedding fervour was no less strong here (that morning in the local paper, I'd read an article advising men to start losing weight and trying out a new beauty regime at least six months before their big day). I still thought that it mattered to raise the question of whether there was more than one way to live and to ask if some ways were freer than others. But for me it seemed that the problem of dangling was solved less by purposefully searching for freedom than by learning to inhabit the present. Though I knew it to be a traveller's cliché, I felt then that I'd become able to open myself to the moment and all it might bring in a way I rarely could at home.

We ate our lunch just in front of the house, looking out at the Great Dyke. People stood watching us, openly curious. The daughter of the house was now holding a small baby and I went to talk to her, learning that she had lived there for fifteen years, since she was twelve. I showed her a picture of my son. Motherhood felt very necessary here, not something to leave behind. It was a vital connection to the people around me, who were perplexed by my stories of crossing the world in search of a writer who'd once lived here but seemed reassured by the picture of the smiling boy, proudly eating an ice cream.

Sitting back down, I asked my guide if he thought I could pay the family to stay there. It had come to feel urgently necessary to stand looking at these hills as the sun set that evening and rose the next morning. I walked back to the girl, and it was all said quickly. The answer was yes, though she would not let me pay, but she would have to ask her father first. A phone call, then I had to call him; a long conversation dominated by linguistic incomprehension on both sides. He was suspicious about my 'research' and I couldn't allay his fears on a bad line with neither of us able to understand the other's accent and his daughter unable to convince him that I seemed genuine. Eventually he told her that it was all right but I'd have to go to the local police station to register my presence.

The police station was a hut, where they seemed to warm to us after a few moments of doubt. They took my details, apparently reassured by my university affiliation. Just as they were about to grant me a licence of some kind, the officer came in to say that the Councillor had called to announce a change of mind; he didn't wish me to stay. My guide telephoned this time, man speaking to man, and convinced the Councillor that we should come to the town where he worked to talk to him. When we arrived, it was all settled in minutes. I named his mountains – the Great Dyke, the Hunyani mountains, the Ayrshire Hills – and explained that I had come from London to see them because a writer I loved had watched them turning from blue to pink in the evening light. He seemed prepared to accept my eccentricity and became apologetic for his earlier hostility. We rushed around town buying presents for the children and a toothbrush for me and then we were back on the hill.

After my guide departed, my host showed me round the house. I was to share a room with her and her baby. The house was dark; the curtains all resolutely drawn, some even sewn shut. Most of the rooms were empty but there was a large living room with sofas grouped around a television, which she suggested I might like to sit and watch. These were not bush worshippers; it had become a nostalgic, European activity to sit staring out at the dying light. But I said that I wanted to go off to see the sun, now low in the sky, and I was followed by three children from the neighbouring house, warm and eager to talk to me now it was known that I was allowed to stay, telling me how glad they were that I was there.

The sun was setting over the Hunyani mountains, known in Shona as the Muchekawakasungabeta. It was hanging low in the sky, turning the yellow grass a glittering gold. The black earth where a fire had been was darker by contrast; the outline of the trees was stronger. It was so beautiful that it was also sad, because my time there was so brief, and because it felt inadequate that all I could do was to look.

The children hung around watching me, curious but bored. I led them back to the house where my host entrusted me with her baby, who immediately fell asleep in my arms. The sun was already lower now so I suggested that we should all go back to see it. It was hard to feel much as the sun set, the twelve-year-old girl next to me eagerly admiring my rings and necklace, impatient for me to go back and do something else. But there was a feeling of astonishing rightness that I should be there, on the Taylers' farm, accepted by all its new inhabitants, holding a tiny black baby.

The evening was long and I started to feel the adolescent Doris's sense of the painful contrast between the freedom of the landscape and the constraint of the house. We sat watching Indian soap operas in the darkened room, waiting for the Councillor to come home. I went out periodically to look at the restless stars, which were indeed unlike anything I had seen before: brighter and more numerous. When the Councillor appeared, I found that he'd become a generous host, and we had learnt to understand each other. There were things that, talking to a white woman at this troubled point in Zimbabwean history, it seemed important to him to explain.

He'd been given the farm, they had not stolen it; as a war veteran, he had fought against an unjust system, not against the white people themselves; now he wished for us to live in racial harmony, sharing the land. He moved on to the current political situation, making me uneasy. Of course, demonstrations needed to be countenanced as part of the democratic process, but these had been getting out of hand. Shops had been looted and neighbourhoods terrorised; it had been necessary for the police to step in and protect the people.

Soon I went to bed, where I spent a disbelieving, wakeful night, enjoying the sound of the baby suckling periodically in the bed next to mine, irritated by the insistence of the guinea-fowl squawking outside in their pen. At dawn there was a shout from the Councillor, rousing the household. I walked out to the back of the house, where the sky was already pink in preparation for the sun that would soon emerge over the Great Dyke. Doris Tayler awoke to this every morning. Her bed looked across the bush to the mountains and when she left her door open she could see the hills changing colour as the sun appeared.

The Councillor joined me, dignified and gracious, suggesting that he would show me around after we had watched the sun rise. Was this a frequent ritual for him? It seemed that it might be. He described where the sun moved on its journey towards the equator, marvelling at the strange fact that it was we who were moving rather than the sun. Then that ball appeared and rose up fast in front of us. Within seconds it was high above us, the sky a blend of blue and pink. We wandered around, looking at the fields of new bush shimmering in the morning light.

'The fields were a timid intrusion on a landscape hardly marked by man,' Lessing wrote in *Martha Quest*. It seemed right to me that after all this time the farm was returning to bush, but it did not seem right to the Councillor, who was ashamed of his failed efforts. Twenty-two of them had arrived fifteen years ago and if they had failed to turn it into a profitable venture, it was because they were struggling for money and water. The water supply had been cut off some years earlier, following an unpaid bill. He had no tractor so couldn't plough the fields, though he did his best when he could. Now he had almost paid the sum required and the water would return that autumn; he'd be able to plant crops again. 'This is the bread basket of Africa,' he said, wonderingly, perhaps using that insistent Rhodesian phrase for my benefit.

I tried to explain that it had always been hard. When he showed me the ruins of a brick house that he thought might once have been the Taylers', I told him that in fact they'd lived in a building made of mud. He found this difficult to believe but I explained that Alfred Tayler had been a failed farmer as well. He'd done his best, but he'd been hindered by his own weakness: he had a wooden leg from the war. The Councillor mused on his defeated, war-wounded predecessor. 'All these wars,' he said. 'Why do we do this to each other?'

After he left for work, I sat talking to his daughter and to a neighbouring child, a twelve-year-old-girl who informed me that she was the best in her class at English. I told them a little about my life in London, finding it hard to describe it in these surroundings. My host told me that she was longing to escape the bush to the city; there was nothing for her here; she wanted to finish her degree and become a teacher in town. I told her that she might miss the bush after she'd gone, like Lessing had, and she agreed that it was hard to leave the place where you had grown up. My twelve-year-old friend didn't want to let me out of her sight so I gave her some colouring pencils I'd bought the previous day and sat reading *African Laughter* while she drew pictures next to me, her crossed legs touching mine. I had not found solitude in the bush. I had not even found that I could remain in the present moment. I was already thinking longingly about the shower I'd have once my guide had picked me up and returned me to the bounty of my hotel, where the water ran so plentifully that even the lawn facing the street was a lurid shade of green. But it still felt as though a ghost of mine or Lessing's had been appeased simply by my being there so easily and happily.

I decided to climb Koodoo Hill. It had never been farmed; the mix of dry vegetation and granite was probably the same as it had been in the Taylers' day. I set off on my own and was joined, silently, by an adolescent girl who seemed not to speak much English but was apparently prepared to accompany me. At first I minded the company and worried that I was taking her further than she'd go by choice, but then I grew used to it, enjoying the silence and accepting that she wanted to walk with me. We wandered on, and the ground turned suddenly from red to white as we left the farm. The vegetation here was different; there was a series of yellow flowering trees I hadn't seen before. The hill was further away than I'd realised and, as we left behind the protection of the farm, I was grateful that my companion would talk to anyone we encountered and show me the way back. Then we reached the hill, and ascended it easily, using the granite stones as footholds. At the top, I reached down and touched the granite, which was warm and smooth under my hands, and thought of Doris standing where I stood, in command of the landscape, looking for the animals that had long since departed. Walking back, I felt a sense of pleased recognition when the ground became red again. It is strange how quickly we can identify a place as ours. We reached a fork on the path and I turned to my companion, asking which track we should take. 'Shall we go home?' she asked me.

During the anti-climactic period after the Second World War, Lessing found that the bush was not enough to make her feel free. She was longing for the sea. This was the only time I'd come across her craving water like this, but it was a consuming desire. 'I envy you the sea,' she wrote to Smithie in May 1945. 'Am aching for the sea. I dream about it. I don't know why. I talk about it in my sleep.'

I could see now why she should have yearned for it so strongly. This was a landlocked country. None of the children at Kermanshah had ever seen the sea. I'd had months on the coast in Suffolk before arriving in the bush, but I was already starting to feel its pull again. Swimming in the sea, I'd be able to merge into the landscape, rather than just looking at it. This longing increased when we went to see the lake at Mazvikadei on the way back from the farm. It was beautiful – a reminder of the lack of water in the other landscapes we had seen – and I found it frustrating that the threat of disease prevented me from swimming.

The sea remained an image of freedom. The bush would never be as freeing for me as it had been for Lessing, if only because I'd never be able to roam around it so easily. It's hard to feel free when you're dependent on someone else for your safety and coordinates or when you are such a figure of interest to the locals that you are never on your own. But though I longed for the sea, I wasn't as drawn to freedom as I had been. I could see that after those years in the bush, Lessing would dream of the long grasses and empty skies as a lost vision of freedom, but I could no longer see freedom itself as an attainable goal in life.

In her novel *Transit*, which I'd read on the plane there, Rachel Cusk observes that 'freedom is a home you leave once and can never go back to'. This was certainly what it had been for Lessing. She never again found the freedom that she yearned for, except at brief moments when she was happy in nature. Indeed, in many ways, she remained less free than I was: more constrained by motherhood, more guilty about the wreckage her freedom had entailed. This didn't negate her efforts. They still seemed a useful corrective to the narrowness of the permissible hopes and desires that confronted her, and sometimes seemed to confront me. But Cusk was probably right that it was childish to seek our own illusory freedom above all else. Interviewed in 1984, Lessing rejected the notion of myth in relation to her portrayal of the African bush: 'I don't see the veld as a myth but a fact'. Nonetheless 'myth' was a term she used frequently herself and she would soon associate it with Africa. Did she know that her personal myth was freedom?

On my final day in Zimbabwe, my guide drove me out to some granite hills an hour from Harare at Ngomakurira. I was expecting to find a clump of Koodoo hills but encountered instead something on a much vaster scale. These were enormous sheets of rock, towering above us, and as we climbed up through foresty rocky paths, we could survey the hilly bush beyond. At the top there were bushmen paintings: evocative stick figures hunting for animals or making fires. My guide went on further, leaving me to sit in front of the paintings on the rock face and look out at the trees and hills in the afternoon light. There were mountain acacias beside me, their sparse branches entwining with each other, and a canopy of bushy green waterberry trees below. The granite slab opposite was dotted with clumps of white grass, miraculously attached to the vertical rock face. And there were the same combretums there had been in Lessing's bush: trees from which yellowish four-winged pods hung, sparkling like jewels in the sunlight.

I was pleased that I'd found a landscape that Lessing hadn't described. She had brought me to the bush and taught me how to look at it, but now I needed to discover it on my own. It may be true that we cannot regain the unconscious freedom of our childhoods, but it's also true that we remember what it feels like and can recognise it again when it occurs: that quality of still, expansive happiness. Getting out my notebook, I wrote that perhaps I had been seeking peace as much as freedom, as I learnt to dangle. After all, dangling is the opposite of striving.

'I am interested only in stretching myself, in living as fully as I can.' At those weddings, two years earlier, I'd been troubled by a feeling of claustrophobia. I didn't have an answer to the question of how to live differently; for a while, that summer, I had found contentment in motherhood and marriage, liberated not by a radical new way of life but by a country cottage. But perhaps I'd found the answer to the claustrophobia in seeing these choices as provisional and asking what it might feel like to be freer than I was, and how much freedom I could bear. Now it seemed that I'd been released simply through seizing the freedom to leave my husband and child behind and spend the night in a small and very particular spot of the Zimbabwe bush; to assert this as a need more pressing than those of the people I lived with, even if I had remained responsible enough to fit it in between the end of the summer and the start of my son's new school.

As the pen I'd bought in Banket began to run out, I wrote that there was a colossal selfishness simply in my marshalling so much effort and funding in order to sit there looking out at the changing light on the acacia trees, which were now becoming more coppery as the sun lowered in the sky. But in my enjoyment of this selfishness I was also forging a necessary form of independence. It felt like a minor triumph that I should be happy to do this alone; should wish that I had the confidence to repeat the whole walk unguided and be grateful that similar expeditions in Britain could take place unaccompanied. I wondered if it was my months in Suffolk or the intense unexpected sociability of my trip to Kermanshah that had taught me the value of solitude, showing me the way that being alone can be a form of freedom. For now, I had found in this enjoyment of lone wandering an answer to the problem of dangling. And I had found that admitting my need for this had shown me a way to escape the expectations that made me so stifled at weddings.

It didn't seem to matter that those were expectations that were if anything more present in Zimbabwe. Several people had asked openly at the farm why I hadn't brought my son with me. I had excused myself with the question of expense, unable to say that this was something I needed to do alone. They had asked me too about whether I was going to have more children. Sitting on the warm stones at the front of the house as we waited for my guide to whisk me back to first-world comfort, I had told my host about my difficulties with pregnancy. I offered her this as a sign of my fallibility as I'd offered her father Alfred Tayler's mud house and wooden leg.

Now I found that my desire for a child floated outside me – identifiable, but not felt urgently from within. Pleased to be sitting on my slab of granite, I was appreciative of the freedom of having only one easy child whom I could leave behind at home. Holding the baby as the sun set over the

Hunyani mountains, I had been moved by the contact with sleeping flesh but hadn't longed for this child to be my responsibility; had been contented to hand her back and retreat into the irresponsibility of my own thoughts.

I thought that there might be a freedom simply in recognising that what I had already might be enough and in accepting some kind of fateful force. I could see that I'd been slow to appreciate this. If I had initially regarded the first miscarriage as teaching me a lesson about failure and about our inability to plan the future, then it was a lesson I had evaded through embarking on IVF. Now I felt that I needed to sink deeper into the possibility that I might not have another child and felt that this knowledge was rendered bearable by my sense of awakening into surprisingly joyful knowledge of my own powerlessness. What dangling really involved was an awareness that you could not prepare for what life might present you with; that you had to endure the tragedy and be open to the happiness, in whatever unexpected form it came your way. We do not, as I believed in my twenties, create our own luck. I had seen this in my two friends, dying of arbitrary cancers; I had seen it in Lessing, whose life had narrowed despite all her energy and talent. But I had failed to accept it in my own life.

'Africa gives you the knowledge that man is a small creature, among other creatures, in a large landscape', Lessing once wrote. Was that the lesson I'd needed her to teach me? I sank back into the rock, closing my eyes in the sunlight, laying my hands on the granite beside me. I had arrived less than an hour earlier and would soon be gone, my presence unnoticed by anyone except the man at the entrance of the mountain, waiting fruitlessly for custom. The rocks had been there for billions of years.

* * *

Doris Lessing dreamt about the sea for a whole year before she finally reached it in March 1946, three months pregnant with Peter. The train journey to Cape Town took five days, and when she finally saw and then smelt the sea through the train window, she began to feel drunk with pleasure. She expected immediately to plunge into the water, but she was waylaid by communists demanding her help in canvasing for a by-election. It wasn't till her second afternoon that she could escape:

> I firmly broke the ranks and told them to go to hell,
> and spent an ecstatic three hours leaning over a rail and
> looking at it, and putting my feet into it, and testing it,
> and feeling the feel of seaweed, and watching the way the
> waves gather and come in and curl over, till emotionally
> and physically exhausted I tottered back to bed.

A few weeks later, she began the affair with Gregoire Boonzaier, the painter who 'so passionately loved the woman-ness of woman'. This was a sensual relationship in which the sea itself played a part. They spent weeks living in a hut just by the water, listening to the waves as they slept. 'We made love and listened to the sea, made love and listened, our bodies as slippery as fishes.'

I saw it as the plane landed and then again as my taxi swerved around the bend to my hotel. This was the first time I'd slept within sight and sound of the sea for two years. I was on the cliffs, looking down on to the Atlantic, and the waves crashed as I fell asleep and were the first sound I heard in the morning. It was too cold to swim here, so it was lucky that I'd found my own painter to take me to the warmer waters of the Indian ocean, on the other side of the Cape. Like all the white people I'd met in Africa, he was the friend of a friend of a friend. He also turned out to have been friends with Boonzaier in his old age. They'd even drawn each other and his drawing, of a wise and weathered old man, hung in his study.

The beach was cold by the time we arrived and the southeaster gale had descended on the water, creating fierce waves. We changed out of our clothes and edged towards the wall of a tidal pool that looked safer than swimming further out. I felt mad and English and fairly sure that Lessing wouldn't have swum in this weather. But I was having my own adventure now; it was time to let her go.

The waves bounced unpredictably from the sea into the tidal pool and then over the wall of the pool to the beach, so we were swept in before we'd had a chance to pause and contemplate the temperature of the water. The painter only lasted for a few seconds, enough to generate some watery adrenalin and launch me on my way. I lasted for longer, habituated enough to cold seas to be able to keep moving.

Swimming fast, up and down the tidal pool, I eventually became warm or numb enough to look around me, gazing up in renewed wonder at the vast sky. We were surrounded by the hills of the Cape, steep rocks shrouded in green grass. Across the bay it was just possible to see the more majestic snow-capped Hottentots Holland mountains, emerging through the mist. I knew that I wouldn't last long in the water and that I'd be even colder when I emerged. But for those seconds, jumping over Indian waves in an African pool while a man I had just met held out a pink stripy towel towards me, I wanted nothing more than to dangle.

Afterword

Time has passed since the two years of my life described in this book. That August when I went to Zimbabwe, I was left with two embryos. We tried another one in October, without success. The strain was becoming unbearable and it had become clear that having a second child might not be the way to save our marriage. I offered my husband his freedom, suggesting that perhaps he should have a child with someone else. Was I seeking my own freedom in the process? I don't know. Either way, shortly afterwards, he started a relationship with another woman and started talking about divorce. In January the doctors declared me ready for the third embryo and, as in the old wives' tales, just when we had given up hope and he had lost the desire to have a new child with me, I became pregnant.

Now we are no longer together but we have a daughter, who seems to me all the more miraculous for the struggle involved in her creation. I am tied to this new creature by the kind of love that makes freedom seem less urgent. Yet I would say that now, unable to leave the house without my child, unable to quest after new places or new lovers, I do feel freer than I did in the period described in this book. I think this is because I have become more honest and because I have discovered that it's possible to live and to write honestly even in the public sphere, even at the risk of shame. This, more than anything, has been a lesson I have learnt from Lessing.

The book that has resulted from my strange, selfish but nonetheless urgent quest to understand freedom has made painful reading for my now ex-husband and I am grateful for his forbearance. I hope that everyone who knows us will see that the love I describe for him in the book is real. Certainly, though he may not always like it, I would not be the complicated and convention-fearing person I am today without his influence during the many happy years we spent together. This book may also one day make difficult reading for my children and I ask for their patience and understanding when they come to read it. I hope, again, that the love is as palpable as the dissatisfaction with my life at that time.

It has made more enjoyable reading matter for my friends, many of whom have helped me with love, encouragement and good humour during the period of living and writing this book, assuring me that I am strong enough to live and to write in the way that I have. Several friends have read drafts of the manuscript; others are mentioned in these pages. You know who you are.

Looking back in old age on her years as a single woman, Lessing told an interviewer that what mattered to her most were 'real friendships, not just acquaintances. You can have thousands of acquaintances, but I think friendship is hard and takes a long time.' This book is dedicated to my friends.

Acknowledgements

I am happily indebted to the Leverhulme Trust for awarding me the Philip Leverhulme Prize, which made the travel involved in researching this book possible, and to my colleagues in the English department at King's College London for supporting the project. Thank you to everyone at Bloomsbury but particularly to my editor Michael Fishwick and to Marigold Atkey, Jasmine Horsey and Sarah Ruddick. Grateful thanks to my agent, Tracy Bohan.

Notes

Where quotations are from Lessing's novels or non-fiction books, searchable editions of these exist and the provenance is made clear in the text, references are not given; such quotations are featured by kind permission of Jonathan Clowes Ltd., London, on behalf of The Estate of Doris Lessing. Letters from Lessing to John Whitehorn and Coll MacDonald are housed in Special Collections at the University of East Anglia, while those from Lessing to Leonard Smith are housed in Special Collections at the University of Sussex. Letters from Lessing to Joan Rodker and to Clancy Sigal, together with Sigal's own papers (essays, diaries, notebooks) are in the Harry Ransom Center at the University of Austin.

ONE
'THIS INFINITE EXCHANGE OF EARTH AND SKY'
THE BUSH

I won't: I will not be like that	DL, *Under My Skin* (HarperCollins, 1994), p. 120
childhood, girlhood and youth	DL, *Under My Skin*, p. 186
Sometimes I stopped the car	DL, *Going Home* (Flamingo, 1992) p. 145
they are beautiful	DL, *Under My Skin*, p. 173
latent always	DL, preface to *Collected African Stories*, volume 1, 1964 (Flamingo, 2000), p. 8

TWO
'SHE WAS FREE. FREE!'
WOMANHOOD

My fourteenth was	DL, *Under My Skin*, p. 155
apprentice love	DL, *Under My Skin*, p. 186
raped the first time	DL to John Whitehorn, Aug 1947
nice boys who wouldn't	DL to Whitehorn, 22 Mar 1946
combined the most	DL to Whitehorn, 29 Sep 1947
meet and merge	Th. H. Van de Velde, M.D., *Ideal Marriage: Its Physiology and Technique* (Heinemann, 1930) pp. 249, 153
local (genital)	Van de Velde, *Ideal Marriage*, pp. 165, 159
The first time I was	DL to Whitehorn, 29 Sep 1947
crops touched by it	Pliny the Elder, *Natural History*, bk 7, ch 15, 64–5

THREE
'I'M SETTING YOU FREE'
ESCAPE

a free woman	Angela Carter, *The Sadeian Woman* (Virago, 1979) p. 27
they could not do	DL, *Under My Skin*, p. 219
Obedience in infancy	F. Truby King, *Feeding and Care of Baby* (revised edition, Whitcombe & Tombs, 1940), pp. 224, 12–13
I remember those afternoons	DL, *Under My Skin,* p. 185
We would embrace	DL, *Under My Skin*, p. 227
The mother, however	D.W. Winnicott, 'Hate in the Counter-Transference', 1949, reprinted in the *Journal of Psychotherapy Practice and Research*, vol 3, Fall 1994, p. 355
She could be herself	Virginia Woolf, *To the Lighthouse* (Longman, 1984) p. 54
like a catastrophe	D.H. Lawrence, *Sons and Lovers* (Cambridge University Press, 1992) pp. 50–51

My children cause	Adrienne Rich, *Of Woman Born* (Norton, 1996), p. 21
The only thing	Jane Lazarre, *The Mother Knot* (Virago, 1987), p. ix
both child and parent	Rachel Cusk, *A Life's Work* (Faber & Faber, 2008) pp. 5, 14, 13, 141, 215
I would give up	Kate Chopin, *The Awakening* (Penguin, 1986) p. 97
A child who	Truby King, *Feeding and Care*, p. 147
The experience of ambivalence	Cusk, *A Life's Work*, p. 4
Writing just passes	Geoff Dyer, 'Over and Out', in Meghan Daum (ed.), *Selfish, Shallow and Self-absorbed: Sixteen Writers on the Decision Not to Have Kids* (Picador, 2015) p. 202
extraordinary satisfaction	DL to Whitehorn, 1 Feb 1946
experimenting idiotically	DL to MacDonald, 18 Feb 1946
I now begin to spread	DL to Whitehorn and MacDonald, 2 May 1946
a vivid picture	DL to MacDonald, 25 Aug 1946
thrilled to bits	Dl to Whitehorn, 24 Sep 1946
never under any	DL to Whitehorn, 11 Oct 1946
My baby, if you are interested	DL to Whitehorn and MacDonald, 26 Oct 1946
it is difficult to believe	DL to Whitehorn, 31 Dec 1946
A stinking carcass	DL to Whitehorn, 29 Sep 1947
On mature consideration	DL to Whitehorn, 24 Feb 1948
always full of anxiety	DL to Leonard Smith, 27 Oct 1947
monstrous baby	Jenny Diski, *In Gratitude* (Bloomsbury, 2016) pp. 203, 236

FOUR

'IT WAS LIKE A REBIRTH'

COMMUNISM

I remember reading	DL to Whitehorn, 21 Mar 1945
The authenticity	John Strachey, review of *The Soviet Trials*, 1938 in John Callaghan and Ben Harker (eds.), *British Communism, A Documentary History* (Manchester University Press, 2011) p. 51

had begun to intrigue	Beatrice and Sidney Webb, *Soviet Communism: A New Civilisation* (Longmans & Co, 1942), p. xxxiv
smoothness of transition	Arthur Koestler, *The Yogi and the Commissar and Other Essays* (Cape, 1985), p. 118
The magnitude of the horror	Victor Kravchenko, *I Chose Freedom* (Scribner's Sons, 1946), p. 303
in order to strengthen	*History of the Communist Party of the Soviet Union*, 1939 translation (Cobbett Publishing, 1943) p. 316
maximising of opportunity	Webb, *Soviet Communism*, p. 1035
very shattered	DL to Whitehorn, 15 Aug 1945
in a world that is sick	DL to Smith, 6 Sep 1945
reign of terror	DL to Smith, 15 Oct 1947
We are in the middle	DL to Leonard Smith, 15 Oct 1947
freer, more democratic	DL, *Going Home*, p. 82
combatants in an	Eric Hobsbawm, *Interesting Times: A Twentieth-Century Life* (Allen Lane, 2002) p. 139
Lessing is out	Memo, 23 Nov 1956, in Lessing's MI5 file (The National Archives, Kew)
What Isaiah Berlin	see Isaiah Berlin, *Four Essays on Liberty* (Oxford University Press, 1969)
bourgeois individuality	Karl Marx and Friedrich Engels, *The Communist Manifesto*, ed. Jeffrey C. Isaac (Yale University Press, 2012) p. 87
only in community	Karl Marx and Friedrich Engels, *The German Ideology*, ed. C.J Arthur (Lawrence & Wishart, 1970) p. 83
the liberal claim	Randall Swingler, 'Is the Individual Losing his Freedom' in John Lewis (ed.), *The Communist Answer to the Challenge of Our Time* (Thames Publications, 1947), p. 37
I wish to speak	Henry David Thoreau, 'Walking', 1862, *The Major Essays of Henry David Thoreau*, ed. Richard Dillman (Whitston Publishing Company, 2001) p. 161
That government is best	Henry David Thoreau, 'Civil Disobedience', 1849, *The Major Essays*, pp. 47, 54
the straitjacket	Lessing to E.P. Thompson quoted in DL, *Walking in the Shade* (HarperCollins, 1997) p. 195

FIVE

'I CANNOT IMAGINE MYSELF NOT LOVING SEVERAL
PEOPLE AT ONCE IN VARIOUS WAYS'
FREE LOVE

Owing to my unfaithfulness	DL to Whitehorn, Jan 1945
all for adultery	DL to Smith, Oct 1944
stylised love affair	DL to Whitehorn, 9 Jan 1945
The essence of	DL to Whitehorn, 1 Feb 1946
Through sleep I know	enclosed DL to Whitehorn, 14 Aug 1946
I cannot imagine	DL to Whitehorn, 28 Nov 1948
an excellent institution	DL to Smith , 10 Jan 1946
I have never met any	DL to Smith, 17 May 1946
how much narcissism	'I was *almost* able to sink myself into being found a treasure of pleasure – and narcissism does have its part to play, how much you learn only when you are old' (DL, *Under My Skin*, p. 356)
Yes, I am a free lover	Victoria Woodhull, 'And The Truth Shall Make You Free: A Speech On The Principles Of Social Freedom', 20 Nov 1871 (http://gos.sbc.edu/w/woodhull.html)
fix by law	Havelock Ellis, *Sex in Relation to Society* (Heinemann, 1910) pp. 494–496
familiarity dulls	Bertrand Russell, *Marriage and Morals* (Routledge, 2009) pp. 85, 175
more and more widely realised	Irene Clephane, *Towards Sex Freedom* (John Lane, 1935) pp. 230, 224
Code on Marriage and S. la Vol'fson	see Wendy Z Goldman, *Women, The State and Revolution, Soviet Family Policy and Social Life 1917–1936* (Cambridge University Press, 1993) p. 1
individual sex love	see Goldman, p. 39
two people to make love	see Goldman, p. 8
neither morality nor	see Goldman, p. 7
I heartily approve of all	DL to MacDonald, 18 Jul 1945
One must throw everything	D.H. Lawrence, *Women in Love* (Cambridge University Press, 1987) pp. 132, 254, 320
futile years	DL to Smith, 30 Nov 1947

the love or sweetness	see Elizabeth D. Harvey, 'Anatomies of Rapture: Clitoral Politics/Medical Blazons', *Signs*, 2002 (27), p. 315
the true female organ	Female development 'is a process of transition from the one phase to the other', Sigmund Freud, 'Female Sexuality', *International Journal of Psychoanalysis*, 1932 (13), p. 282
wriggling and shouting	DH Lawrence, *Lady Chatterley's Lover* (Penguin, 2006) p. 202
men fear that they	Anne Koedt, 'The Myth of the Vaginal Orgasm', in *Notes from the Second Year* (New York Radical Feminists, 1970) p. 41
every couple	NMGC, *Sex Difficulties in the Wife*, 1958, p. 8
One wonders just	Germaine Greer, *The Female Eunuch* (MacGibbon & Kee, 1970) p. 306
One isn't only	Graham Greene to Catherine Walston, 14 Dec 1949 (Greene archive, Georgetown University).
erotic centre	Simone de Beauvoir, *The Second Sex*, trans. Constance Borde and Sheila Malovany-Chevallier (Alfred Knopf, 2009) pp. 384–5, 390, 405, 410, 415
What happens in marriage	DL to Smith, Mar 1947
an inter-subjective	De Beauvoir, *The Second Sex*, p. 467
his desire transformed	Simone de Beauvoir, *The Mandarins*, trans. Leonard M. Friedman (Harper Perennial Modern Classics, 2005) p. 410. Reprinted by permission of HarperCollins Publishers Ltd © 2005 Simone de Beauvoir
dry and lonely	DL, preface to *The Mandarins*, 1984, in *Time Bites* (Harper Perennial, 2005) p. 207
some gay men	see Maggie Nelson, *The Argonauts* (Melville House, 2016) p. 91
the freedom of surrendering	Deborah Anapol, *Polyamory in the Twenty-First Century* (Rowman & Littlefield, 2010) p. 5

SIX

'IT IS POTENTIALLY LIBERATION AND RENEWAL AS WELL
AS ENSLAVEMENT AND EXISTENTIAL DEATH'

MADNESS

It is potentially	Laing, *The Politics of Experience*. Reproduced by kind permission of the R.D. Laing Estate. © The R.D. Laing Estate
A woman opens	see DL, *Walking in the Shade* and *The Golden Notebook*
A man climbs	see Clancy Sigal, 'How to live with a lady writer, first lesson don't call her a lady writer', *The Secret Defector*, 'May 19 1957', 'The sexual history of Jake Blue', (Open Road ebook, 2013)
Something about Doris	Sigal, 'How to live with a lady writer, first lesson don't call her a lady writer'
Except for the FBI	Sigal, *The Secret Defector*
I Had a Lover	DL to Joan Rodker, 27 Oct
You've never enjoyed	Sigal, diary, 4 Mar 1959
I do not look	Sigal, diary, 14 Aug 1958
Rage, pain	Sigal, untitled undated article
My cock an	Sigal, *The Secret Defector*
Nothing I say	Sigal, diary, 13 Jan 1958
I'm not your mother	DL to Sigal, undated
persistent scission	R.D. Laing, *The Divided Self* (Routledge, 2001) p. 82
denial, splitting	R.D. Laing, *The Politics of Experience* (Penguin, 1984) pp. 23, 105, 110
The truth is	Sigal, diary, 14 Aug 1959
freedom and breathing	Sigal, diary, 4 May 1963
My hands ink-spattered	Sigal, notebook, undated
heroic undertaking	Laing to Sigal, 12 Feb 1963
No woman can	Sigal to Laing, 21 Sep 1963
freedom, from	Sigal, *Zone of the Interior* (Open Road ebook, 2013)
a poor substitute	Sigal, 'The rebellious games of a divided self', *Independent*, 30 Aug 1989

Get your ass	Sigal, article on Laing for *Dazed and Confused* (in Sigal archive)
sun rising	DL interview with Roy Newquist, 1964, *Putting the Questions Differently* (Flamingo, 1996) p. 12
He rejoiced	Lawrence, *Women in Love*, p. 108
One of Diski's	For more details about the model for Watkins see 'Writing Autobiography' in *Time Bites* p. 97
split off from	Laing, *The Politics of Experience*, p. 27. Reproduced by kind permission of the R.D. Laing Estate. © The R.D. Laing Estate
so lonely when	DL to Joan Rodker, undated
It's necessary to	DL to Sigal, undated
Sometimes, awaking	Sigal, untitled, Sep 1959
How can I explain	Sigal, diary, 29 Dec 1963
an act of victory	DL to Sigal, undated
I am lost	Sigal to Laing, 25 Jun 1963
Rock and no water	T.S. Eliot, 'The Waste Land', *The Waste Land and other Poems*, Faber & Faber, 2002. Reproduced by kind permission.

SEVEN

'I WAS ABLE TO BE FREER THAN MOST BECAUSE I AM A WRITER'

WRITING

she was intensely	Virginia Woolf, 'Professions for Women', 1931, *The Crowded Dance of Modern Life* (Penguin, 1993) p. 102
Sometimes I feel	Chris Kraus, *I Love Dick* (Serpent's Tail, 2016) pp. 65, 195, 56. Reproduced by kind permission.
flaring with shame	Karl Ove Knausgaard, 'The shame of writing about myself', *Guardian*, 26 Feb 2016

EIGHT
'A SICK SWEET SUBMERSION IN PAIN'
THE DARK

the difference between	DL interview with Josephine Hendin, 1972, *Putting the Questions Differently*, p. 55
The Sufis was	Review of *Knowing How to Know*, 1998, *Time Bites*, p. 228
improbably but	DL to Joan Rodker, undated
Soon afterwards	This information comes from Suzette Macedo
one has to accept	DL interview with Nissa Torrents, 1980, *Putting the Questions Differently*, p. 65
break out of	DL, 'If you knew Sufi', *Guardian*, 8 Jan 1975
new guy	Sigal, *The Secret Defector*
an infinitely elevated	Sigal, 'Lunch with Rose'
I suppose there's	Sigal, *The London Lover* (Bloomsbury, 2018)
Real freedom is	Iris Murdoch, *The Sandcastle* (Vintage, 2003) p. 213
To be oneself	Murdoch to David Morgan, Jan 1972 (in *Living on Paper, Letters from Irish Murdoch 1934–1995* (Chatto & Windus, 2015) p. 397
touched by the	De Beauvoir, *The Second Sex*, p. 620
no longer a	De Beauvoir, *The Mandarins*, p. 101
flabbergasted, at	De Beauvoir, *Force of Circumstance*, trans. R. Howard (André Deutsch, 1965) p. 656
There are positive	Germaine Greer, *The Change*, pp. 2, 12, 7, 9
a slave	Plato, *Republic I* 329
It's out on loan	Idries Shah, *The Sufis* (ISF Publishing, 2015) p. 96
mainly desiccated	Sigal, 'Lunch with Rose'
I'm glad we could	Philip Glass, *Words without Music* (Faber & Faber, 2015) p. 321
I'll not forget	DL, 'Philip Glass', *Time Bites*, p. 145
never had one	DL interview with Thomas Frick, 1987, *Putting the Questions Differently*, p. 166
Words are our	DL, 'Opera', 1996, *Time Bites*, p. 370
Doris was then	Glass, *Words without Music*, W. W. Norton & Company (Liveright imprint), 2016, p. 321
It was the counter tenor	DL, 'Philip Glass', p. 146

| *I breathe the sweet breath* | 'Akhnaten' – words by Robert Israel, Richard Riddell & Shalom Goldman. Music by Philip Glass. © Copyright 1983 Dunvagen Music Publishers Incorporated. Chester Music Limited. All Rights Reserved. International Copyright Secured. Used by permission of Chester Music Limited. |

NINE
'FULL OF RESTLESS STARS'
THE BUSH

big, cool, empty	DL, *Going Home*, pp. 8, 28; 30
They were her	DL, 'The de Wets come to Kloof Grange', *Collected African Stories*, volume 1, (Flamingo, 2000) p. 84
night after night	DL, *African Laughter* (Flamingo, 1993) pp. 12, 28, 313, 315
Twenty-three years	DL, 'The Tragedy of Zimbabwe', 2003, *Time Bites*, pp. 231, 233
at some point	DL, 'Old', 2015, *Time Bites*, p. 215
I am standing	DL, 'On Not Winning the Nobel Prize', 2007 (https://www.nobelprize.org/nobel_prizes/literature/laureates/2007/lessing-lecture_en.html). © The Nobel Foundation 2007.
I envy you the sea	DL to Smith, 7 May 1945
freedom is a home	Rachel Cusk, *Transit* (Jonathan Cape, 2016) p. 210
I don't see the veld	DL interview with Eve Bertelsen, 1984, *Putting the Questions Differently*, p. 122; in an interview with Stephen Gray in 1983 Lessing had stated that 'there *was* this mythical consciousness about' when asked about her portrayal of Africa (p. 114)
Africa gives you the	DL, preface to *African Stories*, p. 8
I firmly broke	DL to Whitehorn, 22 Mar 1946
We made love	DL, *Under My Skin* p. 356

Index

A Note on the Author

Lara Feigel is a Reader in Modern Literature and Culture at King's College London. She is the author of *Literature, Cinema and Politics, 1930–1945* and the editor (with Alexandra Harris) of *Modernism on Sea: Art and Culture at the British Seaside* and (with John Sutherland) of the *New Selected Journals of Stephen Spender*. She has also written journalism for various publications, including the *Guardian*, the *Financial Times* and *Prospect*. *The Love-charm of Bombs* (2013) and her most recent book, *The Bitter Taste of Victory* (2016), were both published to critical acclaim. Lara lives in London.

www.larafeigel.com
@larafeigel

A Note on the Type

The text of this book is set Adobe Garamond. It is one of several versions of Garamond based on the designs of Claude Garamond. It is thought that Garamond based his font on Bembo, cut in 1495 by Francesco Griffo in collaboration with the Italian printer Aldus Manutius. Garamond types were first used in books printed in Paris around 1532. Many of the present-day versions of this type are based on the *Typi Academiae* of Jean Jannon cut in Sedan in 1615.

Claude Garamond was born in Paris in 1480. He learned how to cut type from his father and by the age of fifteen he was able to fashion steel punches the size of a pica with great precision. At the age of sixty he was commissioned by King Francis I to design a Greek alphabet, and for this he was given the honourable title of royal type founder. He died in 1561.